Essentials and Assessment of Risk Management

THE FERMA-RIMAP® SERIES

The FERMA-rimap® Series serves as a proactive, continuous and dynamic learning and research platform to respond to risk managers' present and future educational and professional needs. The volumes set a flexible and dynamic measurable standard taxonomy for European Risk Managers and essential reading for students gaining their qualification. The scope of *The FERMA-rimap® Series* is to reach out to experienced or junior risk professionals, whatever their background is, and wherever their career is heading. All risk professionals have a duty to stay in contact with the evolution of the risk landscape.

Essentials and Assessment of Risk Management

EDITED BY

SIMON GRIMA
University of Malta, Malta

MARÍA ISABEL MARTÍNEZ TORRE-ENCISO
Universidad Autónoma de Madrid, Spain

AND

MAURIZIO CASTELLI
Augustas Risk Services SpA, Italy

emerald
PUBLISHING

United Kingdom – North America – Japan – India – Malaysia – China

Emerald Publishing Limited
Emerald Publishing, Floor 5, Northspring, 21-23 Wellington Street, Leeds LS1 4DL.

First edition 2025

British Library Cataloguing in Publication Data
A catalogue record for this book is available from the British Library

ISBN: 978-1-83662-303-8 (Print)
ISBN: 978-1-83662-302-1 (Online)
ISBN: 978-1-83662-304-5 (Epub)

INVESTOR IN PEOPLE

Contents

Preface

Risk management has become an indispensable function in modern organisations, playing a critical role in safeguarding assets, ensuring regulatory compliance, and enhancing decision-making processes. In an era characterised by increasing complexity and uncertainty, the need for structured, dynamic, and forward-thinking risk management frameworks has never been more pronounced. This volume, *Essentials and Assessment of Risk Management*, is a comprehensive resource designed to provide both aspiring and seasoned risk professionals with a robust understanding of risk management principles, frameworks, and practical applications.

This book is part of the *FERMA-rimap® Series*, which aims to create a dynamic, continuous learning platform for risk professionals across Europe and beyond. The content has been meticulously curated to align with the evolving landscape of risk management, drawing from best practices, established methodologies, and contemporary challenges faced by organisations. It serves as a valuable reference for those preparing for the FERMA-rimap® certification, as well as for practitioners seeking to deepen their expertise in enterprise-wide risk management.

The structure of this book reflects a holistic approach to risk management, beginning with foundational concepts and progressing towards more complex topics, such as strategic risk management, financial models for risk analysis, and emerging trends in risk governance. Through detailed discussions on frameworks such as ISO 31000:2018 and COSO ERM, we aim to equip professionals with the knowledge required to implement effective risk management strategies that integrate seamlessly with organisational objectives.

We extend our sincere gratitude to the contributing authors, industry experts, and academic professionals who have shared their insights and expertise in shaping this publication. Their dedication ensures that this book remains a valuable resource for risk managers, corporate leaders, policymakers, and students alike. This book series is a testament of FERMA's (Federation of European Risk Management Associations) unwavering commitment to promoting excellence in risk management through education, research, and professional development.[1]

[1]To know more FERMA's commitment to risk management, please visit www.ferma.eu

As you engage with this material, we encourage you to approach risk management not merely as a compliance exercise but as a strategic enabler of business resilience and value creation. We hope this book serves as a guiding tool, inspiring you to adopt proactive and innovative risk management practices that contribute to the long-term success of your organisation.

Acknowledgements

ISO 31000:2018 Risk Management – Guidelines reproduced under licence from SAI Global Ltd

The structure of the following document is based on the FERMA rimap® Body of Knowledge developed in 2015 by a team of European risk managers representing their national risk management associations, members of FERMA, to serve as a basis for a European Risk Management certification. The FERMA rimap® Body of Knowledge was designed under the supervision of Prof. María Isabel Martínez Torre-Enciso, Doctor in Business and Economics by UCM, Professor of Corporate Finance in UAM, MBA, RIMAP.

Prof. Jean-Paul Louisot, Docteurès Sciences de Gestion de la Sorbonne, MBA, ARM, FIRM, acted as FERMA's subject matter expert to ensure greater consistency among the numerous chapters of the Body of Knowledge, the FERMA existing learning materials and the new content developed to enrich the document.

Disclaimer

This subject matter is provided by FERMA for study, on the understanding that no person should act on the basis of the material contained in this publication without considering and taking professional advice. In particular:

- FERMA, its directors, authors, or any persons involved in this publication expressly disclaim any and all contractual, tortious, or other forms of liability to any person in respect of the publication and any consequences arising from its use, including any omission made, by any person in reliance upon the whole or any part of the contents of this publication.
- FERMA expressly disclaims any and all liability to any person in respect of the consequences of anything done or not done by any person in reliance upon the contents of this subject material.

Chapter 1

Introduction to the FERMA rimap® Certification (4 Pillars System)

Introduction

This chapter describes the role of the Federation of European Risk Management Associations (FERMA) in risk management in Europe and the aims of the FERMA rimap® certification system.

It describes the four-pillar approach of the certification and outlines who is eligible to seek certification.

There are no learning outcomes for this chapter.

FERMA and Risk Management Associations

FERMA was established in 1974 under the name of the 'European Association of Industrial Insureds' (AEAI) as an international association with the aim of representing the interests of commercial insurance buyers and exchanging ideas and experiences.

Today, FERMA brings together 22 risk management associations in 21 European countries and represents more than 4,800 risk managers across a wide range of business sectors, from major industrial and commercial companies to financial institutions and local government bodies.

FERMA provides the means of coordinating risk management and optimising the impact of its membership associations outside their national boundaries on a European level. FERMA promotes communication among its members and also within IFRIMA (International Federation of Risk and Insurance Management Associations), of which FERMA is a member.

FERMA rimap® Certification

FERMA has developed the FERMA rimap® certification scheme as an attempt to organise and re-structure the risk management industry. Its aim is to give a

Essentials and Assessment of Risk Management, 1–3

Published under exclusive licence by Emerald Publishing Limited
doi:10.1108/978-1-83662-302-120251002

strong identity to the profession, making sure executives, boards, human resource departments and academics value the profession as it really is.

FERMA rimap® will provide formal recognition of the competence of the risk professionals who undertake the certification.

Why Should Risk Professionals Be Certified?

To be resilient, organisations need more than ever to ensure their assets are protected and therefore to go beyond insurance. This requires risk managers to have a particular set of skills and experience – as listed in our Body of Knowledge. The role of FERMA rimap® is to provide assurance to all organisations that the certified risk manager they employ is appropriately skilled and has sufficient knowledge to help protect their organisation.

For individual risk professionals, FERMA rimap® will:

- increase your credibility and competitive advantage over peers;
- provide international recognition, which will enable opportunities in multinational organisations;
- increase the opportunities for you to grow your responsibilities;
- assist you to develop your career;
- provide independent recognition to top management of your professional status.

The Four Pillars of FERMA rimap® certification

FERMA rimap® certification is based on four pillars to ensure that the skills essential to risk managers are equally valued and can be equally employed. The premise is that knowledge should always be cross-checked against experience and ethics to ensure that the knowledge being applied is not theoretical in nature but fully applicable to the relevant situation. Continuous professional development (CPD) will guarantee that risk managers continue to learn and stay up to date with the latest trends through the many available risk management and insurance events.

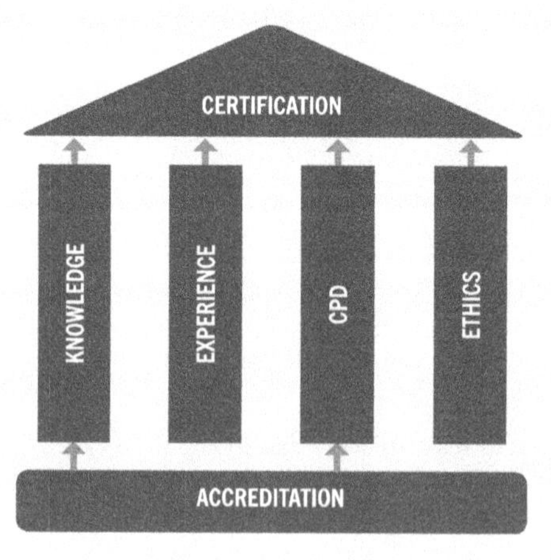

The four pillars can be defined as follows:

- *Knowledge* – the overall and comprehensive knowledge base that risk managers should be familiar with in their professional careers.
- *Experience* – the measure of the significant experience that risk managers have obtained over the course of their careers.
- CPD – the common requirement for qualified professionals to ensure they continue to learn and develop throughout their careers.
- *Ethics* – the sound basis for a code that can be expanded and updated over the coming years.

Eligibility Criteria

Depending on the combination of education and experience, FERMA rimap® certification will be accessible to risk managers who fulfil the following criteria:

FERMA rimap® Certification

	Education	Experience
	Master	Min. 3 years
Level	Bachelor	Min. 5 years
	High school	Min. 5 years

Chapter 2

Principles and Aims of Enterprise-Wide Risk Management

Introduction

The need to manage risk is increasingly featured in legislation and regulations. The need to integrate risk management into the general management practices of organisations is fast becoming a key organisational objective as shareholders, stakeholders and public interest groups become more interested in how organisations manage their risk exposures. In addition, the drive to improve corporate governance is compelling organisations to examine the manner in which they manage the risks facing them at strategic, tactical and operational levels.

To be most effective, risk management should become part of an organisation's culture. It should be embedded in the organisation's philosophy, practices and business processes rather than viewed or practised as a separate activity. When this is achieved, everyone in the organisation becomes involved in the management of risk (ISO 31000:2018).

The introduction of an enterprise-wide risk management framework is the most effective means available for organisations to support the principal objectives of informed risk taking, good corporate governance, compliance with increased regulation and an improved relationship with the organisation's stakeholder community.

Risk management is the foundation of the control environment (i.e. the environment in which an organisation's internal control procedures operate) and sound corporate governance, and affects all of the organisation's activities. For this reason, the implementation of an effective enterprise-wide risk management framework requires careful planning.

Essentials and Assessment of Risk Management, 5–13

Published under exclusive licence by Emerald Publishing Limited
doi:10.1108/978-1-83662-302-120251004

This chapter describes the principles of risk and enterprise risk management (ERM) and the aims and benefits of effective ERM. It explores what risk is and its prevalence in daily life as well as the key factors that should be accounted for when creating a plan for responding to risks.

Learning Outcomes

By the end of this chapter, you should be able to:

- describe what risk is and what constitutes risk management;
- describe the aims of enterprise-wide risk management;
- understand the benefits that sound risk management can bring to organisations.

Risks in Daily Life

Whatever you do and however you do it, there are always elements of risk in your daily life that you need to manage, whether you're at home, at work or at play.

Examples of ways in which you take risks in your life may include:

- driving a car
- mowing the lawn
- developing a general project
- dealing with clients or colleagues
- establishing work priorities
- purchasing new equipment or systems.

Activity | Risk management in your life

Consider the following two scenarios then answer the following questions.

Mowing the lawn

1. Did you check for stones in the grass before you started to mow the lawn?
2. Did you wear solid shoes or boots, or were you barefoot?

Driving a car

1. How much care do you take when you drive a motor vehicle?
2. Why do you service your motor vehicle?

Enterprise Risk Management

Your answers to the questions in the previous activity may have highlighted that you seek to minimise the consequences of risks in your daily activities, whatever they may be. With these consequences in mind (whether you're aware of them or not), you probably aim to effectively manage your risk exposures in life.

Like you in your everyday life, organisational stakeholders also aim to minimise the consequences of an organisation's activities in terms of the risks it is exposed to. The overall management of the risk that organisations accept to achieve their strategic objectives is known as enterprise-wide risk management.

All organisations are exposed to many risks, whether they be losses (such as damage to an asset or poor investment earnings) or failure to achieve a planned positive outcome (such as failing to break into a new market or execute a government policy effectively). Simply by conducting everyday business, an organisation is exposed to risk, but organisations must also take risks. Therefore, in some cases, risk-taking is deliberate and in others it cannot be avoided. It makes sense for organisations to manage all risks in a co-ordinated and planned manner. Risk management is a tool that enables an organisation to do this.

Risk Management

Risk management is a combination of organisational systems, processes and procedures that identify, assess, evaluate and mitigate risks in order to protect the organisation and its strategies and objectives. An effective risk management system plays a significant role in reducing exposure to potentially unfavourable events.

Within a corporate context, risk is managed through a range of formal and informal systems that are a reflection of the corporate culture, the type of industry in which they operate, and external factors such as jurisdictional laws and regulations, and the forces of competition.

Many organisations follow an ERM model, which is one that operates across an entire organisation.

The ERM model, as described within ISO 31000:2018, is the framework for managing risks that:

- Is iterative and assists organisations in setting strategy, achieving objectives and making informed decisions.
- Is part of governance and leadership and is fundamental to how the organisation is managed at all levels. It contributes to the improvement of management systems.
- Is part of all activities associated with an organisation and includes interaction with stakeholders.
- Considers the external and internal context of the organisation, including human behaviour and cultural factors.
- Is based on the principles, framework and process.

Risk Management Principles

ISO 31000:2018 specifies eight risk management principles that an organisation should address to effectively manage its risks and achieve its objectives.

The organisation's board and senior management need to consider these principles when establishing a mandate and commitment to manage risk. According to these eight principles, in addition to preserving and creating value risk management should be:

1. Integrated
   Risk management is an integral part of all organisational activities.

2. Structured and comprehensive.
   A structured and comprehensive approach to risk management contributes to consistent and comparable results.

3. Customised
   The risk management framework and process are customized and proportionate to the organisation's external and internal context related to its objectives.

4. Inclusive
   Appropriate and timely involvement of stakeholders enables their knowledge, views and perceptions to be considered. This results in improved awareness and informed risk management.

5. Dynamic
   Risks can emerge, change or disappear as an organisation's external and internal context changes. Risk management anticipates, detects, acknowledges and responds to those changes and events in an appropriate and timely manner.

6. Best available information
   The inputs to risk management are based on historical and current information, as well as on future expectations. Risk management explicitly takes into account any limitations and uncertainties associated with such information and expectations. Information should be timely, clear and available to relevant stakeholders.

7. Human and cultural factors
   Human behaviour and culture significantly influence all aspects of risk management at each level and stage.

8. Continual improvement
   Risk management is continually improved through learning and experience.

Source: ISO 31000:2018, pp. 3–4.

Risk Management Objectives

The principles outlined above provide guidance to organisations about what considerations need to be incorporated into organisations' planned responses to risk.

The common objectives of these principles, and risk management more broadly, are to:

- manage uncertainty (both upside, opportunity, and downside, threats);
- minimise waste and loss;

- manage capital effectively;
- take advantage of opportunities through an understanding of the associated risks;
  - The upside of risk is that risk-taking can provide opportunities that can help achieve an organisation's strategies and objectives. This means taking risks to generate a positive outcome rather than just protecting or maintaining what already exists.
- avoid major adverse incidents.

Failing to effectively manage risk can expose an organisation to adverse events, such as:

- damage to or loss of assets
- injury to staff
- damage to reputation
- reduction in earnings or turnover
- poor investment earnings
- property damage.

These financial, reputational and regulatory events can also have negative secondary effects. Managing uncertainty is a particular issue for publicly listed companies with many shareholders (current and future). Their dependence on external sources of capital means that they need to provide a perception of stability and predictability in order to support share price and cost of lending.

In an organisational context, management can ask the following two key risk management questions to assist them in minimising the downside and maximising the upside of risk:

1. What could stop us from achieving a strategy?
2. How do we control that threat?

These questions enable management to consider how they can use risk management to better achieve the outcomes to which they aspire.

Risk and Reward

It is almost impossible to function without taking any risks, and there can be no reward or progress without risk.

As the following picture illustrates, the aim is to achieve a balance.

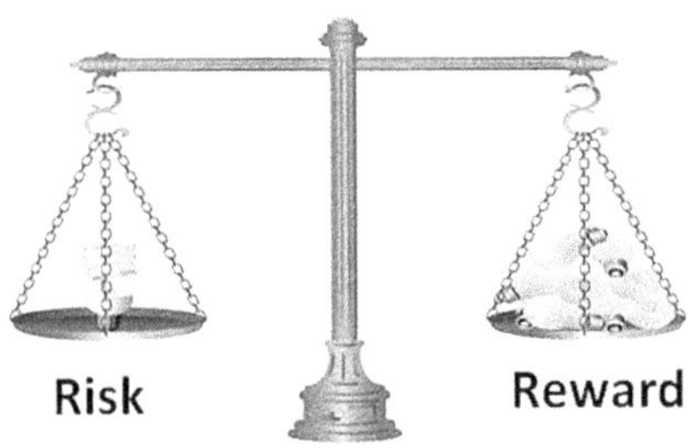

Similarly, because risk taking can be a source of profit or reward, the co-ordinated management of all risk exposures plays an important part in the ongoing wellbeing of:

- organisations
- individuals
- society as a whole.

Increasing Global Complexity and Risk

The world is becoming more complex and with the increasing complexity comes more risk. Organisations cannot ignore these increasing risks; rather, they must establish risk management systems to manage this complexity. Examples of this increasing complexity include increased:

- regulation
- politics
- competition
- customer demands
- employee expectations
- stakeholder demands
- supplier requirements
- economic conditions
- legal actions
- globalisation.

An example of the relationship between increasing world complexity and risk management is the mortgage-backed securities that sparked the global financial crisis (GFC). People purchasing these complex financial products did not understand their inherent risks.

Another example is the ever-increasing complexity of laws and regulations, which raises the risk of these rules being broken.

Finally, in the retail space, the introduction of the internet has created a major risk for retailers who have invested heavily in bricks and mortar as a key outlet for selling their products. More and more, people are now shopping online.

Self-Help Question 2.1

In your own words, what does risk management seek to minimise and what does it seek to increase?

Answers to self-help questions are provided at the end of each section.

Case Studies in Poor Risk Management

Many local and international organisations have suffered considerable losses (or ceased to exist) because they:

- failed to identify the risks to which their organisation was exposed;
- adopted a poor risk management approach.

These risks were all foreseeable and the affected organisations could have used sound risk management to either prevent or minimise the consequences.

International organisations

The following is a list of cases involving international companies that failed to effectively manage risks in recent years.

Company Name	Company Description	Ineffective Management of Risk
Japan Meteorological Agency	Disaster mitigation and prevention agency	The agency underestimated the size of the 2011 tsunami in Japan that killed 19,000 people. It issued a warning for a 10-foot tsunami, but the tsunami reached 131 feet in places.
Toyota	Multinational automaker	Toyota has recalled significant numbers of vehicles over the years due to various issues. In 2016, Toyota recalled 340,000 Prius cars due to faulty brakes. The defect caused a number of crashes, injuries and deaths.
BP/Transocean	Oil company/ offshore-oil drilling company	An explosion on the Deepwater Horizon oil rig caused a huge marine oil spill. It was found that a series of risk management failures combined to cause this massive disaster.

(*Continued*)

(*Continued*)

Company Name	Company Description	Ineffective Management of Risk
Volkswagen	Multinational automaker	In 2015, Volkswagen recalled thousands of cars after it was found that the levels of nitrogen oxide emissions were much higher than testing had suggested. The levels of emissions exceeded regulated limits.
Samsung	Mobile phone manufacturer	In 2016, Samsung recalled its Galaxy Note 7 phone after a manufacturing defect in the battery caused the phone to overheat, triggering fires and explosions.

Summary

Please keep the following points from this chapter in mind:

- Risk management is the use of an organisation's resources and activities to reduce exposure to potentially unfavourable events.
- ERM models aim to integrate risk management into an organisation's broader processes and therefore operate across an entire organisation.
- ISO 31000:2018 Risk Management – Guidelines contain a set of principles, a framework and a process for effectively managing risks on a global and integrated basis (ERM).
- Risk can be positive (generating opportunities) or negative (potential for adverse events).
- Two key risk management questions are:
  - What could stop us from achieving a strategy?
  - How do we control that threat?
- Poor risk management can have significant and far-reaching consequences.

Answers to Self-Help Questions

Self-help question 2.1

Risk management seeks to minimise the risk that the organisation will experience events which result in a loss of value or other damage.

Risk management also seeks to increase the likelihood that strategies will be successfully delivered by identifying those things that threaten execution and either reducing or eliminating them.

Chapter 3

Risk Management Frameworks and Standards

Introduction

The management of risk is an essential aspect of the overall management of an organisation. It contributes to making the organisation's strategic vision a reality by reducing losses and providing the opportunity to take greater risks.

The introduction of an enterprise-wide risk management framework is the most effective means available to organisations to underpin the principal objectives of:

- informed risk taking;
- good corporate governance;
- compliance with increased regulation;
- an improved relationship with the organisation's stakeholder community.

This chapter describes risk management frameworks and standards that are available to organisations today, including global and local ones. It outlines why these standards and frameworks were developed, and what they aim to achieve.

Learning Outcomes

By the end of this chapter, you should be able to:

- enforce the applicable risk management framework;
- identify key features of risk management standards;
- implement recommendations from the frameworks and standards;
- manage the effects of material risk exposures.

Essentials and Assessment of Risk Management, 15–26

Published under exclusive licence by Emerald Publishing Limited
doi:10.1108/978-1-83662-302-120251007

Risk Management Frameworks

ISO/Guide 73:2009 – Risk management – Vocabulary defines a risk management framework as 'a set of components' that provide the foundations and organisational arrangements for designing, implementing, monitoring, reviewing and continually improving risk management throughout the organisation'.

The key aspect of this definition is the imperative to embed the risk management framework within the broader organisational strategy.

The risk management framework within an organisation should encompass strategic, tactical and operational planning, decision-making and processes and practices for dealing with risk exposures. A well-defined risk management framework establishes the parameters within which an organisation will manage its risk exposures. It sets the scope for the entire risk management process and determines how systematic risk management can be established and maintained within an organisation.

An organisation's risk management framework should fully support the organisation's overall objectives. For an organisation to successfully manage its risk exposures, it is necessary for the board, senior management and operational management to support and commit to the risk management framework.

The risk management framework establishes how the organisation will view its exposure to risk as well as the administrative, human and financial resources necessary to enable those exposures to be managed effectively, while meeting the organisation's objectives.

Note: The term *risk management framework* is sometimes used interchangeably with the term *risk management program*. This module uses a risk management framework in line with the international standard.

Benefits of an Effective Risk Management Framework

Embedding a risk management framework is beneficial for a number of reasons, as described below.

More Effective Strategic and Operational Planning

By applying the risk management process to the process of objective setting, at all levels of the organisation, it becomes effectively integrated as an enterprise-wide process. In addition, controls and strategies are integrated and linked with the organisational objectives as the unifying focus.

Risk management therefore ensures that the risks associated with an organisation's strategic and operational objectives are identified and addressed by appropriate controls that also function as strategies.

An effective risk management framework will ensure that all strategic and business objectives implemented are mindful of the risks involved and the opportunities that exist.

Greater Confidence in Achieving Planned Operational and Strategic Objectives

Organisations that identify and treat risks when planning have a far greater chance of achieving the planned outcomes than an organisation that does not.

Risk management applied to the planning process provides confidence regarding performance in two ways:

1. Applying the following formula develops strategies that provide reasonable assurance that an organisation will achieve its objectives within an acceptable degree of residual risk:
   strategies = objectives + risk management
2. Developing an enterprise-wide risk management culture that supports capability and commitment to the management of risks therefore supports the achievement of objectives.

Enhanced Organisational Resilience

Risk management develops a framework for anticipating and professionally managing risks, therefore reducing the time and energy spent in crisis management.

This benefit is further enhanced by incorporating risk management throughout the workforce, which can facilitate a rapid organisational response to unexpected threats and to take advantage of opportunities.

Greater Confidence in the Decision-Making Process

Risk management plays multiple roles in evaluating opportunities. The decision-making process involves asking the following questions:

- What are the risks of not taking up the opportunity?
- How are these risks balanced by those associated with taking up the opportunity?
- Once the decision has been made to take up the opportunity, what are the risks involved in managing the opportunity effectively?
- In an organisation focused on performance the overall question should be, 'Are we taking enough risks?'

These questions assist in strategic decision-making processes, including those surrounding major investments or mergers and acquisitions.

An additional advantage of an embedded risk management process is that it documents the decision-making process thereby enhancing accountability and traceability of decisions in the overall governance setting.

Greater Stakeholder Confidence and Enhanced Capital Raising

Demonstration of a sound risk management framework (applied throughout the organisation as part of normal business practice) gives confidence to investors, lenders and insurers, facilitating capital raising and protection.

Director Protection

Embedding an enterprise-wide risk management framework, and developing capability and commitment in this regard (among all members of the organisation), enhances the quality of information contained in documents such as reports.

This enterprise-wide risk management framework is complemented by the development of an effective organisational information framework – promoting clarity of roles, responsibilities and accountabilities. Such frameworks can provide directors with confidence in the information they receive (for their decision-making purposes) and the scope of their due diligence responsibilities.

Activity | Benefits of implementing a risk management framework

Review the current status of your organisation and list some of the ways that you believe implementing a risk management framework would benefit the organisation. In doing so, consider such aspects as:

- the effectiveness of the existing risk management framework (if one exists);
- the manner in which risk management currently contributes to the achievement of the organisation's goals and objectives;
- the way in which risk management is perceived within the organisation (i.e. is it a compliance activity or something that is embedded into the management practices of the organisation).

Relationship Between the Risk Management Framework and Risk Management Process

The relationship between a risk management framework and the risk management process is depicted in the diagram below:

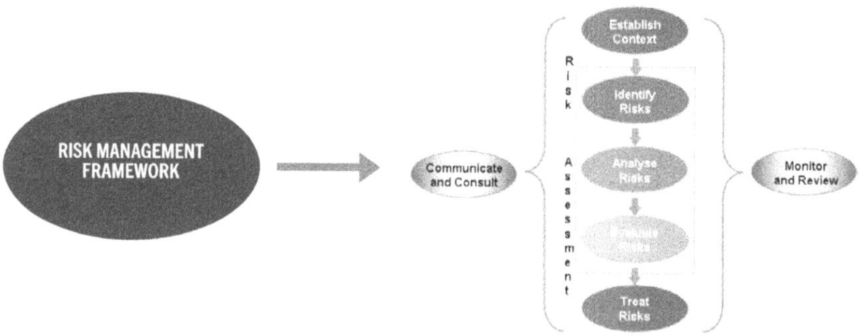

©2008, Rod Farrar, reproduced with permission.

It needs to be recognised that while the risk management process can be undertaken within an organisation, it will be nowhere near as effective if the elements of the framework are not in place to support those undertaking risk management activities.

Different Frameworks

Across the world, a number of risk management standards have been published in order to guide the application of risk management. These standards include (but are not limited to):

- *Enterprise risk management – Integrating with Strategy and Performance* (Committee of Sponsoring Organisations of the Treadway Commission [COSO] – USA).
- ISO 31000:2018 Risk Management – Guidelines (International Organization for Standardization).
- JIS Q31000:2010 *Risk management – Principles and guidelines* (Japanese Standards Association).
- BS 6079-3:2000 *Project management – Guide to the management of business related project risk* (British Standards Institute).
- *King IV report on governance* (Institute of Directors in Southern Africa).

Some of these standards focus on the risk management process. Others provide guidance as to the elements required to implement a risk management framework within an organisation.

This section of the module will explore the following standards in detail:

- *Enterprise risk management – Integrating with Strategy and Performance* (COSO).
- ISO 31000:2018 Risk Management – Guidelines (International Organization for Standardization).

COSO Enterprise Risk Management – Integrating with Strategy and Performance

The Committee of Sponsoring Organizations of the Treadway Commission (COSO) develops frameworks and guidance on enterprise risk management, internal control and fraud deterrence designed to improve organisational performance and governance and to reduce fraud.

In 2004, in response to a demand in North America for better guidance in enterprise risk management, COSO developed *Enterprise risk management – Integrated framework*. This framework was updated at the end of 2016 to incorporate guidance on aligning risk with strategy and performance.

On 6 September 2017, a new COSO ERM Framework: Enterprise Risk Management – Integrating with Strategy and Performance was released. The new title is meant to better distinguish enterprise risk management from internal control.

COSO focuses on the links between strategy and performance. It relies on a new framework structure based on five components that support 20 principles to reflect the different viewpoints and operating structures of an organisation. By enhancing strategies and decision-making, embedding the ERM throughout an organisation would support the creation, preservation, and realisation of value.

The different benefits of ERM (loss mitigation, strategic advisor) are detailed in line with the design of a risk framework. Diagrams showing 'risk curves' are included to identify and assess the relationship between the amount of risk and the level of performance.

Business Scandals and Failures

The framework was originally developed during a period when a series of high-profile business scandals and failures occurred. Investors, company personnel and other stakeholders suffered tremendous losses during these events.

In the aftermath, calls were made for enhanced corporate governance and risk management, which resulted in new laws, regulations and listing standards (for example, the *Sarbanes-Oxley Act 2002)*.

COSO undertook the ERM framework project to develop a framework that would be readily usable by management to both evaluate and improve their organisations' ERM.

COSO's Enterprise Risk Management Framework

The 20 principles follow the lifecycle of an organisation (whatever the size or the sector) and do not consider the risk management process in isolation. It is aimed at providing a certain level of assurance to the board and leadership of an organisation that risks are managed in accordance with the strategy and the objectives.

The five components are:

1. Governance & Culture
2. Strategy & Objective-Setting
3. Performance
4. Review & Revision Information
5. Information, Communication & Reporting

The 20 principles are:
Governance & Culture

1. Exercises Board Risk Oversight
2. Establishes Operating Structures
3. Defines Desired Culture
4. Demonstrates Commitment to Core Values
5. Attracts, Develops and Retains Capable Individuals

Strategy & Objective-Setting

6. Analyses Business Context
7. Defines Risk Appetite

8. Evaluates Alternative Strategies
9. Formulates Business Objectives
10. Identifies Risk

Performance

11. Assesses Severity of Risk
12. Prioritizes Risks
13. Implements Risk Responses
14. Develops Portfolio View

Review & Revision

15. Assesses Substantial Change
16. Reviews Risk and Performance
17. Pursues Improvement in Enterprise Risk Management

Information, Communication & Reporting

18. Leverages Information and Technology
19. Communicates Risk Information
20. Reports on Risk, Culture and Performance

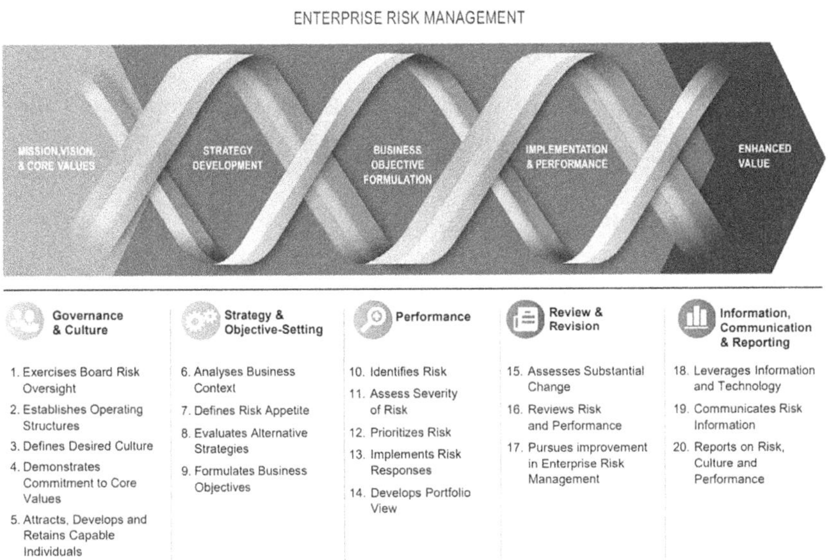

In increasingly complex, global and technologically driven business environment, organisations are seeking to attain better value from enterprise risk management. The objective of the COSO ERM Framework is to provide a full picture of the potential risks as well as an understanding of the opportunities in order to evaluate the strategic options and put the capabilities to create advantage.

Risk, risk appetite, targeted level of performance, and variation in performance are presented according as a "risk curve" to reflect the dynamic nature of risk. Strategy is incorporating the risk appetite by setting certain objectives. Risk appetite is then managed to respond to deviations in performance during the execution phase.

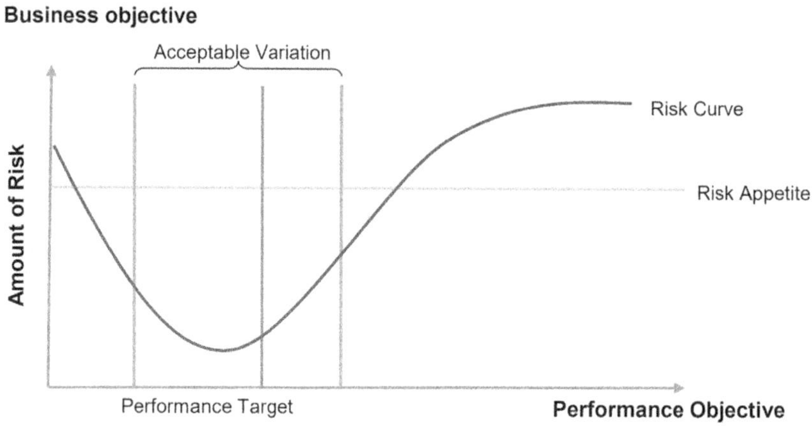

> **Activity | ERM framework**
>
> Read an executive summary of the ERM – Integrating with Strategy and Performance at: https://www.coso.org/Pages/erm.aspx.

ISO 31000:2018 Risk Management – Guidelines

Published by the International Organization for Standardization (or ISO), ISO 31000:2018 is considered the definitive guide on risk management and a core reference for professionals involved in the management of risk.

ISO 31000:2018 provides guidelines, not requirements, and does not contain any normative references. This gives managers the flexibility to implement the standard in a way that suits the needs and objectives of their organisation.

It places a greater emphasis on creating and protecting value as the key driver of risk management and features other related principles such as continual improvement, the inclusion of stakeholders, adaptability to the organisation and consideration of human and cultural factors.

To help organisations use risk management principles in their planning and decision making, ISO 31000:2018 focuses on leadership by top management who should ensure that risk management is integrated into all organisational activities, starting with governance.

It puts a greater emphasis on the iterative nature of risk management, using new experiences, knowledge and analysis for the revision of process elements, actions and controls at each stage of the process. This open system model allows regular exchanges of feedback with its external environment.

The Risk Management Process

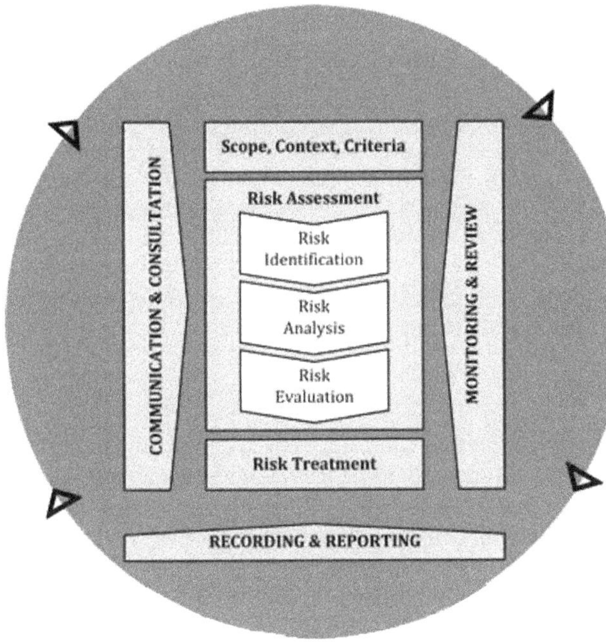

The elements of the risk management process outlined in ISO 31000:2018 are explained in detail in the Standard itself.

For more information, view ISO 31000:2018.

Note: FERMA's licencing agreement allows you to access a secure online version only. You may not print or distribute the Standard. You can purchase this Standard and others from www.iso.org.

A Contemporary, Fully Integrated Approach

ISO 31000:2018 provides excellent guidelines for establishing a risk management program within the overall strategic and operation levels of the management of an organisation.

Risk managers deem ISO 31000:2018's integrated and holistic approach to be an integral component of good management practice and an essential element of good corporate governance.

With the continued pressure on the bottom line performance of all kinds of organisations, risk management has become a vital tool in the armoury of techniques used to manage organisational performance.

In contrast to the traditional silo-based approach (for example, considering insurance and workplace health and safety as separate areas), the contemporary approach to risk management takes a proactive, holistic approach to material risk exposures.

Note: Material risk exposures are risks that could cause significant damage to an organisation. All other risks are business as usual (BAU) risks.

This modern risk management approach seeks to provide solutions by managing the effects of all material risk exposures in the context of the overall management of the organisation.

The management of risk is now widely considered an integral function of general management. It is about managing exposures to risk through planning, organising, directing and controlling the resources or activities of individuals or organisations.

Importantly, organisations cannot manage risk exposures without embedding risk management within the overall management system.

Management Integration

ISO 31000:2018 does not prescribe a risk management system as separate from the overall management system. Rather, ISO 31000:2018 advocates a risk management framework designed to embed/integrate risk management through all levels of the overall management system, which are listed in the following diagram.

Essentially, an organisation's risk management program should be firmly embedded throughout the organisation's management system and fully support the organisation's overall objectives.

Comparing the COSO and ISO Frameworks

While COSO and ISO are calling for quite similar actions, they have different labels and sequencing which may prove confusing for a first-time reader.

The ISO *"Establishing the context"* includes the *internal* and *external* environment and sets *objectives* aligned with *strategy*, taking into account the "risk factor".

ISO *risk assessment* includes the three steps of the risk mapping exercise (*identification, analysis, evaluation*) whereas for COSO, *"identification"* is a separate entity, hence *"assessment"* is really *quantification*.

When ISO includes under *"Risk treatment"* all tools to reduce or finance risk, COSO has a different approach with a *"Risk response"* which means continuity/crisis/protection, and *"Control activities"* which involves prevention.

COSO ERM–Integrating with Strategy and Performance	ISO 31000:2018
Internal environment	Establishing the context
Objective setting	
Event identification	Risk identification
Risk assessment	Risk analysis and risk evaluation
Risk response	Risk treatment
Control activities	
Information and communication	Communication and consultation
Monitoring	Monitoring and review

In line with the global approach with ISO 3100, a number of working groups have been established to explore areas of risk management, the main efforts underway include:

Legal risks – ISO 31022 currently circulated for final revision
Travel risks – ISO 31030 currently circulated for final revision
Resilience and Emerging risks – ISO 31050 currently under review
Consumers' risks – ISO 31040 stalled for the time being, but strong support from Chinese delegation to relaunch it
Supply chain – currently in standby
Guidance Handbook still in progress (ISO 31004).

Other Standards

Uncertainty is a hot topic in all organisations as the world becomes more complex and more volatile. There is currently a flurry of research and debate around the possibility of including risk management considerations in all management-related international standards.

The International Organization for Standardization is inviting experts to include risk management in all Standards as they become due for updating, such as ISO 9001:2015, *Quality management systems*.

Activity | Local frameworks

Although there is a comprehensive international standard, countries still have their own nationally applicable frameworks to provide guidance on issues specific to that country.

- What frameworks apply in your country?
- Where do they differ from the international standard and why?
- Why isn't the guidance provided in the national framework suitable for inclusion in the international Standard?

Summary

Please keep the following points from this chapter in mind:

- ISO/Guide 73:2009 – Risk management – Vocabulary defines a risk management framework as

  > *a set of components that provide the foundations and organizational arrangements for designing, implementing, monitoring, reviewing and continually improving risk management throughout the organisation.*

- The key aspect of this definition is the imperative to embed the risk management framework within the broader organisational strategy.
- The risk management framework within an organisation should encompass strategic, tactical and operational planning, decision-making and processes and practices for dealing with risk exposures.
- Two key risk management standards are:

  – Enterprise risk management – Integrating with Strategy and Performance (COSO)
  – ISO 31000:2018 Risk management – Guidelines (International Organization for Standardization).

- Material risk exposures are risks that could cause significant damage to an organisation.
- This modern risk management approach seeks to provide solutions by managing the effects of all material risk exposures in the context of the overall management of the organisation.

Chapter 4

Risk Management in the Organisation

Introduction

Risk management has a long history. It has its roots in the development of probability theory in the 17th century and has been continually developed since then.

A major component of early risk management was insurance, which would be purchased for any element of an organisation that was seen as susceptible to loss. This method identified risk and provided a means to compensate for the associated losses.

What this approach lacked was a means to prevent losses from occurring in the first place, and it wasn't until 1956 when Russell B Gallagher theorised that by controlling risk, organisations could control insurance costs and therefore increase profits. Since then, modern risk management techniques have been further developed, beyond North America and beyond insurable risk, to address optimising organisations' management through uncertain times.

Since the beginning of the 21st century, the development of ERM has meant dealing with strategic, tactical and operational issues and making sure that risks, both threats and opportunities, are taken into account at all levels of decision-making.

This chapter describes the historical foundations of risk management, how the profession has changed and developed over the years, how risks are managed in contemporary organisations and the models that are used. It details the three lines of defence model, which is an important tool for integrating, co-ordinating and aligning all support and assurance functions within an organisation.

Essentials and Assessment of Risk Management, 27–43

Published under exclusive licence by Emerald Publishing Limited
doi:10.1108/978-1-83662-302-120251009

Learning Outcomes

By the end of this chapter, you should be able to:

- describe the contemporary approach to risk management;
- explain why insurance as a risk management tool is no longer sufficient;
- encourage executive support for risk management within an organisation;
- develop a risk management policy;
- describe and implement the three lines of defence model.

The History of Risk Management

The status of risk management has grown over the years, giving way to changes in the way risk management functions are structured and the approaches that are used.

As little as 50 years ago, the term risk management was still relatively unknown, infrequently used in organisations and risk management itself was seen as an informal discipline.

Risk management has now evolved into a discipline that uses numbers and past information to assist in quantifying and predicting the future. Although risk management is a useful tool, it is not an exact science because the future can never be totally known and remains in part unpredictable.

Risk Management Versus Buying Insurance

Prior to the implementation of modern risk management practices, organisations were fairly unscientific in how they identified their risk exposures. This unscientific approach offered little more than reactive solutions by adopting what is now regarded as a traditional insurance-focused approach.

Organisations using this approach purchased insurance for insurable exposures, thereby sharing the organisation's potential losses with an insurance company for an agreed price (premium).

However, certain problems with the insurance-focused approach soon became obvious. It was realised that the proceeds from insurance did not cover all the costs a company might incur from a loss. In addition, insurance is not able to provide finance to offset the downside outcomes of all of an organisation's exposures to risk. Managers began to see that it was equally as important to prevent losses from occurring as it was to insure against them.

The beginnings of risk management lay firmly in game playing, gambling and, consequently, probability and statistics. The following is an outline of how the foundations of risk have developed since the seventeenth century, adapted from Peter Bernstein's book, *Against the Gods*.

Historical Foundations of Risk Management

1654: Theory of Probability

In 1654, a French nobleman named Chevalier de Méré challenged the mathematician Blaise Pascal to solve a puzzle related to a game of chance. The puzzle revolved around how to divide the stakes of an unfinished game of chance between two players when one of the players was leading the game. The outcome of this challenge led to the discovery of the *theory of probability* by Pascal and Fermat, which allowed people to make decisions and forecast the future by using numbers. Over the years, mathematicians and scientists advanced the probability theory, taking it from a gambling aid to a powerful instrument for analysing data. This theory remains as the mathematical core of the concept of risk as we know it today.

1700s: Law of Large Numbers

Over time, other quantitative techniques of risk management emerged. In 1713, the Swiss scientist and mathematician, Jacob Bernoulli, proved the *law of large numbers*. This law states that as the number of variables increases, their sample mean (the average of the numbers) approaches their theoretical mean, meaning essentially that the accuracy of predictions will improve as the amount of source data increases. This law is fundamental to insurance underwriting and methods of statistical sampling. Indeed, by 1725, mathematicians were devising tables of life expectancies and the English government was able to finance itself through the sale of life annuities.

1730: Law of Averages

In 1730, Abraham de Moivre developed the structure of normal distribution (now commonly known as the *bell curve* or Gauss distribution) and also discovered the concept of *standard deviation* to measure the dispersion. These two concepts form the *law of averages* and are fundamental to modern techniques for quantifying risk.

1750s: Bayesian Probability

The theories and laws that had been developed by the middle of the 18th century enabled marine insurance to emerge as a prosperous business.

In the 1750s, an English minister named Thomas Bayes advanced statistics and risk management further by demonstrating how decision-making could be improved by mathematically combining new information with old information (Bayesian networks).

1875: Regression to the Mean

In 1875, Francis Galton, a lay mathematician, discovered regression to the mean. This means that whenever someone makes any decision based on the expectation that things will return to normal, they are using the idea that things will actually regress to the mean (average).

1952: Diversification

Harry Markowitz, when a graduate student at the University of Chicago, demonstrated mathematically why it is unwise to 'put all your eggs in one basket' and that diversification is a necessary risk management strategy that should be employed.

1956: The Advent of Risk Management

The concept of risk management first appeared in an article written by Russell B Gallagher for the *Harvard Business Review*, in which Gallagher urged corporate insurance buyers to focus on the cost of dealing with the effects of exposure to risk rather than on getting the most insurance for their money.

Managers also began realising it was equally important (and cheaper) to prevent losses from occurring as it was to insure against them. They realised insurance was only one form of risk mitigation to be considered as part of systematic management of risk.

1995: AS/NZS 4360

In 1995, *AS/NZS 4360:1995 Risk Management* was developed. This was the first true risk management standard providing meaningful guidance on how to structure a risk management process. This standard was revised in 1999 and again in 2004 and at that stage it was decided that an international risk management standard should be developed. The International Organization for Standardization established a working group that used AS/NZS 4360:2004 as its first draft. The process for managing risk remains as was described in AS/NZS 4360:2004, but updates were made to the definition of risk, how the principles were explained, and the amount of guidance around how to implement and integrate risk management provided.

AS/NZS 4360 has now been superseded by ISO 31000:2018.

A Contemporary Approach

Risk management has evolved over the years, as the operational risk management structures of organisations as well as the approaches to risk management have changed. With the continued pressure on the bottom-line performance of organisations, risk management these days takes a proactive, holistic approach to risk exposures by seeking to manage the effects of all risk exposures. Management of risk has become a vital part of a fully integrated approach to organisational management and very important to organisational resilience. A resilient organisation is one that is able to recover from or adjust to a state of disturbance, including a crisis, or change. This is key to an organisation's survival.

The management of risk is now about managing exposures to risk through planning, organising, directing and controlling the resources or activities of individuals or organisations. This cannot be done without embedding risk management within the overall management system of an organisation.

While some organisations employ independent specialist risk management consultants, other organisations have a dedicated risk management structure within their operations. Whatever structure is adopted, the role and accountabilities of modern risk management operations are always to maximise any opportunities and reduce any threat of failing to meet organisational objectives.

Risk Management in the Organisation

For an organisation to successfully manage its risk exposures, it is necessary for the following key stakeholders to actively support, commit to and understand the part they play in the implementation of the risk management program:

- the board
- senior management
- operational management.

Implementing risk management begins with the board approving a mandate and committing to the implementation of a risk management policy.

It is vital for all levels of management to take ownership of all of the risks to which their particular division of the organisation is accountable.

The Board

Corporation boards representing the organisation's owners are responsible for the overall governance and risk management of the organisation. The actual management of risk is delegated to management but the board provides oversight and ensures that the process and its outputs are suitably rigorous.

Boards seek reassurance on risk through the following measures:

- management reporting and attestation
- internal and external auditing
- oversight by board subcommittees
- board interrogation of risk matters related to strategy, operations, projects and change management.

Depending on complexity and size, an organisation's board may establish a number of board committees to assist with the organisation's governance, including the management of risk. These subcommittees then advise and recommend actions, approvals and strategies to the board.

Typical board committees include:

- *Audit committees:* These oversee and monitor audit processes, including internal control activities.
- *Risk committees:* These focus on risk oversight, risk management and internal control.
- *Remuneration committees:* These advise the full board on pay issues, and recommend, monitor and review remuneration decisions.
- *Nomination committees:* These assist the full board with selection and appointment practices.
- *Human resources committees:* These support the development of human resource (HR) strategies, remuneration policies and ensure legal compliance.

Audit and risk committees are often combined into a single committee and given the role of providing assurance on a range of risk related controls.

Management of the risk management program is delegated from the board to the chief executive officer (CEO) or equivalent. Responsibility for managing the operational aspects of the risk management program is delegated to a risk manager, sometimes referred to as the chief risk officer (CRO). In larger organisations, it is typical for the CRO to have their own risk management department and to report directly to the CEO with separate reporting accountabilities to the board and board subcommittees.

Depending on the size of the organisation and the associated risk management department there may also be a hierarchy of risk managers at regional or business unit level.

CROs are not responsible for managing risk. Their responsibilities are to communicate, co-ordinate and administer policy for risk management, but the job of actually managing the risks falls to those that are in the best position to manage them – the risk owners; for example, managers and staff.

In their role of co-ordinating the organisation's ERM program, CROs must maintain strong relationships with key personnel within the organisation including executive management, department managers, and operations managers.

Example Risk Structure

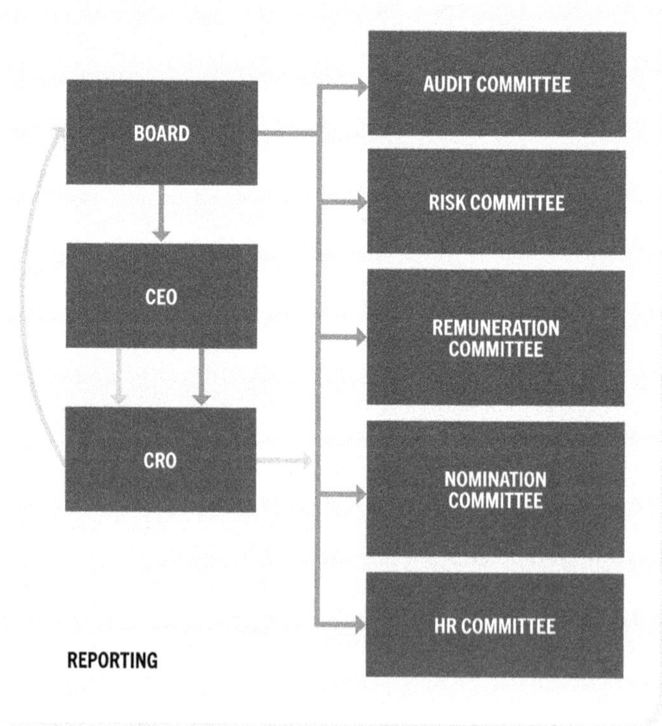

Ensuring the Support of Senior Management

To ensure the success of the risk management framework, it is critical from the outset that there is active and ongoing support for risk management from the organisation's directors and senior executives.

It is important to develop an organisational risk management philosophy that promotes awareness of risk and the impacts of exposure to risk at both a board and senior management level. For that reason, it is vital that all levels of management in the organisation take ownership of all the risks to which their particular parts of the organisation are exposed.

There are a number of ways that senior management support for the risk management framework can be demonstrated:

- development of the risk management policy for the organisation;
- communication with the organisation on risk matters;
- involvement in the risk management process for enterprise level risks;
- allocation of sufficient resources;
- establishment of a risk committee or a senior manager as the risk champion within the organisation;
- empowerment of staff to manage risks effectively;
- acknowledgement, reward and publicity of effective risk management.

Developing a Risk Management Policy

For risk management to be successful, it is critical that the organisation creates a well-drafted risk management policy.

An organisation's risk management policy should be a high-level document that provides guidance about managing risk by outlining the organisation's approach to risk management and situating the risk management program firmly within the management structures of the organisation.

Key issues that the risk management policy should address include:

- the purpose of the risk management program and its aims – the objectives, philosophy, culture and structure of the organisation should be clearly reflected in, and supported by, the risk management program;
- which risk exposures will be managed within which parts of the organisation;
- the organisation's tolerance or appetite for exposure to risks;
- clearly designated responsibility, accountability and authority for the overall risk management program and specific areas within it – including performance measurements and reporting processes and accountabilities;
- resources required to implement and maintain the risk management program – including people, talents, skills, information systems and financial resources;
- clear documentation of the risk management process and overall program;
- a plan for regular monitoring and review of the implementation and maintenance of the risk management program.

Implementing risk management is a difficult task and for it to be successful it is critical that a well-drafted policy is produced and that the implementation has the support, commitment and sponsorship of senior management.

When the risk management policy has been crafted, it should be communicated to all stakeholders to ensure everyone has the same information.

Activity | Risk management policy

Find out whether your organisation has a risk management policy.

If it does, read through the policy and determine whether the document covers the areas outlined above. Think about whether the policy could be improved to strengthen the organisation's approach to risk management.

Activity | AusNet Services' risk management policy

View a sound example of a risk management policy at the following hyperlink or follow the steps below: https://www.ausnetservices.com.au/-/media/Files/AusNet/About-Us/Corporate-Governance/Risk-Management-Policy-Statement.ashx?la=en

1. Navigate to www.ausnetservices.com.au.
2. Enter risk management policy into the **Search** field.
3. Click the Corporate Governance result.
4. Click Risk Management Policy under the **Risk Management** heading.

A Risk Management Champion

It is important that senior management appoints a risk champion among the senior leadership team or, if the size of the organisation warrants it, the risk committee.

A risk management framework that has a *figurehead* will have more chance of succeeding because there will be a committed individual (or committee) with sufficient standing driving the framework.

It is not enough that the organisation simply appoints an individual or a committee. This figurehead needs to be seen to be proactive in implementing and maintaining the framework, and needs to be in constant communication with all parts of the organisation and the wider stakeholder community on risk matters.

Other Initiatives

Other initiatives that may stimulate management support are including risk management responsibilities in executive job descriptions, and including risk management and compliance with the group risk policy as key performance indicators (KPIs) in the performance management system.

For example, the organisation could have KPIs requiring executives to:

- effectively manage and promptly report all material foreseeable risks;
- manage the business according to its stated risk appetite.

The Three Lines of Defence Model

It can be difficult for the governing bodies of organisations to get a clear opinion on risk management functions and avoid work and cost overloads. An accumulation of separate functions can lead to the risk of thinking in silos and poor integration of the various roles.

There might also be redundancies between various functions, for example, teams from different areas (e.g. risk management, quality and internal audit) may visit the same unit at the same time. There could also be gaps and blind spots: activities or units not assessed by anybody.

A lesson learned from the financial crisis is the need for a cohesive, co-ordinated approach to risk. Limited risk and control resources may not be deployed effectively and significant risks may not be identified or managed appropriately if efforts are not coordinated.

Accordingly, FERMA endorses the three lines of defence model as an important tool for integrating, co-ordinating and aligning all support and assurance functions (internal audit, control, compliance, quality, safety, security, etc.) within an organisation.

The below outlines the basic structure of the model, but companies may organise the various lines differently depending on the maturity, resources and staffing of the second and third lines.

The three lines of defence are:

1. **Operations and business units that design and enforce risk management controls**
   The line managers have ownership, responsibility and accountability for assessing, controlling and mitigating risks. They design the risk controls that the second line implements.

2. **Internal governance groups that monitor risk management controls**
   Internal governance functions, such as group support and control functions, monitor and facilitate the implementation of effective risk management practices as determined by the first line and assist risk owners in reporting adequate risk-related information throughout the organisation.

3. **Independent audits that assess risk management controls**
   Independent audits (internal and external) provide assurance to the governing body and senior management about the organisation's effectiveness in assessing and managing its risks and related internal control systems, including the manner in which the first and second lines operate.

The First Line of Defence

As previously discussed, risk management departments or full-time managers are responsible for ensuring the organisation executes the risk management framework and providing effective risk management outcomes for the organisation. However, they are not responsible for the day-to-day management of risks.

Responsibility for the management of each risk rests with designated risk owners. Risk owners are the staff members formally assigned to manage each risk on a daily basis. They should be organisational stakeholders (most often line managers) with a corporate or legal liability for their decisions. Because of their position on the front-line of risk, risk owners are the most important source of information regarding risk in an organisation.

Risk owners need to:

- regularly review assigned risks to ensure the risk treatment plan is still applicable;
- identify current control deficiencies;
- ensure risk information is updated as required;
- escalate the risk when the risk is increasing in likelihood or consequence to senior managers with greater knowledge and/or authority (in extreme cases, the CEO and/or board may need to be informed);
- provide information about the risk when required, often in the form of regular reports that summarise the information for the CEO and senior managers.

The risk owner may delegate tasks associated with the risk treatment plans in the case of complex risks if they can ensure these tasks are performed properly and on a timely basis.

As listed in the following table, specific employees may be responsible for providing advice to managers on specialised risk exposures.

Specific Role	Specialised Risk Exposure Advice to Line Managers
HR manager	• Staff morale
	• Welfare
	• Retention
Security manager	• Personal safety
	• Loss prevention
IT manager	• IT disaster recovery
	• Data security

The Second Line of Defence

The second line of defence involves monitoring and facilitating the effective implementation of the risk management practices determined by the first line.

The organisation's support functions, including risk management, financial control, compliance, business continuity, quality, security and legal, are responsible for this.

Each function operates within the scope of its specific mission with its own tools and processes and assists risk owners to report risk information to the organisation using regular reports and, when appropriate, the risk register.

The Third Line of Defence

The mission of the third line is to enhance and protect organisational value by taking risk into account and by providing stakeholders with objective and independent assurance, advice and insight. As both the second line and the third line may report to the board, it is important that upper management clearly defines the role and scope of each line. This information should be kept in the risk register and be clear enough so that the differences in responsibilities can be understood throughout the business.

Organisations may employ risk management specialists to coordinate or facilitate the risk management plan. Organisations often employ external risk management specialists to:

- assist with the risk management process;
- undertake a cost-benefit analysis.

Risk management specialists undertake a variety of tasks, including those listed in the following table.

Area	Tasks
WHS activities	• Ergonomic review and recommendation • Analysis of public safety • Safety audits • Environmental audits • Works system management • Safety training • Construction risk review • Hazardous substance review
Property loss control activities	• Property loss control programs • Motor vehicle risk analysis • Security system review • Fire protection design and review • Property regulatory review • Construction risk review

(*Continued*)

(Continued)

Area	Tasks
Business analysis	• Credit analysis and review • Market analysis • Risk exposure analysis • Strategic planning
Business continuity (disruption-related risk)	• Business impact analysis • Crisis/emergency management planning • Business continuity planning • Disaster recovery planning
Legal	• Compliance programs • Legal opinion • Contract drafting and review
Audit	• Fraud prevention • Governance and assurance programs • Effectiveness of risk treatment programs
General risk management activities	• Major event management • IT security • Self-assessment programs • Corporate reporting • Risk manuals and procedures • Major projects/project management • Engineering standards

Activity | Risk management specialists

1. List the different types of risk management specialists your organisation employs/has employed.
2. Outline the tasks the risk management specialists undertake/undertook.
3. Categorise these tasks as being able to be undertaken by either:
   - o Internal staff
   - o External staff.
4. Consider whether your organisation needs to extend its specialist base. If so, in what areas?
5. Document the value of the skills the identified specialists will bring to your organisation.

External specialists	Value provided

Internal specialists	Value provided

Benefits and Limitations of the Three of Lines of Defence Model

The three lines of defence model involve a first line, the operational function that owns and manages the risk, a second line in charge of the risk management function and compliance monitoring (including risk management, financial control, compliance, inspection, business continuity, quality, security and legal) and a third line that provides independent assurance that all significant risks are identified, quantified and managed.

The CEO and the executive team are ultimately responsible for the management of risks and internal controls and they are held accountable for this by the board, which approves the overall risk appetite and the philosophy of risk taking. Regular meetings between the CRO, the chief compliance officer and the chief audit executive are essential to ensure that all assurance functions are well co-ordinated and consistent across the organisation. At the end of the day, the success of the model is dependent on a well-managed first line.

The three lines of defence model have been an essential component of many organisations' risk management efforts and strategies since the late 1990s. However, this model is now being challenged as it is defensive, and its main aim is to keep an organisation out of trouble. However, the speed with which the environment is changing requires swift and decisive action on the part of all decision-making risk owners. Confronted with the technological revolution, customer empowerment and lower barriers to entry for potential competition, or substitution, organisations can no longer hope to survive only by defending themselves. A more proactive approach, involving embedding risk management at all levels of decision-making – strategic, tactic, and operational – is needed. This is the aim of ERM in general.

It is possible to implement the three lines of defence in a more proactive way, by using predictive analysis and a multi-risk approach to verify risk interactions. This makes risk management more relevant to the executive team and contributes to value creation for shareholders. This new approach to the model is essential in supporting organisations to increase their resilience and enable them to face the challenges of the new complex and rapidly changing business environment.

Developing a Risk Aware Culture

A risk-aware culture is one in which there is a mutual understanding of risk. This means that every person within an organisation, from the employees to the board members, has shared values, beliefs, knowledge and attitudes about risk.

Such a culture can be developed by:

- determining the organisation's risks;
- clearly describing risk management practices;
- defining roles and responsibilities;
- encouraging all staff members to identify and report risk.

The three lines of defence model supports the development of a risk aware culture as it is a framework that includes all disciplines, uses common language and definitions and provides a clear understanding of the roles and responsibilities of employees.

Organisations with an effective three lines of defence model in place are likely to also have a risk aware culture; however, this is not guaranteed. No matter which risk management model an organisation employs, the organisation should ensure a focus on clarity and reward to fully support a positive risk culture.

Activity | A sound risk culture

Read more about risk aware cultures on page 6 of IRM's 'Risk culture: Under the microscope Guidance for Boards' at www.theirm.orglre-sourceslfind-a-resourcelrisk-culture-under-the-microscope-guidance-for-boards

How does IRM's description of a good risk culture intersect with the three lines of defence model? Think about the risk culture at your organisation.

- What sort of risk culture do you think there is?
- Do you see any ways to improve the culture based on this document?

Case Study – GPG's Risk Management Program

GPG is a 50-year-old government-owned medium-size business that prints a range of quality materials on behalf of government organisations including:

- annual reports
- marketing materials
- information fliers
- newsletters.

The current risk management program

The organisation has just appointed Mike Trigg as a new independent director. During Mike's first board meeting, he inquires about how GPG is managing the risks to which it is exposed.

One of the senior managers, Sarah Refergo, explains that GPG has an extensive insurance program so the company is effectively managing all the risks to which it is currently exposed.

Mike becomes concerned that this narrow insurance-based approach will not be able to address all of GPG's risk exposures. In particular, Mike refers to how GPG's enviable reputation for quality outcomes is being damaged by some recent unfortunate events, including:

- printing errors in annual reports;
- the late delivery of materials for a key government public awareness campaign.

These issues have created considerable concern among their key customer base, which includes a variety of departments and agencies.

Mike believes that GPG needs a more comprehensive approach to managing risks.

Convincing the board

Following extensive discussions with board members, Mike manages to convince the board that buying insurance cover is insufficient protection from all risks (for example, quality and timeline issues). The board approves developing and implementing a risk management program on the basis of Mike's argument that a more comprehensive view of risk at GPG is critical.

Implementation

The organisation delegates to GPG's finance manager, Marjorie Crawford, the responsibility of assisting the organisation's management team to implement an enterprise-wide risk management process.

Self-Help Question 4.1

What should Marjorie Crawford determine before establishing the risk management context step for GPG?

Answers to self-help questions are provided at the end of each section.

Summary

Please keep the following points from this chapter in mind:

- Early risk management techniques focused on purchasing insurance or managing specific high-risk areas; for example, workplace health and safety (WHS).
- Risk management has evolved over the years as the operational risk management structures of organisations as well as the approaches to risk management have changed.
- Risk management is now about managing exposures through planning, organising, directing and controlling the resources of organisations.
- Embedding risk management within the overall management system of an organisation is essential.
- Active and ongoing support for risk management from an organisation's directors and senior executives will ensure success.
- To align the vision and objectives with the organisation's overall strategic vision, mission and objectives, the organisation needs to develop and communicate a risk management policy.
- The risk management policy is a simple statement of the organisation's risk management intent and commitment.
- The three lines of defence model is an important tool for integrating, co-ordinating and aligning all support and assurance functions within an organisation.
- The three lines of defence model consists of a first line, the operational function that owns and manages the risk, a second line in charge of the risk management function and compliance monitoring and a third line that independently ensures that all significant risks are identified, quantified and managed.
- The success of the three lines of defence model depends on a well-managed first line.

Answers to Self-Help Questions

Self-help question 4.1

Before establishing the risk management context, Marjorie should:

- obtain the management team's support;
- establish the risk management framework for the organisation;
- examine existing risk management besides the company's insurance program;
- set up a communication process with all relevant stakeholders;
- establish how GPG will document the risk management process.

Chapter 5

Organisation Strategy, Objectives, Responsibilities, Structure and Programme

Introduction

The risk management framework is the overarching structure of risk management within an organisation. It should be specific to an organisation's size, activities, risk exposure and risk appetite and should outline the organisation's reporting structure, risk managers, risk owners and the requirement for all staff to be involved in risk management.

This chapter describes the various activities that are involved in organisational risk management and the different personnel who are responsible for each. It also describes the steps involved in establishing a risk management framework. The importance of monitoring risk management and formally reviewing the processes at regular, specified intervals is explored.

Learning Outcomes

By the end of this chapter, you should be able to:

- describe different risk management responsibilities;
- differentiate between the risk management policy and the risk management plan;
- develop a risk management framework;
- document a risk management framework;
- implement a risk management framework.

Risk Management Responsibilities

In general, directors and senior management are responsible for managing the broader risks to which the organisation is exposed, and departmental personnel are responsible for managing the risk exposures within their areas of control.

Essentials and Assessment of Risk Management, 45–62

Published under exclusive licence by Emerald Publishing Limited
doi:10.1108/978-1-83662-302-120251011

Persons Responsible and Accountable

Establishing responsibilities, accountability and authority for risk management entail specifying those persons who are responsible and accountable for the following tasks:

- management of the risk management framework at the strategic level;
- management of the risk management framework within functional areas;
- management of particular risk exposures;
- implementation of specific risk treatment strategies;
- maintenance of risk controls within the organisation.

It is also important to establish performance measures and reporting processes for the specific areas of the risk management framework.

In addition, it is vital to the effectiveness of the risk management framework within any organisation that any person, who is responsible for any part of the risk management framework, be provided with the necessary authority to undertake those responsibilities.

Appointing Risk Co-ordinators

One of the most pivotal roles within the risk management framework both at the organisational level and within functional areas is that of risk co-ordinator.

The responsibilities of a risk co-ordinator include:

- providing risk management advice to managers and staff at all levels when required;
- assisting with facilitating risk identification workshops when requested;
- co-ordinating the analysis and evaluation of identified risks in conjunction with the managers;
- assisting managers to implement the identified risk treatments;
- ensuring that identified risks are documented in the risk register.

Appropriate risk co-ordinators need to be identified as early as possible and, where possible, receive intense training prior to commencing their duties.

In many organisations, risk co-ordination is seen as a secondary duty and is therefore assigned to junior staff members. However, better results are achieved when skilled and experienced personnel are appointed.

A risk co-ordinator should be someone who has:

- extensive knowledge in the fundamentals of risk management including how to customise and apply the process in different contexts;
- enthusiasm for the management of risk;
- the ability to communicate with employees in relation to risk;
- the ability to provide sound advice and, where required, facilitate the risk management activities of the functional areas within the organisation.

The importance of risk co-ordinators throughout the implementation and ongoing maintenance and review stages cannot be overstated.

Where Risk Management Responsibilities Will Be Detailed

The two major avenues for communicating the risk management roles and responsibilities within an organisation are the:

1. risk management policy
2. risk management plan.

The Risk Management Policy. As previously explored, the risk management policy describes the broad responsibilities of those with a management and oversight role within the risk management framework.

The Risk Management Plan. A risk management manual or plan (described for the remainder of this section as the risk management plan) defines exactly how risk management activities will be undertaken, not only for those with a management and oversight role, but also for those with an operational role.

It is of little consequence that the organisation has developed a policy that provides guidance on what is to be done and why this policy is not supported by a document that details how it is to be done. This is the key difference between the policy and the plan.

The aim of the risk management plan is to entrench risk management within the organisation's existing business practices, procedures, systems and policies (at both management and operational levels). This will ensure that risk management has the best chance of succeeding within the organisation and that it is capable of being sustained.

The plan generally encompasses elements of the organisation's:

- risk management policy;
- context established for risk management;
- scope and objectives of risk management activities;
- functions of risk management within the organisation;
- person/s responsible for implementing the functions and activities.

Although there is no set format for risk management plans and each organisation will be different, the following are some of the issues that should be addressed in the plan:

- benefits of risk management to the organisation;
- risk management organisation;
- risk management key performance indicators;
- risk management roles and responsibilities;

- risk reporting requirements;
- risk criteria for the organisation;
- risk management funding arrangements;
- application of the risk management process to the organisation.

It should be noted that, for larger organisations that undertake a diverse and complex range of activities, risk management plans may also need to be developed at lower levels within the organisation.

EXAMPLE

GPG's Risk Management Plan

The following are examples of risk management roles and responsibilities that may be found in an organisation's risk management plan.

Board of directors

The board of directors for GPG, while not having an active role in the management of individual risks, does have an important role to play in the risk management framework. Some of the responsibilities of the board include:

- approving the risk management policy;
- overseeing the establishment and implementation of the risk management framework;
- reviewing the effectiveness of the framework on a regular basis.

Risk management committee

Overall management oversight of the risk management framework within GPG is the responsibility of the risk management committee. Specifically, the risk management committee is responsible for:

- continually reviewing the robustness of GPG's risk management framework to ensure that risks are being adequately identified, assessed, managed and retired;
- identifying, analysing and treating enterprise-level risks;
- ensuring that the level and extent of consultation with external stakeholders on risk matters is appropriate;
- ensuring that the risk management framework is resourced appropriately;
- continually reviewing the effectiveness of the risk management organisation within GPG;
- ensuring that the risk management reporting regime provides an effective overview of the significant risk exposures to GPG and an understanding of the measures that are being taken to mitigate the identified risks.

General manager

The general manager or CEO has a significant role to play in providing the leadership necessary for the risk management framework within GPG to flourish. The specific responsibilities of the general manager include:

- chairing of the risk management committee;
- providing regular reports to the board on matters arising from risk management committee meetings;
- providing guidance to the divisional heads through the development of GPG's risk management policy.

Divisional heads

Divisional heads have an important role in ensuring that the management of risk within their divisions is afforded the appropriate priority in line with the expectations detailed in the risk management plan. The specific roles and responsibilities for each of the divisional heads include:

- ensuring that the risk management processes documented in the risk management plan are adhered to;
- ensuring that managers within their division are effectively managing risk within their areas of responsibility;
- reviewing risk assessments made by functional areas within their division, including the risk treatments;
- ensuring that functional areas within their division are conducting regular risk reviews;
- ensuring that all risks are maintained in a risk register and that they are updated after each risk review;
- monitoring the risk treatments to ensure they are completed in accordance with the timeframes specified;
- ensuring that risks that are outside of the responsibility/capability of the division are escalated to the risk management committee;
- completing the monthly risk report for presentation to the risk management committee.

GPG's risk co-ordinator

The emergency management officer for GPG is the nominated **risk co-ordinator**. The risk co-ordinator's primary responsibility is the day-to-day co-ordination of the risk management framework for GPG on behalf of the general manager.

The specific responsibilities of GPG's risk co-ordinator are as follows:

- acting as secretary to the risk management committee;
- providing risk management advice to managers and staff at all levels when required;

- promoting the acceptance of risk management techniques;
- assisting with the facilitation of risk identification workshops when requested;
- co-ordinating the analysis and evaluation of identified risks with GPG's managers;
- providing assistance to managers in the implementation of identified risk treatments;
- ensuring that identified risks are documented in the risk register.

Where possible, the risk co-ordinator should not be involved in the management of individual risks.

Risk owners

The risk owner is the person assigned the responsibility for the day-to-day management of a risk or set of risks. The risk owner is chosen based on their role within the functional area, and their ability to competently analyse and treat risks. Risk owners are responsible for the following:

- ensuring that each risk assigned to them is handled in accordance with the risk management process defined in GPG's risk management plan;
- ensuring treatment actions are completed in a timely manner;
- ensuring all reporting requirements are met;
- ensuring any indication that the risk has, or is about to, eventuate is reported immediately.

Other staff

All GPG staff are responsible for identifying risks within their functional area. If a risk is identified, in the first instance, staff are to report it to their functional manager. Those risks that are assessed as *extreme* or *high* are to be reported to the divisional head as appropriate.

Elements of a Risk Management Framework

There is no one size fits all approach to the introduction of a risk management framework. Every organisation will differ depending on its size, its activities and its appetite for risk.

From the frameworks detailed, a group of elements has been developed. Not all of these elements will be appropriate to every organisation. However, by analysing them all, organisations will have the ability to develop and implement a framework that suits their particular environment.

These elements can be refined further, and broken into three distinct categories.

1. Developing the framework

Developing the framework is concerned with the supporting elements that ensure the framework will be appropriately established. It sets the pre-conditions for the documentation and implementation of the framework.

The activities include:

- ensuring the support of senior management from the outset;
- integrating risk management into strategic and business planning;
- reviewing the current risk management systems (if any exist);
- determining how risk exposures will be managed at each level of the organisation;
- communicating risk matters with relevant stakeholders;
- establishing responsibilities, accountability and authority;
- customising the risk management process for the organisation;
- providing training to staff;
- resourcing risk management within the organisation;
- establishing how the risk management framework will be monitored and reviewed;
- establishing how risk management will be reported within the organisation.

2. Documenting the framework

Documenting the risk management framework, within an organisation, is a vital enabler in ensuring its effectiveness. Without documentation to strengthen the development of the framework, there will be a lack of:

- understanding within the organisation as to what the risk management framework is to achieve;
- consistency in the approach to risk management across the organisation;
- ability for decisions made within the organisation to be justified on the basis of risk management;
- understanding of the key risks facing the organisation;
- visibility of the treatments developed to mitigate the identified risks within the organisation;
- understanding of the risk exposure of the organisation;
- ability within the organisation to communicate to its external stakeholder community in relation to the management of risk.

Documenting the risk management framework will include developing some or all of the following documents:

- developing the organisation's risk management policy;
- developing and establishing organisational-level risk management plans;
- capturing risks in a risk register;
- developing risk treatment plans;

- capturing performance data on the risk management framework in monitoring, review and audit documentation;
- developing cost of risk documentation;
- developing an incident database.

3. Planning and implementing the framework

The implementation of a risk management framework into an organisation will involve two phases:

- an initial phase where the implementation plan is developed and board and senior management support is generated;
- an ongoing phase by which the framework is embedded throughout the organisation and maintained through monitoring and reviewing risks, controls and changes to the internal and external environments.

It needs to be realised, that the goal of implementing a risk management framework is not only to embed the individual physical elements of the framework into the organisation (change), but also to enable the transition of the organisation. This involves far more than the documented aspects of the framework. It involves moving the organisation:

- from risk naïve to risk aware;
- from reactive to proactive;
- towards a different mindset/paradigm.

Developing and implementing the elements of the risk management framework will no doubt change the organisation, but for the change to be long lasting, this transition also needs to occur–and that takes significantly more effort.

The Implementation Plan

The initial phase of implementation involves the development of an implementation plan. The breadth and depth of the plan depends on:

- the size of the organisation;
- the extent of the framework elements to be implemented;
- the current level of risk management within the organisation (e.g. whether this framework simply formalising much of what already exists in the organisation);
- the time over which the implementation is to occur;
- the resources available.

Someone within the organisation needs to be assigned responsibility for the development of the plan and for the implementation activity itself.

Implementation Plan Contents

A suggested format for an implementation plan is shown below:

Part		Information contained
1	**General information/introduction**	
1.1	Overview	This part of the implementation plan contains: introduction to the risk management framework within the organisation purpose of the plan objectives of the risk management framework ownership of the plan within the organisation.
2	**Implementation overview**	
2.1	Implementation objectives	Lists the specific objectives of the implementation, which differ from the objectives of the framework.
2.2	Assumptions	Details any assumptions that have been made in preparing the implementation plan.
2.3	Expected outcomes	Details the end state of the implementation plan.
2.4	Risks to success	Details the risks that have been identified as integral to the success of the implementation of the framework.
3	**Responsibilities and organisation**	
3.1	Responsibilities	Outlines all of the responsibilities for implementation of the framework.
3.2	Organisation	Details the organisational structure in relation to implementation.
4	**Implementation approach**	
4.1	Common risk management methods and tools	Details the identification and assessment/analysis methods that are to be used when implementing the framework.
4.2	Pilot frameworks	Details any pilot frameworks that may take place as part of the implementation, such as proof of concept frameworks for introducing a commercially available risk register.
4.3	Integration with existing processes	Details how the framework will integrate with current processes, such as the strategic planning process.

(*Continued*)

(Continued)

Part		Information contained
5	**Implementation work plan**	
5.1	Summary of activities	Details all of the activities that are to take place as part of the implementation.
5.2	Timelines and milestones	Details when all the activities are to be completed and the milestones along the way.
5.3	Key performance indicators	Details how the success of the implementation will be measured.
6	**Communications strategy**	
6.1	Communications objectives	Details the communications objectives related to the implementation. Provides an overview of the objectives for both internal and external communication.
6.2	Target audience	Identifies the target audience for the communications related to the implementation of the framework.
6.3	Key messages	Details the key messages to be communicated to the target audience in regard to the implementation. Key messages may include: that the implementation will reap significant benefits from a corporate perspective that implementing the framework will better equip all functional areas to meet or exceed their objectives that the framework is not onerous and that being more proactive will provide time savings for all that the organisation will help transition staff to a fully developed risk management culture through extensive training, mentoring and coaching support.

Communicating the Implementation Plan

The implementation plan needs to be endorsed by the CEO and/or the board of the organisation. After the plan has been endorsed, it needs to be enacted. As implementation often involves change, the plan is best communicated through a series of information sessions.

Information sessions should begin with functional managers. Functional managers manage the processes of functional areas (or silos) within organisations. They may not necessarily directly manage people but they will implement the framework throughout the organisation. If they do not agree with the plan or the framework, they may become barriers to successful implementation.

Functional managers, therefore, should be consulted from the outset on the understanding that changes can be made before the framework is fully implemented. Briefing the functional managers serves as a trial of the implementation plan and the framework itself. If problems arise, the implementation plan may need further refinement.

If the plan and/or the framework cannot be changed in line with functional managers' expectations, they should be told why this is the case. Additionally, what is expected of them in terms of supporting the implementation plan should be discussed.

Once the functional managers have been briefed, and have demonstrated that they can follow the plan, the plan can be implemented throughout the organisation.

It is important that when any part of the organisation is being briefed their functional manager is present and openly voices their support for the framework and its implementation. If staff see any hesitation on the part of functional managers, the framework could be in jeopardy from the start.

One of the most important aspects that needs to be stressed when briefing any group is **what's in it for them** (WIIFT). If staff can appreciate how they will benefit, both professionally and personally, from the implementation of a risk management framework, it will have a much greater chance of success.

Activities During the Implementation Phase

Implementation generally includes the following activities:

- reviewing the current risk management systems (if any exist);
- determining how risk exposures will be managed at each level of the organisation;
- communicating risk matters with relevant stakeholders;
- establishing responsibilities, accountability and authority;
- customising the risk management process for the organisation;
- providing training to staff;
- establishing the risk management framework monitor and review mechanisms;
- establishing the risk management reporting guidelines;
- developing the organisation's risk management policy;
- developing and establishing organisational-level risk management plans;
- setting up the organisation's risk register;
- developing an incident database.

It is not possible to implement all of these activities at the same time. The implementation plan therefore needs to provide a realistic schedule as to the introduction of the elements of the framework.

Organisations should be aware that change involves significant uncertainty and difficulty. Those driving change therefore need to plan for potential difficulties and challenges.

Change should be seen as a journey towards a goal with the potential for many wrong turns and missed opportunities. No matter how much thought has gone into the change effort, there will be unforeseen external uncontrollable forces that will have a profound impact on the success of the change effort.

Activity | Risk management framework

Identify whether your organisation has a risk management framework.

If it does, identify whether it incorporates the elements detailed in this section.

Self-Help Question 5.1

From your reading of this section, discuss how you see risk management contributing to:

1. compliance
2. internal audit
3. assurance
4. corporate governance.

Answers to self-help questions are provided at the end of each section.

Monitoring

Section 3.8.2.1 of ISO/Guide 73:2009 Risk management – Vocabulary defines **monitoring** as:

> continual checking, supervising, critically observing or determining the status in order to identify change from the performance level required or expected.

Note: Monitoring can be applied to a risk management framework, risk management process, risk or control.

The above definition makes it clear that monitoring the risk management process should be done regularly at each step of the process. Monitoring includes supervising all activities in the risk management process and looking at individual exposures to risk to ensure changing circumstances do not alter the parameters that were used to develop the risk strategies and priorities.

Monitoring also involves constant upkeep and management of risk information, and should:

- record any changes in risk profiles;
- identify risk treatment measures and strategies;
- track progress and completion of risk control actions;
- allow progress against the risk management plan to be measured;
- allocate and track accountability for risk exposures, treatment measures and control actions;
- trigger monitoring and assurance activities;
- provide a way to measure and report on risk management activity and progress generally.

Changes that occur to organisations and the environments in which they operate may affect risk exposure profiles, and treatment and financing programs. Continual monitoring and review enable organisations to fine-tune and alter their risk management programs so as to achieve the best possible outcomes.

For example, if an organisation starts selling its products to new overseas markets, then it is likely that the risks that the company is exposed to will change. There needs to be a monitoring process in place to ensure that the risk management program accounts for such changes.

Therefore, it is important to consider the why, what, who, when and how of monitoring:

- Why do organisations need to monitor?
- Who does the monitoring?
- What should be monitored?
- How should the monitoring be conducted?
- When should the monitoring be done?

Why Monitor?

The most common reasons for monitoring are:

- **Meeting performance targets** – risk management processes should have performance targets and these targets need to be set with the organisation's objectives, its current exposures to risk and its claims history in mind.
- **Allocating funds** – there are considerable costs associated with risk exposures and programs that manage those exposures. Monitoring provides ongoing information to enable such costs to be properly allocated, to justify the basis for allocating these costs, and to prove the benefits of the risk management program.
- **Statutory reporting** – monitoring can provide statistics and data that may be required to satisfy statutory obligations; for example, workers' compensation reporting requirements and environmental legislation.

- **Identifying new/changed exposures** – exposures often change in the course of business and new exposures constantly arise. For example, an organisation may decide to outsource the operation and maintenance of its motor vehicle fleet, thereby changing the nature and extent of its motor vehicle risk exposures, or it may decide to go into a new market, thereby changing its market risk exposures. All new and changed risk exposures need to be promptly identified and reported on.
- **Defending the risk management program** – if risk management practices are questioned, particularly in regard to exercising duty of care, contractual obligations and legislative responsibilities, monitoring and review can provide information to defend an organisation's actions.
- **Performance review** – the performance of the risk management process needs to be constantly monitored and regularly reviewed.

Who Does the Monitoring?

Risk management is the responsibility of every employee in an organisation, with the only difference being the scope, breadth or accountability assigned to specific persons. However, the risk owners, who have clear accountability, authority and resources for managing risk exposures, should both monitor and report on key exposures as outlined above. Responsibilities were outlined in detail at the start of this section.

What Should Be Monitored?

Each activity in the risk management process needs to be monitored, especially changes to context; that is, changes to things like:

- organisational objectives
- operating environments
- legislative changes
- business plans
- stakeholders.

New and emerging risks should also be monitored in terms of context to ensure that existing risks remain relevant. Generally, the focuses of the monitoring process are people, products and activities, such as:

- new activities and changes in operating structure;
- staff changes/training;
- customer/product reports;
- work accidents and incidents involving injury to people;
- property and business interruption exposures – for example, purchase and sale of assets, aggregation risks;

- machinery breakdowns – for example, a record of the number of times mechanical breakdowns occur on specified pieces of machinery;
- incidents and near misses;
- security breach incidents;
- motor vehicle costs – the costs of motor vehicle accidents versus the cost of insurance is often monitored and considered. Motor vehicle insurance is typically one of the first risk exposures that an organisation self-insures.

How Is Monitoring Conducted?

A risk management program needs both formal and informal monitoring and review processes. Formal monitoring involves establishing reporting systems such as monthly or quarterly claims reports associated with insurable risks. Informal monitoring can include discussions with staff, reading reports, inspecting the site and making general enquiries.

Some examples of formalised monitoring systems for hazard-type risks are:

- claims databases/registers
- property loss reports
- motor vehicle accident reports
- workplace health and safety reports
- operating licence renewals.

Recording the cause, time, place and amount of losses as well as other information that may be used for analysing any unexpected events/losses should be a fundamental part of any monitoring system.

Most of the above monitoring systems involve an actual event or loss and some can be (and often are) budgeted for by the organisation. They can be measured and planned for, and the results for a period can be compared to the previous time periods.

Examples of informal monitoring systems are:

- log analysis – some businesses typically compile logs in areas such as security, visitors, breakdowns and phone calls;
- staff meetings where incidents are raised and discussed;
- customer complaints.

When Should the Monitoring Be Done?

Informal monitoring occurs on a daily basis and formal monitoring programs are generally dictated by the organisation's structure, activities and markets.

Risk exposures are continually changing and therefore the risk management process needs to be applied on an ongoing basis to ensure optimum results are obtained.

Reviewing

In addition to ongoing monitoring, regular formal reviews of risk management processes should be conducted to assess and document:

- the effectiveness of the risk treatment plan, strategies and management system;
- the effectiveness of and adherence to risk treatment measures;
- the relevance of the risk management plan to the organisation's objectives;
- factors that may affect the likelihood and consequences of a risk exposure;
- factors that affect the suitability or cost of particular treatment options;
- board and management commitment to the risk management process.

Mechanisms need to be developed and implemented to ensure that regular reviews take place. The board and management of an organisation should take responsibility for making sure that a formal review of the organisation's risk management system, in accordance with the organisation's risk management plan, is carried out at regular intervals.

When reviewing risk management activities, it is essential that:

- the decisions made and the actions taken are checked to ensure that they are logical and effective;
- the actions taken (including any measures implemented) are working as expected and bringing about the desired results;
- remedial action is taken to address the decisions or actions that are not working or not having the desired effect – this remedial action should correct the situation.

To review the management of risk, it is important to record details of:

- how often individual risk exposures and the risk management program will be reviewed;
- the outcomes of the review and any other monitoring procedures;
- how review recommendations will be actioned.

Review Questions

The review should ask the following questions:

- Are the risk management objectives aligned with the organisational performance objectives and values?
- Do the risk management initiatives reflect the realities of the environment in which the organisation in question operates?
- Can the outcomes of risk management be effectively measured?
- Do the risk management initiatives generate value for the organisation?

- Does the information provided allow senior management to make decisions about whether to expand or contract resources and effort in managing risk exposures?
- Is clear and concise information provided for evaluation by management and the board?

Summary

Please keep the following points from this chapter in mind:

- There is no one size fits all approach to the introduction of a risk management framework.
- All staff are responsible for identifying risks within their functional areas and reporting them to their functional managers.
- The risk owner is the person assigned the responsibility for the day-to-day management of risk.
- For risk management to be successful and add value there must be the board/ senior management team's mandate and commitment.
- The three categories for a risk management framework are:
  - developing the framework
  - documenting the framework
  - planning and implementing the framework.
- Monitoring the risk management process should be done regularly at each step of the process.
- In addition to ongoing monitoring, regular formal reviews of risk management processes should be conducted.

Answers to Self-Help Questions

Self-help question 5.1

1. Compliance

Risk management contributes to compliance in that compliance is an activity like any other activity undertaken within the organisation.

To that end:

- there will be objectives associated with the compliance program;
- within the compliance program there will be a number of activities required to achieve the objectives of the program;
- each of these activities within the compliance program will have potential risks.

→

→

It is therefore extremely important that the risk management framework applies to the activities involved in the compliance program.

This is even more vital considering the potential impact of non-compliance.

2. Internal audit

Internal audits are implemented, in most organisations, to ensure that emerging problems are detected before they develop into full blown issues.

Risk management complements the internal audit program as it identifies those programs, activities or processes that represent the greatest risk to the organisation's objectives. In doing so, the internal audit program can be developed to account for this level of risk.

3. Assurance

Risk management contributes to organisational assurance programs in that:

- there will be objectives associated with each assurance program;
- within each assurance program there will be a number of activities required to achieve the objectives of the program;
- each of these activities will have potential risks.

It is therefore extremely important that the risk management framework applies to the activities involved in each of the assurance programs.

4. Corporate governance

Risk management contributes to good corporate governance by providing reasonable assurance to boards and senior managers that the organisational objectives will be achieved within a tolerable degree of residual risk.

In its focus on positive outcomes, risk management provides a major contribution to those aspects of corporate governance directed to enhancing organisational performance.

Chapter 6

Strategic Risk Management

Introduction

This section describes the importance of strategic management in helping to steer the organisation along a path of growth and success. The section explains:

- the importance of strategic planning in achieving effective management;
- the role of risk management at the strategic level;
- how to integrate risk management within the strategic planning and management processes.

Learning Outcomes

By the end of this chapter, you should be able to:

- state the drivers behind strategic management;
- define risk appetite;
- define risk tolerance;
- write a risk appetite statement;
- define creeping and emerging risks;
- define strategic planning;
- define the corporate risk profile;
- recall some typical risk categories;
- describe the risk accountability framework;
- define the reporting framework;
- recall some of the factors influencing an organisation's positive risk culture.

Essentials and Assessment of Risk Management, 63–99

Published under exclusive licence by Emerald Publishing Limited
doi:10.1108/978-1-83662-302-120251015

The Strategic Direction of Risk Management

For an organisation to manage risk in an integrated fashion, it must first establish an infrastructure that aligns risk management objectives with:

- overall strategic objectives
- operating practices
- organisational culture.

This alignment enhances the organisation's understanding and communication of risk both horizontally (across the organisation) and vertically (bottom-up and top-down).

Key Elements

Integrated risk management requires a healthy risk culture, leadership and innovation. Effective management through integrated risk management will not be created successfully without commitment, drive and allocating the necessary resources.

The organisational infrastructure should also include the following elements:

- management direction on risk management
- building capability/capacity.

The following table further describes these elements.

Element	Description
Management direction on risk management	Communicated, understood and applied by means of: • mandate • commitment • policies and procedures • operating principles
Building capability/ capacity	Developing learning plans and tools for use throughout the organisation

Activity | Risk management improves organisational share price

The AON Risk Maturity Index has found a statistically significant correlation between more sophisticated risk management practices and stronger financial performance.

Undertake the following steps to learn more:

1. Navigate to the following URL: www.aon.com.au.
2. Enter Risk management improves company share price into the Search field.
3. Click the relevant search result.

Risk Appetite and Risk Tolerance

The organisation's risk appetite and tolerance determine the type and amount of risk an organisation is willing and able to accept in the pursuit of its objectives.

The organisation's interpretation of its risk appetite denotes how the board or senior executives:

- set organisational objectives;
- pursue those objectives with regard to the degree of the environment's volatility.

Risk Appetite: Definition

ISO/Guide 73:2009 Risk management – Vocabulary (3.7.1.2) defines risk appetite as:

> – the amount and type of risk an organisation is willing to pursue or retain.

In a slightly different way, Crowe Horwath (2011) defines risk appetite as:

> – the amount of risk an organisation is willing to seek or accept in the pursuit of its long-term objectives.

The organisation's risk appetite is determined and set at the level of the board, secretary, CEO and the executive level.

Risk Tolerance: Definition

Risk tolerance is:

> – the level or amount of risk the organisation is willing to bear.

Crowe Horwath (2011) differentiates between risk appetite and risk tolerance, by stating that risk tolerance is:

> – the boundaries of risk-taking outside of which the organisation is not prepared to venture in the pursuit of its long-term objectives.

EXAMPLE

Risk Appetite and Tolerance Interpretation

A context analysis aims to provide the organisation with a better appreciation of its operating environment.

The outcome of this context analysis informs the organisation about whether it is having a conservative, neutral or progressive year. In summary, an organisation's risk appetite and tolerance inform the kind of objectives the board sets.

Risk appetite

Depending on the type of year the board decides the organisation is having, the board will consult the risk appetite to convey the tone about how the organisation should proceed.

For example, the board would set very conservative objectives if it decides it is a conservative year (for example, due to budgetary constraints). Conversely, the board may 'stretch' the organisation's objectives if it decides the organisation is having a progressive year (because of the appetite to consume more risk in the pursuit of the organisation's objectives).

Risk tolerance

In a progressive year, the organisation might be able to tolerate a larger loss in the pursuit of its objectives due to the environment being more prosperous.

Conversely, in a conservative year, an organisation would endeavour to reduce any loss due to the less prosperous environment.

The Risk Appetite Statement

The board determines the organisation's risk appetite and tolerance in the risk appetite statement. The risk appetite statement reflects the board's view on what degrees of risk are acceptable (or unacceptable) to the business to meet its stated strategy.

The following table defines:

- acceptable and unacceptable risks;
- the tolerance levels risk appetite statements assigned to the risks by way of tolerance (or target) levels.

Risk Type	Definition	Allocated Tolerance Level
Acceptable	Forms part of the necessary strategic elements required to meet the organisation's vision or goals	Rated on a sliding scale
Unacceptable	Does not realise the strategic vision of the company	Little tolerance level

Design

The design of the risk appetite statement is based on the existing risk management framework. The key difference is that thinking about risk has moved from a **risk is bad and should be minimised** approach to a **portfolio management, pick risks**

that are good advisory function. The risk appetite framework should align risk with the elements in the following table.

Element	Description
Shareholder expectations	Align the target risk and earnings profile with: shareholder demands; or the board's performance expectations
Strategy	Align capacity and tolerance for risk taking with capital allocation for profitable growth
Finance	Shape aggregate risk levels through decisions on balance sheet structure (leverage) and risk transfer (hedging or insurance)
Business operations	Aligning the acceptability and volume of risks actually taken by business lines with the desired risk profile
Regulatory standing	Ensuring business activities align with licensing and legislative obligations

Strategy

Success in establishing an integrated risk management program depends on the organisation's ability to communicate its risk management message throughout the organisation. One way the organisation can achieve this is by including risk management in the strategic planning process. When informed by integrated risk management, organisations can use strategic planning to:

- recognise risks;
- incorporate measures to embrace opportunities for innovation;
- avoid adverse consequences.

Self-Help Question 6.1

Record your ideas about why organisational strategic goals need to be closely connected to operational capabilities.

Answers to self-help questions are provided at the end of each section.

The word strategy is derived from the Greek word for a military general and the verb **stratego** which means to:

> [...] plan the destruction of one's enemies through the effective use of resources
>
> Bracker, 1980, p.219

Activity | The secret origins of corporate strategy

Watch *Harvard Business Review*'s video titled *The Secret Origins of Corporate Strategy* on YouTube for more information on the origins and benefits of corporate strategy.

Strategic Management

Strategic management involves the following three steps:

1. identifying opportunities for market growth;
2. determining which of those opportunities to pursue;
3. allocating resources to support the achievement of the opportunity.

There are various consequences attached to implementing the strategic plan, which may have a positive or negative impact on the business. A well-considered strategic plan anticipates these consequences and evaluates the potential benefits.

Effective risk management, as part of the organisation's strategic approach, informs the senior management team about where to invest their resources to mitigate negative risks and achieve growth and progress.

Strategic management involves determining key organisational objectives by developing and implementing policies and plans aimed at providing direction to the entire organisation to enable it to survive in a challenging environment and deliver value to its stakeholders.

Key Determinants and Implementers

For organisations to be successful, it is critical they have effective strategic management that is:

- determined by the board;
- supported by effective operational management;
- implemented by the senior management team.

Essentially, the board sets the strategic direction of the business, while the CEO and the senior management team implement it.

Resources to Implement the Strategic Direction

To effectively implement the strategic direction of the business, the organisation needs to possess the appropriate combination of:

- capabilities
- resources
- skillsets.

Strategic management is about arranging the functional resources of the business to maximise organisational competitiveness and improve shareholder value.

Risks (Threats and Opportunities)

When implementing the strategic direction of the business through the corporate plan, managers need to consider risks (threats and opportunities) the organisation might encounter. The ability to identify and manage the size of the potential risk is an essential part of setting strategy.

The key risks of which management needs to be aware include:

- creeping risks
- emerging risks.

Creeping Risks

The World Economic Forum Global Risks report (2010) defines creeping risks as:

> [...] risks linked to big shifts that are recognized and which will roll out over many years, even decades. For example, global population growth, ageing and the ensuing rise in consumption have implications for resources, climate change, health and fiscal policy.
>
> [...] Because these failures and risks emerge over a long period of time, their potentially enormous impact and long- term implications can be vastly underestimated.

Emerging Risks

Reto Schneider, Swiss Re's Head of Emerging Risk Management (2012) defines emerging risk as:

> [...] new or already known risks which are difficult to assess. I prefer a definition which focuses on faint, initial signals that may or may not further develop into real emerging risks. We investigate these risks because of their potential impact on our business and that of our clients.

Self-Help Question 6.2

Brainstorm five strategic concerns in a modern corporate context (for example, to achieve a high level of customer satisfaction).

Answers to self-help questions are provided at the end of each section.

Activity | Develop a strategy as a team

Watch *Harvard Business Review*'s video titled *Develop Strategy as a Team* on YouTube to learn more about the importance of developing a strategy.

The Strategic Risk Management Framework

A strategic approach to the management of risk involves a holistic view of the potential risks. To successfully manage these risks, it is necessary to ensure the risk management process is integrated throughout the organisation.

One role of **strategic risk management** is to identify and analyse risk against the corporate risk appetite, which involves:

- understanding where major areas of risk exist across an organisation;
- ensuring levels of acceptable risk exposure given the corporate risk appetite.

Organisations need to manage both singular and aggregate risks to be able to function efficiently. An example of a singular risk could be a major hazard.

An example of an aggregate risk could be the same type of risk existing across different functional areas (for example, a loss of corporate knowledge).

Essentially, strategic risk management aims to assist management to achieve organisational performance and profitability targets while preventing:

- a loss of resources;
- damage to the organisation's reputation;
- other associated consequences.

In summary, strategic risk management assists an organisation in achieving its goals and avoiding (or minimise) surprises along the way.

Self-Help Question 6.3

The benefits of an integrated risk management framework align with those of an effective management model.

List five benefits of implementing an integrated risk management framework (for example, improved planning opportunities).

Answers to self-help questions are provided at the end of each section.

The value of strategic management is maximised when management sets strategy and objectives to strike the optimal balance between growth and return goals, and related risks, and efficiently and effectively use resources.

Recognising where things can go wrong enables management to build contingencies into the proposed strategy.

The key success factors of a strategic risk management framework include:

- aligning with the strategic intent and related objectives;
- identifying and managing opportunities while minimising threats;
- including all business risks, not just financial ones;
- integrating risk management into management processes.

In this way, strategic risk management relates directly to an organisation's strategic management processes.

Strategic Management Processes

The main strategic management processes include:

- formulating the strategy
- implementing the strategy.

While these main processes exceed mere planning, they are sometimes referred to as the *strategic planning process* because they relate to developing and executing an organisation's strategic plan.

Self-Help Question 6.4

What do you consider to be the potential capability benefits of strategic management for an organisation? For example, a capacity to be proactive and respond positively to changes in the environment.

Answers to self-help questions are provided at the end of each section.

Formulating the Strategy

The central element of formulating strategy is the board's development of the strategic plan. This document articulates the strategic objectives. The strategic planning process is the process of developing and implementing plans to reach goals and objectives.

Strategic planning may provide overall direction to an organisation or give specific direction in areas such as:

- finance
- human resources
- organisational development
- information technology
- marketing.

Formulating the strategy involves the following three steps.

1. Creating a vision
2. Understanding the environment
3. Creating the strategic plan.

Step 1: Creating a vision

Before developing the strategic plan, the board and senior management need to clarify and agree upon a vision. A risk management vision statement is an aspirational statement that identifies what the organisation will look like with a fully developed and mature risk management framework. It helps staff to understand the aim of the risk management framework and helps the organisation analyse the gap between its current framework and the framework it desires, thus enabling it to develop a plan.

This vision needs to take into account the perspectives of the organisation's key stakeholders, including:

- customers
- suppliers and subcontractors
- staff
- regulatory bodies
- shareholders.

An example vision statement is:

> To be recognised as a world class provider (of a product or service) on a national or global scale.

Note: Vision statements are typically general in nature.

Case Study – A Shared Vision or Purpose for Integration

An organisation's management team decides to move away from silo-oriented mentalities. The first step in establishing integrated management within the organisation is to create a shared vision or purpose for integration. Therefore, the executive management team must be united in its vision of creating cohesion and breaking down silo-oriented mentalities.

Step 2: Understanding the Environment

Conducting an environmental scan enables the board and senior management to gain a better understanding of the organisation's:

- internal strengths and weaknesses (SW)
- external opportunities and threats (OT).

Case Study – The Systems Map

The organisation mentioned in the previous case study can integrate its various management systems by defining these systems through process mapping and analysis. This analysis results in a systems map, which documents the inputs and outputs of each system.

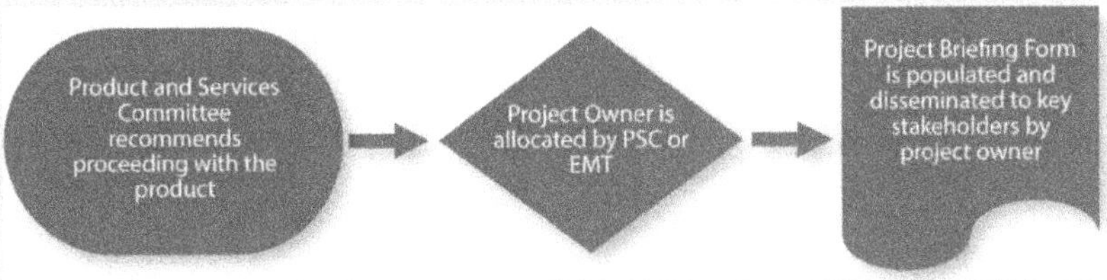

As depicted in the following diagram, organisations can also use the systems map to:

- demonstrate the overlap or dependencies existing between systems;
- reveal opportunities for cohesion that will decrease duplication and increase efficiencies;
- identify how to most effectively embed risk management into the system.

Overlap between systems

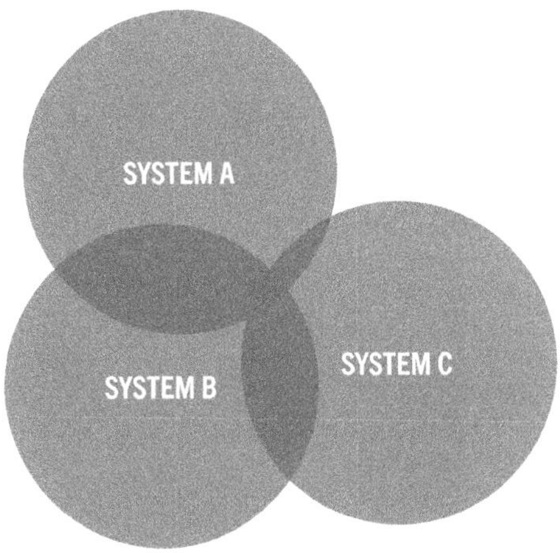

An environmental scan can assist the organisation to:

- identify stakeholders affected by its decisions and actions;
- understand the external environment to inform strategic and risk acceptance decisions.

Each stakeholder group has a different level of tolerance for risk. In general, the higher the level of uncertainty, the lower the risk tolerance.

Risk tolerance levels are higher when there is:

- a greater understanding of the impact of the risk, and its likelihood and consequences; or
- assurance that the control regime is effective.

Activity | Risk management and strategic planning

Access a current (or past) strategic plan within your organisation.

- Is it clear where the organisation has used risk management to inform the strategic decision?
- How has the organisation used this risk information to make strategic decisions?
- Can you identify and explain the company's risk appetite?

SWOT Analysis

Conducting a strengths, weaknesses, opportunities and threats (SWOT) analysis is a standard form of environmental scanning. It is important that an organisation understands its competitive advantages to gain an insight into the likelihood of realising its opportunities. By understanding its strengths in the marketplace, an organisation can establish a strategy to manage its capacity and capability to exploit opportunities.

Porter's Five Forces

There are several strategic management methodologies that can help an organisation to better understand its external environment. One of the more famous methodologies is known as the Five Forces model, which was developed by Harvard academic Professor Michael E. Porter.

The following diagram shows what Porter identified as five forces affecting organisations.

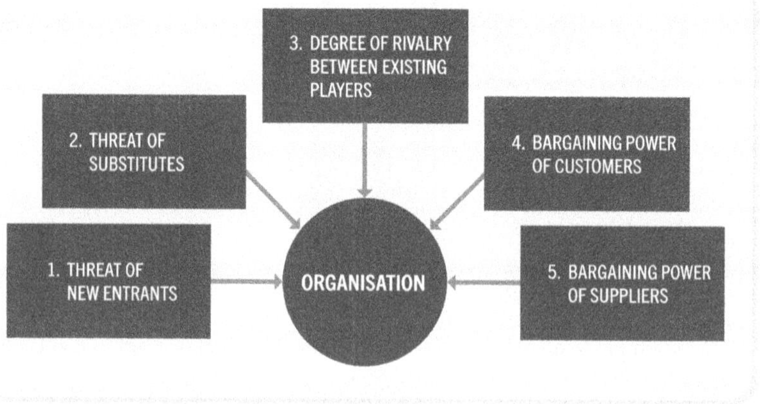

Activity | The five competitive forces that shape strategy

Watch *Harvard Business Review*'s video titled *The Five Competitive Forces That Shape Strategy* (available on YouTube) to view an interview with Michael E. Porter about the five competitive forces that are the basis for much of modern business strategy.

Step 3: Creating the strategic plan

Strategic planning

Strategic planning (or setting organisational strategy) is the process by which an organisation:

- determines its long-term goals/objectives;
- identifies the deliverables necessary to achieve these goals and objectives;
- understand the risks associated with achieving these goals and objectives in line with the organisation's risk management appetite and tolerance.

Note: The public sector also uses strategic planning to maximise service delivery and meet the department/minister's objectives.

The strategic plan

The strategic plan details how, when and what will be done to achieve an organisation's set vision. The plan typically looks ahead from three to five years and communicates the organisation's:

- vision
- mission
- key strategic goals.

The senior management team identifies the tasks the organisation must undertake to meet the strategic goals identified in the environmental scan. The organisation also considers its available resources and organisational competencies when determining these tasks.

Self-Help Question 6.5

List the content areas you would expect to see in a typical strategic plan (for example, an executive statement from the board chairperson or CEO).

Answers to self-help questions are provided at the end of each section.

Self-Help Question 6.6

List what you expect would be critical success factors for strategic plans.

Answers to self-help questions are provided at the end of each section.

Activity | Strategic planning

Strategic planning

Examine your organisation's strategic plan.

- Does it contain the main elements of a strategic plan described previously?
- What mechanisms does the organisation use to communicate and implement the plan?

Implementing the Strategy

Implementing the strategy involves:

- allocating resources, authority and accountability;
- managing strategy implementation.

Allocating Resources, Authority and Accountability

Implementing the strategic plan requires allocation of sufficient resources to ensure the organisation can achieve its strategy. Authority and accountability also need to be assigned to ensure the organisation can achieve its milestones.

Managing Strategy Implementation

Implementing the strategy also involves managing the process, which includes:

- monitoring results;
- comparing to benchmarks and best practice;
- evaluating the effectiveness and efficiency of the process;
- controlling for variances;
- making necessary adjustments to the process.

Organisations can manage strategy implementation through business and operational planning and monitoring, analysis and review.

Business and Operational Planning

The next step in the strategic management process is to translate the strategic plan into the corporate and functional business plan. Organisations use information from the strategic plan to populate the annual business plan. Each functional area develops its own business plan that reflects its contribution to meeting the targets set in the corporate business plan.

The corporate and business plan identifies operational risks relevant to the business and designs tasks with built-in control measures to mitigate the identified risk/s.

Monitoring, Analysis and Review

The organisation needs to define how it will monitor, analyse and review its strategic plan as part of the strategic planning process. Often, the strategic plan includes developing a performance-based management system, which formalises these monitoring and reviewing processes.

By establishing key performance indicators (KPIs) against each milestone, a performance-based management system can facilitate the regular auditing of actual versus expected performance. The organisation can then analyse the results of the regular auditing to determine any relevant trends. The organisation embeds identified areas needing improvement into the business and operational plans, which it regularly reviews.

Important – Monitoring is* not *reviewing

Reviewing and monitoring are two different things. Reviewing occurs regularly but monitoring is continuous.

You may review all the risks in your risk register annually or bi-annually, but you should continuously monitor the risks that are most important to the organisation (for example, how complete the controls are and how effective).

Self-Help Question 6.7

List two ways different organisations may refer to operational plans (for example, action plans).

Answers to self-help questions are provided at the end of each section.

Risk Management and Strategic Planning

Risk management is an integral component of strategic planning because realised and unrealised risks have an effect on an organisation's ability to achieve its objectives. As described in the following table, strategic planning involves **identifying** and **managing** both positive and negative risks.

Element	Description
Identification	Strategic planning identifies: • strengths (S) • weaknesses (W) • opportunities (O) • threats (T)
Management	Strategic planning manages adverse outcomes while leveraging the organisation's strengths

Traditionally, operational managers implemented risk management; however, strategic planning is becoming more sophisticated and is being actively used as a decision-making tool. Strategic risk management identifies risks associated with the strategic objectives of the organisation. Identifying these strategic risks enables an organisation to position itself in such a way to:

- reduce the consequence of negative risks (threats);
- increase the likelihood of positive risks (opportunities).

In executing a strategic plan, an organisation must accept a certain amount of risk in the course of exploiting opportunities – without risk, there can be no innovation or creativity, which are the keys to establishing a competitive edge in the market.

Without a structured approach to understanding the risks organisations face, the organisation may not be able to implement the strategy successfully. It is important to ensure strategic goals are matched by operational competency – to exploit or maximise emerging market opportunities, organisations need to be appropriately resourced to take calculated risks.

There are three main components of risk management at the strategic level:

- managing risk in the pursuit of opportunities;
- the strategic risk management document suite;
- developing a risk management framework.

Managing Risk in the Pursuit of Opportunities

The risk management process can assist the organisation to evaluate a strategic opportunity (and marketplace threats) to determine the likelihood:

- of the organisation achieving its objectives;
- that external threats will interfere with the pursuit of that opportunity.

The need to seize market opportunities is an essential component of the strategic planning process. As illustrated in the following diagram, organisations can enhance this element of the process by integrating risk management methodologies.

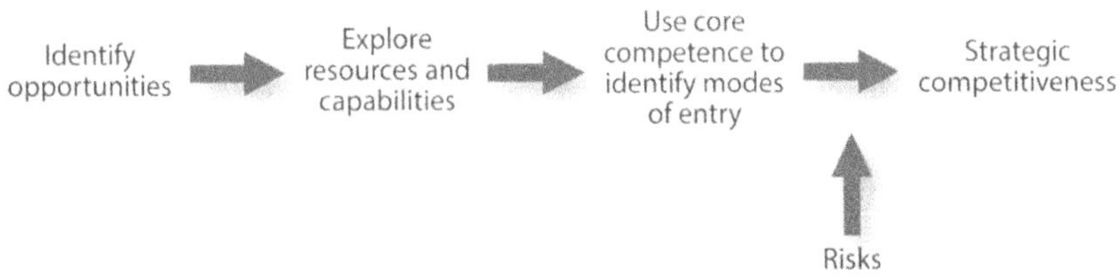

All strategies involve risks of varying degrees that can also be wide-ranging (for example, financial, economic or physical). Being aware of all types of risks that could affect the organisation and appropriately planning for them helps to minimise their impact.

Existing Risks

Although an organisation does not always have control over the risks it faces, it can make provisions in case they arise. There are two key areas organisations need to consider:

- the possibility (risk) that the opportunity will not be realised and the effect it will have on the strategic objectives of the organisation (for example, not anticipating the movement of competitors into a niche area of the market);
- the impact the opportunity may have on existing organisational objectives (for example, a company looking to diversify may lose its focus on existing clientele, resulting in a loss of market share for that part of the business).

By understanding where risks exist in the pursuit of better performance and innovation, the organisation is better positioned to implement controls that bring the risk within an appropriate risk tolerance level.

The Opportunity Matrix

Organisations evaluate threats by:

- using a risk assessment tool; or
- applying more qualitative or quantitative methods of analysis to determine:

  – a realistic likelihood of loss resulting from the threat
  – the impact of the risk if it eventuates.

An opportunity matrix is a simple strategic management tool that involves:

- listing key external factors (which the environmental scan identifies);
- distinguishing between opportunities and threats that may affect the organisation or the industry.

To differentiate between opportunities, the organisation can map the importance of the opportunity to the organisation's capabilities. This helps the organisation to set a strategy so it understands how hard it needs to work to achieve the benefits of that opportunity.

The following table is an example opportunity matrix comparing the importance of an identified opportunity being successful to the organisation's current ability to respond to the opportunity.

Organisational Capability	Importance of the Opportunity Being Successful			
		Little importance	Moderate importance	Essential
	Limited capability			
	Moderate capability			
	Very capable			

Note: When identifying opportunities, the organisation should try to provide specifics; for example, 'we predict the population will increase by 3–5 per cent over the next 10 years'.

Activity | Opportunity matrix

Use the example opportunity matrix to map the importance of three opportunities against your organisation's capabilities.

Case Study – Strategic Alliances and Risk

Many companies try to capitalise on opportunities and minimise risk through strategic alliances. Such strategic moves are often fraught with risk, as highlighted by the following examples.

Piaggio and LML's joint venture

A joint venture between Piaggio (an Italian automobile manufacturer) and Lohia Machines Private (LML) Limited dissolved after nearly 10 years of success after a restructure at Piaggio caused friction between key stakeholders.

According to Legal Service India:

> On June, 23, 1998, Mr. Deepak Singhania [who held a 23.6% equity stake in LML] received letters from Piaggio. The letters curtly informed him that four of the group companies would be merged with Piaggio & Co. SPA on July 1, 1998, under a restructuring plan. There had also been a change in

the shareholding pattern. Mr. Deepak Singhania immediately sensed that the reorganisation and the changing shareholding pattern of Piaggio & Co SPA would strengthen the anti-Singhania faction in Piaggio. Proactively, Mr. Singhania invoked certain articles of the joint venture agreement with Piaggio. Mr. Singhania contended that he had the right to buy out Piaggio's stake in LML.

Goodwill

Other companies have set up alliances based on goodwill, without establishing robust contracts that articulate:

- accountabilities
- roles and responsibilities of each partner
- intellectual property protection.

An unfortunate consequence of a lack of attention to detail could be one partner in the alliance exploiting the opportunity to claim the other's intellectual property as their own.

Case Study – Coffee on Wheels

Coffee on Wheels is a mobile coffee and fast food company, servicing business parks and construction sites in one of the outer suburbs of a major city.

Recognising the growing success of its business, the owners decide to expand their service to other suburbs. Preliminary market research (informed by an influx of residential construction and newly developed business parks) indicates there are three other rapidly expanding suburbs.

Note: Business parks are areas in which many office buildings, including offices and warehouses, are grouped together.

To effectively expand, Coffee on Wheels needs to:

- purchase and equip three new vehicles;
- employ and train six more staff.

Before being able to borrow additional funds to expand, the business owners need to present a three- to five-year strategic plan. As part of this strategic plan, they complete a SWOT analysis and develop a strategic risk management implementation plan.

Self-Help Question 6.8

Identify some of Coffee on Wheels' strategic risks in implementing their business strategy (for example, an inadequate marketing strategy).

Answers to self-help questions are provided at the end of each section.

The Strategic Risk Management Document Suite

The strategic risk management document suite clearly records the organisation's approach to risk management. Organisations should develop the strategic risk management document suite in accordance with the risk management process (as described in ISO 31000:2018).

In particular, the strategic risk management document suite documents the:

- external, internal and risk management context;
- risks identified in the risk identification workshops and escalated from the operational risk profile;
- existing controls to manage strategic risks;
- residual risk exposures;
- additional risk treatment strategies required to further mitigate risks falling outside the organisation's tolerance limits;
- methodology for monitoring and reviewing strategic risks.

The Strategic Risk Profile

The strategic risk profile should reflect the risks the organisation identifies at the strategic level. The executive management team should conduct regular workshops, with the view for the strategic risk profile to reflect:

- major areas of risk escalated from the operational risk profile, which are important to the strategic environment;
- additional areas of risk determined in the strategic planning process.

These areas of risk may include:

- inadequate contracts
- poorly communicated competencies to customers
- poorly established relationships with strategic partners
- reputational risks.

> **Activity | Risk management and the strategic plan**
>
> Obtain a strategic plan from your workplace or from another organisation. Analyse the plan from a risk management perspective and determine how well the organisation has integrated or applied risk management principles and methodologies.

Developing a Risk Management Framework

Defining and implementing the risk management framework is integral to the success of strategic risk management. The risk management framework is the set of elements in the organisation's management system that are concerned with managing risk. It describes the systems and processes to be used and the mandate and commitment needed to successfully integrate risk management with existing organisational management processes to ensure the risk management program can assist a business to achieve its corporate objectives. It is essentially the infrastructure required to ensure the organisation continually identifies and manages risk throughout the organisation.

ISO/Guide 73:2009 – Risk management – Vocabulary defines a risk management framework as:

> a set of components that provide the foundations and organizational arrangements for designing, implementing, monitoring, reviewing and continually improving risk management throughout the organization' and notes that 'the risk management framework is embedded within the organization's overall strategic and operational policies and practices.

The risk management framework sets out how organisations:

- manage risk within specific contexts;
- integrate risk management practices into the fabric of the organisation;
- ensure risk management becomes a sustainable process within the overall management system.

A risk management framework organises and centralises information to be used in the identification and management of risk, including:

- roles and responsibilities
- processes and procedures
- standards
- tools
- facilities
- documentation.

The risk management framework also sets the context in which risks are managed, including how they will be:

- identified
- analysed
- controlled
- monitored
- reviewed.

See Chapter 5 for more detail.

Risk Management Policy

The risk management policy sets out the overarching philosophy, principles, requirements and responsibilities for a sound approach to:

- risk oversight
- management
- ongoing internal control assurance.

The risk management policy should aim to communicate the organisation's approach to the oversight and management of risk.

Definitions of Risk Categories

Establishing risk categories helps to add structure to risk identification within an organisation. Defining key categories of risk also assists in developing key risk management tools (such as risk analysis tools) when establishing consequence descriptors.

Risk categories for an organisation may include:

- strategic
- financial
- human resources
- operational
- reputation
- safety
- security.

Note: The risk categories should reflect the organisation's core business activities. The scope of each category is different for each organisation.

The Risk Appetite Statement

The risk management framework sits under the risk appetite statement. The framework incorporates the provided risk appetite statement guidance in terms of defining risks acceptable to the organisation. Determining risk tolerance is part of the strategic planning process, so the risk tolerance should be regularly reviewed.

Key determinants of an organisation's risk appetite include those described in the following table.

Element	**Description**
Shareholder expectations	align the target risk and earnings profile with: • shareholder demands; or • the board's performance expectations
Strategy	align capacity and tolerance for risk taking with capital allocation for profitable growth
Finance	shape aggregate risk levels through decisions on: • balance sheet structure (leverage) • risk transfer (hedging or insurance)
Business operations	aligning the acceptability and volume of risks actually taken by business lines with the desired risk profile
Regulatory standing	ensuring business activities align with licensing and legislative obligations

An organisation's risk tolerance ranges inform its risk escalation guidelines, which are defined in the following table.

Risk rating	**Level of required management attention**
Extreme	Escalate to the CEO and board
High	Escalate through the risk committee
Medium	Escalate to a senior manager and manage within the department
Low	Manage risk or event within the department

Risk tolerance ranges ensure organisations:

- make decisions regarding any given risk at the correct level;
- introduce new controls if control measures become less effective.

Accountability

Organisations must clearly define accountability for the ownership and management of risk.

Every risk must have an owner; that is, the person with the authority and accountability to make a decision to do or not to do something about the identified risk.

Note: Risk owners are not always superiors and it depends on what level of delegated authority they have to manage the risks. In other words, risk owners are not always the executives (they may be team leaders, for example).

The Risk Accountability Framework

Organisations assign each control measure to an owner. The responsibility matrix is typically detailed in the risk management policy. To put these items into context, the risk management framework encompasses all matters relating to risk management. The risk management policy is contained within the risk management framework and the responsibility is contained within the risk management policy.

The following is an example of a risk accountability framework.

Owner	Accountabilities
Board	• endorsing the organisation's risk management strategy and policy • setting and endorsing the company's risk appetite • monitoring the risk profile • ensuring that organisational risk management systems are effective
Board risk committee (sub-committee of the board)	• recommending the risk management policy and framework to the board • recommending risk tolerance levels to the board • identifying strategic risks • developing a strategic risk profile • requesting the assessment of key enterprise risks in accordance with triggers, such as: – major change to operations – procurement of a new piece of equipment – a new client • overseeing the risk register • overseeing the implementation of risk mitigation strategies for strategic risks • reviewing progress of business unit risk management processes • reporting all extreme and top strategic risks and their management strategies to the board

(*Continued*)

Owner	Accountabilities
Executive managers	Overseeing the implementation of the risk management framework within their business environment, including: • establishing and evaluating an operational risk profile for their area of control • ensuring risks pertinent to the business processes within their control are identified and managed in accordance with the risk management framework • ensuring risks are documented in the operational risk register
Departmental managers	• implementing the risk management framework within their area of responsibility • identifying departmental risks • establishing departmental risk profiles in accordance with the risk management framework • assessing, monitoring and reviewing emerging departmental risks according to triggers identified in the risk framework • recording identified risks and controls on a departmental risk register • contributing to the periodic review of risk management policies and procedures • notifying relevant executive leadership team members of any risks classified as extreme or high for inclusion on the enterprise risk register • providing the risk and compliance committee with reporting on risks and mitigation for the top five risks for the department
Team members	• assisting departmental managers with implementing the risk framework within their work areas • complying with policy and framework requirements • identifying areas of operational risk on a regular basis • reporting incidents, near-misses and other areas of concern to team leader or manager • assisting with implementing and evaluating of risk treatment strategies • complying with policy and procedural requirements to minimise organisational exposure to risk

Source: Keetelaar (2006. Reproduced with permission).

From the previous table, it would seem that there are multiple accountabilities for the same risk. This is not the case for the board level, because there is a responsibility for ensuring there are practices and procedures for the identification, management and continued monitoring of risk. At the lower level, the responsibility is to:

- implement those practices and procedures;
- ensure risks are identified and managed;
- ensure the continuous process of monitoring and review.

The Reporting Framework

The reporting framework provides the infrastructure required for communicating risks throughout the organisation, and is directly related to the risk accountability framework. The following figure presents the risk reporting framework.

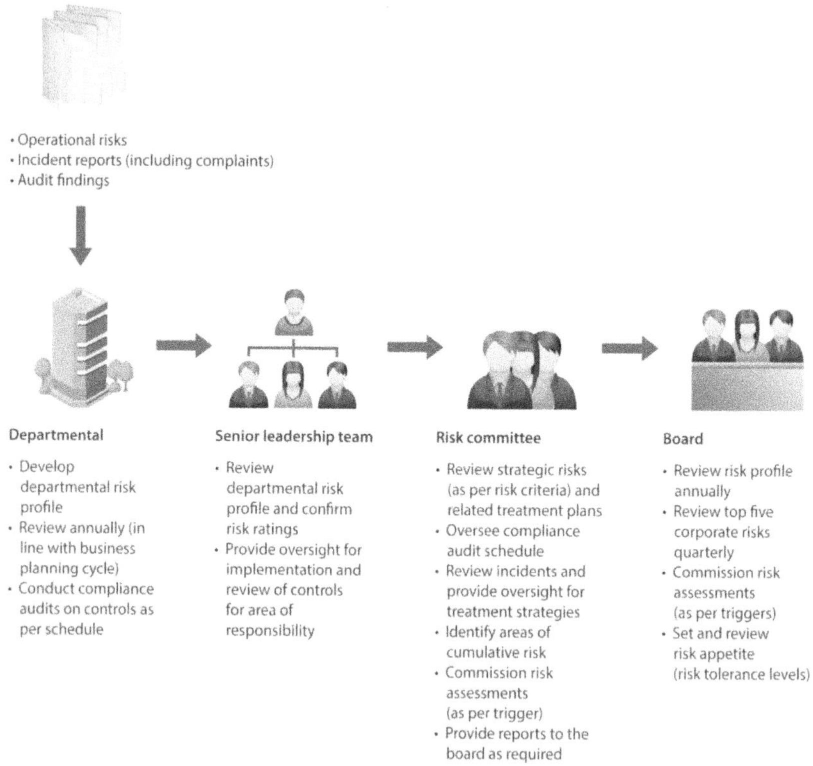

The Risk Management Framework

Inherent in any risk management framework is the allocation of appropriate control resources. A risk management framework includes:

- the structure for risk identification and review
- common language for risk management

- risk analysis tools
- risk management documentation
- the risk management process
- the resources allocated to risk management.

Structure for Risk Identification and Review

The organisation can categorise its approach to risk identification as:

- risk profile development and review
- ongoing risk identification and review.

Risk Profile Development and Review

The organisation should conduct risk identification workshops at the strategic and operational levels, with a view to establishing a risk profile at each of these levels. If a risk emerges as one of critical impacts on the organisation, the frequency of the review may increase as the management of the crisis intensifies.

Ongoing Risk Identification and Review

A corporate risk profile does not remain static. As the organisation changes and evolves, it adds newly emerged risks and retires redundant risks.

Note: Risks should never be deleted; they should be archived for future analysis of lessons learnt.

Implicit in the implementation process is the need to scan the horizon for emerging risks that may undermine the strategic plan.

Organisations may identify new risks as a result of:

- regular team discussions
- changes to business processes
- incident management
- complaints management
- introduction of new policies or other regulations.

All levels of the organisation are required to document newly identified risks in the risk register.

Common Language for Risk Management

To gain a common understanding of risk exposures, it is essential to ensure there is a common understanding of risk and risk management throughout the organisation. This can be achieved by using common organisational terminology and definitions throughout all levels of the organisation.

Risk Analysis Tools

Risk analysis tools assist to understand the level of risk the organisation faces at any given time. These tools combine the potential impact of a risk on the organisation's objectives, with the likelihood of the impact occurring.

Risk Management Documentation

Risk management documentation serves a number of purposes, including:

- creating a record of decisions made in relation to the identification, assessment, evaluation and management of risk;
- providing a means for:

  – communicating risk-based information
  – monitoring and reviewing risks and the actions required to mitigate risks.

Risk management documentation may include:

- risk register templates (for recording risk assessments);
- risk treatment plans;
- risk management implementation plans, enabling the user to document all stages of the risk process for a specific purpose.

The Risk Register

The risk register documents risks identified in the risk management strategy and is a database organisation mine for information by routine review and continuous monitoring. Essentially, the risk register contains the information to put in your report for the board, your audit committee or other stakeholders.

The organisational-wide risk register identifies, consolidates, categorises and records all strategic and operational risks. Key organisational stakeholders use this risk register for:

- developing and managing risk treatment plans;
- board and management reporting.

Tip – Review Frequency

The organisation should set a monitoring and review schedule which best fits the reporting, planning and general organisational review cycles. Essentially, key stakeholders tailor this frequency to the organisation.

The risk register typically:

- identifies risks;
- describes the severity of the consequence, and the likelihood of that consequence occurring;
- assigns accountability to the functional area responsible for the risk;
- describes the control measures the organisation has implemented.

Headings that typically describe the risks and controls contained in a risk register are:

- objective
- risk description

- risk owner
- existing controls
- control effectiveness
- control owner
- treatment plans
- treatment owner.

Note: Each organisation has a different risk profile to use when populating the risk register.

Creating a Positive Risk Culture

To develop and implement a sustainable, effective risk management approach that adds value to an organisation, it is essential to embed the risk management systems and requirements into the culture of the organisation. This is sometimes referred to as creating a **positive risk culture**.

A positive risk culture understands:

- risk factors threatening what the organisation is trying to achieve;
- how to prevent these risk factors;
- opportunities the organisation faces in the pursuit of its objectives;
- how to leverage this knowledge to capitalise on opportunities.

Corporate Governance

Corporate governance involves effectively communicating the organisation's strategy from the top to the grass roots level. It is not sufficient to simply dictate policies and procedures and hope for compliance. The culture of the organisation must be such that effective communication is entrenched throughout the business.

Factors Influencing the Risk Culture

Many factors influence an organisation's risk culture including those in the following table.

Factor	Description
Risk awareness	• awareness levels are based on risks individuals believe they face and their judgements about the significance of those risks • this is a reflection of the organisation's ability to channel undiluted and accurate risk information, from top-to-bottom and from side-to-side within the organisation

(*Continued*)

(*Continued*)

Factor	Description
Risk tolerance	• the decision to act on or accept a risk is based partly on an individual's tolerance of that risk • in the absence of a clear mandate or policy setting out what is and is not tolerable, risk tolerance information is collected and conveyed personally • individuals make up their own minds according to their views, opinions and agendas; their views are then modified by other local factors • an example of this is how managers react when a staff member identifies a risk. If the information is well received by the manager, the staff member feels encouraged and continues to share information. They may also encourage other staff members to do the same
Risk ownership	A measure of an individual's: • authority • acceptance of accountability • willingness to act on available risk information others in the organisation provide

Training, Education and Communication

All organisations develop a distinctive and unique risk culture, which translates as the way they regard and handle operational risk. In the absence of a strong risk culture, the treatment of operational risk becomes a matter of personal interpretation and influence. To avoid potential pitfalls, the organisation needs to build a campaign designed to shape the organisational risk culture.

One method of influencing a positive risk culture is to implement training, education and communication campaigns, which may involve:

- training programs;
- support for key risk champions within operational departments;
- newsletters and other informational material to communicate risk management initiatives.

Activity | Risk management framework

Investigate if your organisation has an established *risk management framework*. If you cannot find one specific document, use the elements of the framework (as described previously) to determine the extent of the framework's development on a less formal level.

The Corporate Risk Profile

When determining its strategic pathway, an organisation identifies and assesses its major areas of risk. This focus on an organisation's major areas of risk ensures the strategic direction it chooses both minimises exposures and exploits opportunities.

Purpose

Competitive organisations have developed the ability to reinvent themselves by examining the following four areas:

- their core business
- the strength of their offerings in the marketplace
- internal weaknesses
- external threats.

Complexity, uncertainty and change are inherent in all business functions. As a consequence, the risk profile of every business needs to change to reflect these uncertainties.

The risk management profile is the organisation's documented understanding of its risk exposures. The senior management team uses the risk management profile to inform decisions about the allocation of resources for the control of identified risks. This improved decision-making leads to:

- good performance measurement
- enhanced accountability
- better management practices
- enhanced shareholder return.

EXAMPLE

Weaknesses in the Production Environment

If the organisation can identify the location of weaknesses in the production environment, it can avoid jeopardising the effectiveness of implemented controls designed to mitigate those risks when it decides to change production resources.

Risk Management Profile Communication

The risk management profile is intended to inform all stakeholders (including staff) about:

- risks emerging from the changing operating environment;
- the associated controls necessary to mitigate emerging risks;
- high priority risk exposures, and how these are to be mitigated and managed;
- the current capacity of the organisation to manage and mitigate significant risks.

The profile's communication is supported by relevant organisational documents (tools and templates); for example:

- the company's risk appetite;
- learning and support needs, structures and actions to sustain the integrated management of risk within the organisation.

Case Study – Systems Solutions

A successful tender

A small technology firm, Systems Solutions, wins a major contract to provide systems support to a large insurance firm. The successful tender is a result of the firm's:

- expertise
- customer satisfaction (from smaller contracts)
- innovative leadership.

Due diligence

Before signing the contract, the insurance company performs its due diligence to ensure System Solutions has the capacity to successfully manage the required IT systems support.

Systems Solutions successfully continues to manage the new systems support contract together with its smaller contracts successfully. Fortunately, Systems Solutions has anticipated the increased workload and resources accordingly.

A new strategy

The newly-appointed leadership team decides to pursue further growth and implements a strategic plan aiming to recruit 10 new major clients within a three- to five-year period. In line with this strategic plan, Systems Solutions wins a number of tenders within the first two years.

Neglecting risk management

As Systems Solutions grows, the leadership team neglects to proactively identify its operational risk exposures. Unfortunately, the risk profile of Systems Solutions changes considerably and the organisation struggles to meet its contractual obligations regarding quality of support and timeliness.

Self-Help Question 6.9

Brainstorm how developing a risk management profile would have helped the management team at Systems Solutions to manage its risk exposures (for example, identifying opportunities as they arose).

Answers to self-help questions are provided at the end of each section.

Summary

Please keep in mind the following points:

- To effectively manage organisational risks, it is critical for key stakeholders to have a common understanding of the concepts and language related to risk and risk management.
- ISO/Guide 73:2009 Risk management – Vocabulary (3.7.1.2) defines risk appetite as:

  ...the amount and type of risk an organisation is willing to pursue or retain.

- Risk tolerance is:

  ...the level or amount of risk the organisation is willing to bear.

- The organisation's appetite and tolerance to risk determines the type and amount of risk an organisation is willing and able to accept in the pursuit of its objectives.
- The risk appetite statement reflects the board's view on what degrees of risk are acceptable (or unacceptable) to the business to meet its stated strategy.
- **Strategic management** involves the following three steps:

  – identifying opportunities for market growth
  – determining which of those opportunities to pursue
  – allocating resources to facilitate realising the opportunity.

- When implementing the strategic direction of the business through the corporate plan, managers need to consider risks (threats and opportunities) the organisation might encounter.
- World Economic Forum Global Risks report (2010) defines creeping risks as:

  ...risks linked to big shifts that are recognized and which will roll out over many years, even decades...

- Reto Schneider, Swiss Re's Head of Emerging Risk Management (2012) defines emerging risk as:

  ...new or already known risks which are difficult to assess...

- Strategic risk management assists an organisation to achieve its goals and avoid (or minimise) surprises along the way.
- The main strategic management processes include:

  – formulating the strategy
  – implementing the strategy.

- Formulating the strategy involves the following three steps:
  - creating a vision
  - understanding the environment
  - creating the strategic plan.
- Implementing the strategy involves:
  - allocating resources, authority and accountability
  - managing strategy implementation.
- Organisations can manage strategy implementation through:
  - business and operational planning
  - monitoring, analysis and review.
- Risk management is an integral component of strategic planning because realised risks have an effect on an organisation's ability to achieve its objectives.
- The three main components of risk management at the strategic level are:
  - managing risk in the pursuit of opportunities
  - the strategic risk management document suite
  - developing a risk management framework.
- Risk management frameworks should address the following elements:
  - a risk management policy including definitions of risk categories and a statement of risk appetite
  - accountability
  - risk management system
  - creating a positive risk culture.
- The risk management profile is the organisation's documented understanding of its risk exposures.

Answers to Self-Help Questions

Self-help question 6.1

The organisation not having the capability to achieve its strategic goals results in consistent frustration and under-performance.

Self-help question 6.2

Five strategic concerns in a modern corporate context are:

- grow the business;
- successfully compete in the marketplace;
- react to a changing market environment;
- ensure that the functional elements of the business work to achieve organisational objectives;
- meet capacity and capability requirements.

Self-help question 6.3

Some of the benefits of implementing an integrated risk management framework include:

- reduced costs through reduced duplication of effort;
- a greater understanding of control requirements (for example, training, delegations, resource allocation and asset management);
- the ability to create unified objectives and to focus on achieving established business goals;
- defined boundaries around roles and responsibilities;
- increased effectiveness of decision-making;
- enhanced levels of organisational harmonisation, leading to increased productivity and quality outcomes;
- enhanced stakeholder satisfaction through more effective communication and confidence in processes to manage risk.

Self-help question 6.4

The potential benefits of strategic management for an organisation include a capacity to:

- optimise organisational performance and results;
- institutionalise a rigorous process of decision-making and environmental analysis;
- identify different levels and types of strategic options;
- identify, prioritise and exploit opportunities and threats;
- develop a framework for improved co-ordination and control of activities;
- reduce bureaucracy and the duplication of work;
- clarification of individual responsibilities;
- encourage forward thinking;
- increased responsiveness to change;
- empower employees.

Self-help question 6.5

The strategic plan may include the following content areas:

- the board chairperson or CEO's executive statement;
- an overview of the strategic plan's development;
- the organisation's:
  - mission and vision statements
  - company values
  - corporate objectives
  - current position in the market (for example, an environmental scan of external opportunities and threats)
  - internal performance (strengths and weaknesses)
  - key result areas (or outcomes)
  - priorities and strategies (by function area).

Self-help question 6.6

The critical success factors for strategic plans include:

- senior management commitment;
- employee commitment;
- an understanding of customer needs;
- the ability to predict the reaction of competitors and other external stakeholders (for example, regulators);
- accurately determining resource capability (for example, are there sufficient staff members and pieces of equipment, or is there appropriate skills management?);
- accurately determining time requirements;
- well-developed reporting and control management systems;
- a flexible organisational structure;
- adequately tracked milestones;
- managing performance measures;
- applying change management principles;
- effective communication plans.

Self-help question 6.7

Other ways different organisations refer to operational plans include:
- annual plans
- management plans
- tactical plans.

Self-help question 6.8

Some of the strategic risks Coffee on Wheels may face include:

- failing to understand market competition (for example, mobile operators or other food outlets);
- failing to understand the strengths of competitors;
- a limited ability to maintain their quality of service and products;
- an increased risk of staff injury as a result of physical threats;
- an inability to provide timely first aid to staff;
- a difficulty in predicting consumables required;
- an inability to meet increased demand (for example, inadequacy of equipment or staffing levels);
- equipment failure;
- a lack of financial protection in the event of:
  - a significant equipment failure
  - the new area(s) not being profitable
- a limited ability to replicate its current success.

Self-help question 6.9

By developing a risk management profile, senior managers at System Solutions would have been able to:

- more effectively identify the organisation's major risk areas, enabling them to ensure they effectively manage key risk exposures;
- have greater confidence they have the capacity to take on new clients as well as manage the needs of existing clients;
- identify new areas of risk going forward;
- anticipate any issues that may threaten achieving their corporate goals.

In addition, new clients would recognise the senior management's increased level of confidence as they conducted their due diligence, which provides the organisation with a market edge over competitors.

Chapter 7

Types and Impact of Risk on Organisations

Introduction

This chapter explores the various definitions of risk, the different types of risk and the different types of hazards that can affect an organisation. It also outlines the importance of risk assessments in managing risks.

Learning Outcomes

By the end of this chapter, you should be able to:

- define risk;
- identify different types of risks and the impacts they have on an organisation;
- define hazards;
- identify different types of hazards and the impacts they have on an organisation;
- document the findings of risk assessments.

Defining Risk

There are countless definitions of risk to be found in published works and there are numerous different types of risk. In the past, risk was commonly seen as the chance of something happening that will have an adverse effect on an organisation or individual. This limited view of risk has now been superseded by a much broader definition and understanding. For example, ISO 31000:2018 defines risk as:

> [...] the effect of uncertainty on objectives.

Essentials and Assessment of Risk Management, 101–115

Published under exclusive licence by Emerald Publishing Limited
doi:10.1108/978-1-83662-302-120251018

In *Enlightened Risk Taking*, George Head and Melanie Herman define risk as:

> [...] the measure of the possibility that the future may be surprisingly different from what we expect.

Risk is all about uncertainty, or more importantly the effect of uncertainty on the achievement of objectives. Without risk, there is no reward or progress, but unless risk is managed effectively opportunities will not be maximised and threats will not be minimised.

All risks have a source – they are generally associated with a particular decision, situation, event or incident – and they have a likelihood and a consequence.

You will notice as you read through the learning material and undertake the questions and activities that the term risk has both a positive and negative connotation. This is because there is both an upside and downside to the risk equation. The downside is the potential for damage to reputation, failure of market or product, reduction in earnings or turnover, property damage or similar type of loss. The upside is the potential for benefit in terms of company profile or credibility, increased profit, reduction in costs, increase in turnover or other similar gain.

Risk Characteristics

There are countless definitions of risk (as well as various risk types) but the shared commonality between these definitions is the components making up risk. All risks have the following three characteristics:

- a source, which is generally associated with a particular:
  - decision
  - situation
  - event
  - incident
- a likelihood (will the risk occur and if so, when?)
- a consequence (what is the impact if the risk occurs?).

EXAMPLE

Building Fire and Company Vehicle Damage

Building fire

For example, the likelihood of a fire in your organisation's building is *very unlikely* but the consequences would be major if it did occur.

Company vehicle damage

Conversely, the likelihood that an employee may accidently cause minor damage to a company vehicle is *likely*, but the consequences are *relatively insignificant*.

Source	Likelihood	Consequence
Building fire	Very unlikely	Major
Company vehicle damage	Likely	Relatively insignificant

Types of Hazards

A hazard is a condition that increases the chance of loss, firstly to the customer and ultimately to the insurer. There are four categories of hazards and each is important in terms of risk acceptance.

Physical Hazards

Physical hazards relate to the condition of premises and the activities that are undertaken. The physical hazards vary according to the class of business operating at the premises.

In commercial property insurance, physical hazards relate to hazards arising under four broad headings:

- **construction of the premises** – e.g. buildings in poor repair or built from inferior materials constitute a hazard;
- **occupation carried on at the premises** – e.g. chemicals or flammable liquids being stored constitute a hazard;
- **protection provided at the premises** – e.g. unguarded machinery or poor fire protection are hazards;
- **location of the premises** – some areas are prone to a high risk of burglary, some areas are earthquake-prone or exposed to regular floods. The occupation of a neighbour can also be a hazard.

You must consider each one of these factors in relation to the perils the insured is being covered against.

With liability risks, the approach is similar when the following are considered:

- insured's activities – these are considered in relation to the legal liabilities that might be faced by the insured;
- insured's premises (whether owned or occupied) – the location and condition of the premises are relevant;
- precautions taken by the insured to minimise possible loss;
- size of the business – the larger the business, the higher the people and property damage exposure.

For the following self-help question, examine the below insurance schedule carefully, particularly in relation to the physical hazards.

Self-Help Question 7.1

Examine the insurance schedule provided below and then answer the following questions:

1. Identify the specific physical hazards in this proposal under the following headings:
    - occupation
    - construction
    - security
    - fire protection.
2. Is there any other information missing that should be included in the insurance schedule? Explain your answer.
3. Are there any items included that should not be included? Explain your answer.
4. Comment on any other aspects of the proposal that need clarification.

FIRE & GENERAL INSURANCE INTERMEDIARIES	
16 Chemin du Feu, Brussels	
Tel: (32) 0876 54321	Fax: (32) 0876 54322
INSURANCE SCHEDULE	
Date:	6 July 2017 Jules
Insured:	Jules Poirot
Situation:	203 Rue des Blancmaisons, Aalst
Occupation:	Property Owners—Vacant Premises
Construction:	Brick walls/concrete floor/iron roof
Security:	
• Front door has a key-operated lock	
• Front windows are double-fronted	
• Rear door has a key-operated lock	
• No rear windows	

→

Fire protection:	Nil
CLASS OF INSURANCE – COMMERCIAL	
Fire	
Building	€ 3,000,000
Removal of debris	€ 30,000
	€ 3,030,000
Business Interruption:	
Gross rental	
*Indemnity period: 12 months	€ 300,000
Plate Glass	
Internal & external glass	Replacement value
Public Liability	
Limit of liability	€ 12,000,000

Answers to self-help questions are provided at the end of each section.

Moral Hazards

A moral hazard depends on the:

- character, qualities and reputation of the insured;
- general nature of the insured's employees and associates;
- subject matter of the insurance, including its vulnerability to changes in fashion, technology, etc.;
- care and efficiency of the insured's management (or the lack of it).

Examples of moral hazards include:

- an employee with a past history of embezzlement;
- a client who has previously been denied insurance, or has criminal convictions.

Poor moral hazards increase the uncertainty in the risk and, unlike physical hazards, adding a premium loading or special terms will not make it acceptable. It is not possible to underwrite around a moral hazard.

Moral hazards are the most difficult to detect and can cause problems. Indicators you can look out for include:

- questionable past losses such as fraudulent and exaggerated claims or questionable business practices;
- a poor financial history or obvious cash flow problems.

Moral and physical hazards are evaluated together via the information you collect. Your good judgement is vital in detecting them.

EXAMPLE

Moral Risk

Piotr wishes to insure a new vehicle valued at €30,000. He completed the proposal form, answering 'yes' to the following question:

> In the past five years, has the proposer or any driver who is likely to drive the vehicle ever:
> a) been charged with or convicted of the following:
> [...] criminal offence, speeding, negligent driving, careless driving, exceeding alcohol limit, driving under the influence, dangerous driving or other?

Piotr discloses one speeding fine and a seatbelt offence. He also discloses a charge for handling/receiving stolen goods for which he was placed on a 12-month good behaviour bond with no conviction recorded. At the time the proposal is put forward, only one month of the bond remains to be served.

Activity | Moral risk

Consider Piotr's disclosure, as outlined in the case study above.

1. Do you think Piotr presents a moral risk? Why/why not?
2. Do you think the proposed risk is likely to fall within an organisation's risk acceptance criteria? Why/why not?
3. Would you accept this risk on behalf of an insurer that handles motor vehicle insurance? Why/why not?

Morale Hazards

Morale hazards are caused by indifference or carelessness – not by the proposer's poor character or integrity. A poor morale hazard increases the uncertainty factor in the risk because, through carelessness, an insured may act in a way that leads to losses.

A morale hazard can be detected in situations where there are poor management practices such as:

- a factory where management fails to keep the floor free of off-cuts and other waste;
- a retail store that does not have enough employees to keep stock in order;
- poor regard for employee safety in a factory, which may result in conditions that increase the risk of employee injury and/or fire hazard;
- poor building and plant maintenance – e.g. frayed wiring, leaking roofs, etc.
- poor security – where the insured's property is not adequately protected from loss or damage.

Hazards like these in one area of a business may indicate similar hazards in other areas. Morale hazards can be good indicators of the insured's attitudes and often follow inadequate financial capital in the business.

Case study – Sky Tower Electronics

Sky Tower Electronics manufactures circuit boards for computers, automobiles, etc. Acid is used in the processing. If the acid escapes into the drainage system it could cause considerable damage to people and property. If it should spill onto skin, employees could be severely burned.

Dieter Schmidt, the owner and manager of the factory, is insured with Global Insurance, which has inspected his premises many times. This time, the insurer's surveyor reports that a number of safety items are not in place, including a hose-down area for employees. This carelessness endangers not only property but also the lives of those who work at the factory.

Legal Hazards

Legal hazards relate to the operation of laws. It is important that you keep up to date with legislation and be aware of court decisions that may affect your work. Higher courts can make findings of negligence in situations where such a possibility had not been previously considered by underwriters.

Like other hazards, legal hazards increase the risk. Areas of insurance most affected by legal hazards include:

- liability – including commercial property insurance that includes liability;
- property insurance – building codes and regulations, local council by-laws and regulations and changing fire brigade or environmental requirements all affect the risk exposure;
- consumer protection legislation can also impact on liability for both customers and insurers.

Types of Risks

Every insurer would prefer to accept only good quality business; however, proposals will inevitably vary from 'above standard' to 'below standard' risks.

Above Standard Risks

Above standard risks are the risks every insurer seeks in order to enhance its portfolio. They are risks that have high loss protective measures in place. For example:

- a modern high-rise office block;
- a fully computerised factory/warehouse of fire-resisting construction;
- premises with a burglar alarm with a central control monitored connection.

These sorts of risks may attract lower premiums and/or improved terms. This is because the good risk reduces the probability of claims to below that of the standard covers.

Below Standard Risks

Less attractive business may be offered to an insurer as part of an overall account, or an insurance intermediary may submit such a risk for consideration, when the majority of business offered is of good quality.

There are occasions when an insurer may feel obliged to quote terms for business that would not normally come within its acceptance criteria. This is called accommodation business. For example:

- burglary cover for the contents of a chemist's shop that stocks 'theft attractive' drugs and has little or no protection;
- domestic contents cover in a high-risk burglary area yet premises have very little or no protection;
- wooden construction of ski lodges in snow country.

Improving Poor Risks

The solution does not always lie in increased premiums. Sometimes, a less attractive risk can be improved by the terms arranged. For example, a large business may be prepared to carry a degree of self-insurance (referred to as deductible or excess) to reduce its costs. It might take the view that it could fund losses up to a certain amount (for example, €600,000) but requires cover for major losses. In these circumstances, the insured would normally undertake risk improvement measures to control losses for the benefit of the business.

Such measures might include:

- the appointment of a safety officer;
- appropriate fire drills;
- possibly, a private fire brigade in large complexes;
- installation of fire protection equipment such as sprinklers, smoke/heat detectors, hydrants, hoses and fire extinguishers;
- management commitment to loss prevention;
- sophisticated security precautions;
- earthquake-resistant design.

Improving poor risks is one solution; addressing them directly (optimising risk) may be another. This involves taking a more active role than risk minimisation and tackling the root causes of risk head on. The following case study shows how creative risk management of this sort can lead to reduced losses.

Case Study – Risk Improvement

A spray painting booth in a motor vehicle assembly plant created a spray 'drift' that clogged up adjacent sprinkler heads.

After investigation, it was decided to put small paper bags over the sprinkler heads to prevent paint penetration without obstructing the activation of the sprinkler. In this situation, the force of the sprinkler's water bursts the paper bag and the sprinkler operates as intended.

Impact of Risks

The primary purpose of risk management is to reduce the impact a risk will have on an organisation and its objectives. Identifying the impact of a risk involves:

- identifying affected organisational objectives;
- establishing the likely effects on the objectives;
- determining where, when, why and how risks are most likely to occur;
- establishing maximum potential consequences or losses.

A risk exposure may have potential sources of risk with financial and non-financial consequences, including:

- property
- reputation and image

- people
- income
- legal liability
- environment.

The measure an organisation uses to record the consequences of a potential exposure to risk largely depends on the organisation's objectives. If the organisation's objective is growth, the organisation would measure its risk exposure in market share or dollar terms.

The organisation would then prioritise the impacts it thinks will have the greatest effect on the business.

Note: The organisation determines the measures of consequence (for example, monetary or frequency of employee injuries) when developing the risk management framework.

Example – Employee Injuries

A good example of the measures an organisation could use to record potential exposure consequences relates to employee injuries, wherein the organisation could choose either the financial or injury measure.

Organisations measure the employee injury risk exposure with regard to the impact on the employee (as the business has a legal and moral responsibility to safeguard them). In this situation, the injury itself is far more important for the organisation to prevent than the resulting financial consequences.

The financial consequences of the injury are often relatively minor due to the worker accident schemes covering the costs.

Recording Risk Assessments

Risk treatment plans facilitate an organisation's documentation of selected treatment options when the risk analysis phase reveals the need for additional control measures.

A well-executed treatment plan should include:

- the proposed actions/activities;
- how to resource the treatment;
- whose responsibility it is to implement the treatment;
- the time frame within which the treatment is implemented;
- measures for determining whether or not the treatment is successful;
- monitoring and reporting requirements.

When there is a material cost involved, it is essential for treatment plans to take into account (and be incorporated into) the overall operational and budgetary management of the organisation.

Planning Documents

The risk register normally has the facility to be able to record and monitor treatment plans. If this is not possible, organisations can create separate planning documents, such as risk treatment schedules and risk treatment action plans.

Document Formality

In practice, the level of document formality depends on the complexity of the risks and the likely costs involved. If the risks are minor, the following items usually suffice:

- a simple action item in the risk register;
- the accountable person and deadlines would usually suffice.

Organisations typically need to systematically develop risk treatment plans in conjunction with people who are familiar with the organisation's processes and procedures.

By using this approach, organisations can usually solve any risk treatment-related difficulties prior to implementation.

Note: It is not the risk manager's decision to implement a risk treatment plan (they can only make recommendations). The risk owner and the executive to whom the risk manager reports need to make decisions concerning risk treatment.

Risk Register

As outlined previously, a risk register provides a record for each identified risk exposure, noting its:

- nature and cause
- existing controls
- consequences and likelihood
- initial risk rating
- assessment of control quality
- accountable manager
- risk treatment plans including responsible persons and time frames.

Risk Treatment Plan

The risk treatment plan:

- documents how the organisation will implement all selected treatment options for any given risk;
- includes how these selected treatment options will work together to treat the identified risk exposures;
- provides a summary of the recommended response and consequences;

- provides an action plan relating to each risk exposure;
- outlines a program for reviewing the effectiveness of the risk treatments.

Contents

The risk treatment plan should:

- clearly identify and prioritise individual risk treatments;
- identify those responsible and accountable for risk treatment implementation;
- provide an outline of the expected outcomes of each risk treatment;
- provide a breakdown of the costs and resources involved in implementing each risk treatment;
- identify risk treatments the organisation cannot implement due to financial limitations;
- include a schedule for implementation (including risk treatments the organisation cannot implement due to financial limitations);
- detail the monitoring and review process the organisation uses to determine the effectiveness of the risk treatments.

Only when an organisation has implemented the risk treatment plan can it add the risk treatment plan as a control in the risk register.

Risk Management Program Development and Implementation

Organisations should not confuse developing and implementing a **treatment plan** with developing and implementing a **risk management program**.

A risk management program takes a much higher level view by:

- selling the concept of managing risk to:

  - developing objectives for the board
  - senior management
  - other stakeholders

- assigning responsibility
- identifying the resource requirements
- setting the risk management policy and other associated policies
- selecting personnel
- communicating policies
- developing the framework.

Residual Risk

Residual risk exposures remain after an organisation has determined risk treatment options and established treatment plans.

Organisations need to inform all stakeholders of:

- these residual risk exposures
- their extent
- what risk these risk exposures constitute for the organisation.

An organisation can inform all these stakeholders by:

- carefully documenting the residual risk exposures;
- regularly monitoring and reviewing them.

Typically, an organisation reports residual risk exposure information to the executive and to the board. The level of reporting depends on the deadline these groups set for receipt of the required information.

Activity | A treatment plan for your organisation

1. Consider how you might develop a risk treatment plan for your organisation (or one of its clients).
2. If possible, develop a risk treatment plan for one of your identified risk exposures.

Summary

- ISO 31000:2018 has clearly shifted the emphasis of the risk management field on creating and protecting value as the key driver of risk management and leadership by top management who should ensure that risk management is integrated into all organisational activities, starting with governance.
- The primary purpose of risk management is to reduce the impact a risk will have on an organisation and its objectives.
- The different types of risk are:

  – above standard
  – below standard

- The different types of hazard are:

  – physical
  – moral

– morale
– legal

- A risk treatment plan documents how an organisation will:

  – implement all selected risk treatment options
  – review their effects.

- The risk treatment plan:

  – identifies and prioritises individual risk treatments to be actioned
  – identifies who is responsible for the implementation
  – identifies the necessary resources
  – includes a schedule for implementation
  – outlines the expected outcomes of each risk treatment
  – provides a breakdown of cost and resources
  – identifies risk treatments an organisation cannot implement due to operational or financial limitations
  – details the review process an organisation uses to determine the effectiveness of risk treatments.

- Organisations need to clearly devise, document and communicate risk treatment plans to clearly understand:

  – the effects of the treatment
  – the reasons the treatment is required.

Answers to Self-Help Questions

Self-help question 7.1

1. The physical risks:

- **Occupation** – additional information is required about how long the building has been vacant, why it is vacant, and what was the previous occupation. Unfortunately, in the current market, underwriters are shying away from writing these types of risks and it is becoming more difficult to place them. The longer the premises have remained vacant, the less likely an underwriter will be to accept the risk. The main problem with this type of risk is the malicious damage that can be caused by trespassers. Should you as underwriter accept the risk, you would impose a very high excess on all classes of insurance.
- **Construction** – construction of the building may be acceptable when the occupation of the risk is known. Physical separation of adjacent premises, age of the building, and divisional walls (such as parapet walls,

→

→ double or single walls between adjoining buildings) are other underwriting considerations.

- **Security of risk** – even though the burglary/theft class of insurance has not been selected, the security of the premises is still very important in the light of potential malicious damage. You should recommend that the insured upgrades security on the front and rear doors to deadlocks, as a minimum. You should also obtain clarification about the construction of the front and rear doors, as it would be pointless to install deadlocks on doors that are frail. Window grilles and a security service are other options.
- **Fire protection** – because the premises are vacant, the installation of fire extinguishers would not help, as any fire occurring in this type of situation would be maliciously ignited, i.e. arson. However, a recommendation could be made to install fire protection, preferably before the premises become occupied – either local or back-to-base at the fire station or a private monitory service. It is also not a bad idea to ask the question about electricity, gas and water, and whether they have been disconnected to reduce any potential loss.

2. Missing information:

- Information is missing regarding the claims experience of the insured. Five years of claims experience is the standard in the industry.
- **Liability** – the main piece of information required for rating public and product liability is the area size of the site that would include the building and any surrounding land.

3. **Business Interruption** – the request is to insure loss of rent for 12 months; however, the premises are vacant. In this case, you would be wise to seek further information. Has a lease been signed? Is a tenant about to move in? The cover should only commence on reoccupation.

   Plate glass – information required to determine a premium for this class is normally the size of the largest pane of glass, e.g. 2sqm or 4sqm, etc. Because of the high excess that would be placed on glass insurance due to the building's vacancy, you should consider whether it would be economical to insure for plate glass, and advise the customer accordingly.

4. Further comments:

Sum insured – you should question the sum insured allocated to removal of debris because it appears quite low in light of the sum insured on the building. Should the building be totally destroyed, the cost to clear the site would certainly be greater than €30,000.

The public liability limit seems too low at 12 million euros. You should question the adequacy of this limit. It is important to guard against underinsurance in all areas including liability.

Chapter 8

Risk Management Process: Identification, Assessment, Treatment, Control, Financing

Introduction

This section describes the risk management process.

Learning Outcomes

By the end of this chapter, you should be able to:

- define risk assessment;
- describe the purpose and benefits of risk assessment;
- recall the three steps of risk assessment;
- suggest reduction and control measures;
- describe the traditional risk financing options and the benefits and limitations of each;
- Select appropriate feedback mechanisms.

The Risk Management Process

To assist with the management of risks, ISO 31000:2018 provides a consistent approach to the risk management process and a framework for the development and implementation of policies and procedures.

The following two important components lie behind the development of a risk management framework and the success of the risk management program:

- communicating/consulting with stakeholders
- establishing the context.

Essentials and Assessment of Risk Management, 117–129

Published under exclusive licence by Emerald Publishing Limited
doi:10.1108/978-1-83662-302-120251021

These two components also form the basis for all subsequent activities in the risk management process.

The Six Major Steps

As depicted in the following diagram, the ISO 31000:2018 prescribed risk management process consists of the following six major steps:

- communicate and consult
- establish the scope, context and risk criteria
- assess risks:
  - identify risks
  - analyse risks
  - evaluate risks
- treat risks
- monitor and review
- recording and reporting.

Guidance

This ISO 31000:2018 guidance for the development and implementation of policies and procedures enables an organisation to:

These six steps consist of a number of activities for assessing and managing risk.

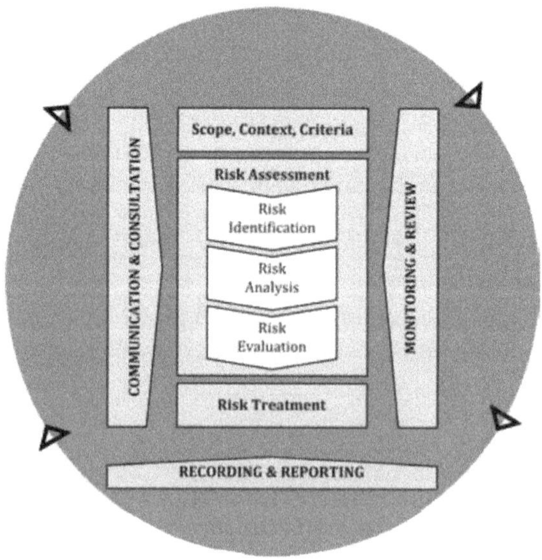

- handle the risks to which it is exposed;
- maximise any opportunities;
- minimise the downsides of risk exposure that could significantly affect the viability of the business.

Note: This guidance must be tailored to the systems and culture of an organisation before it is useful; a one-size-fits-all approach is not effective.

Establishing the Context

Establishing the risk management context is integral to effectively managing risk. An organisation can only establish the context of its risk management efforts once it understands the internal and external context in which it operates. The risk management context includes:

- risk management activity parameters;
- which parts of an organisation these parameters will be applied to.

Parameters

The parameters of the risk management process must be clearly defined, taking into consideration both the costs and benefits of risk management. For example, it is useless to introduce a state-of-the-art risk management initiative if it fails to support the organisation's goals and objectives or if the organisation cannot afford to implement the initiative.

Considerations

According to ISO 31000:2018, the context of the risk management varies according to the needs of an organisation.

The context can involve, but is not limited to, defining:

- the goals and objectives of risk management activities;
- responsibilities for/within the risk management process;
- the scope, and the depth and breadth of the risk;
- management activities, including specific inclusions and exclusions;
- the following items in terms of time and location:
  - activity
  - process
  - function
  - project
  - product
  - service
  - asset

- the relationships between an organisation's different:
  - projects
  - processes
  - activities
- risk assessment methodologies;
- the way the organisation evaluates performance and effectiveness in the management of risk.

The context can also involve:

- identifying and specifying the decisions the organisation needs to make;
- identifying, scoping or framing:
  - required studies
  - the extent and objectives of these studies
  - the resources required for such studies.

In Practice

In practical terms, the risk management context means determining:

- roles and responsibilities with regard to managing each risk exposure;
- the relationship between risk management and the different parts of the organisation.

Organisational Versus Project-Based Risks

Managing an entire organisation's exposure to risk will be quite different from that of a particular project. Organisational risks address an organisation's normal state of operations, in contrast with risks in projects where a short-term set of processes is established.

The Organisational Context

Establishing an organisation's context for risk management involves:

- a single organisation which can present diverse risk exposures;
- a historical review and future strategies;
- speaking with:
  - the CEO
  - the CFO
  - operations management

- understanding the board's mandate and commitment;
- a regulatory environment relevant to the particular industry;
- taking into account competitors.

Project-Based Context

In contrast to the organisational context, the context a project's risk management of a project differs in that it:

- is likely to involve more than one organisation;
- usually has a short duration;
- is often distinctly different from the day-to-day activities of an organisation; thus creating a different risk exposure/profile;
- is in a constant state of change;
- has a different regulatory environment;
- involves speaking with:
  - project staff
  - engineers
  - financiers.

Risk Assessment

Risk assessment aims to identify, analyse and evaluate risks to inform organisational decision-making and actions. Risk assessment involves:

- collecting detailed information using a variety of techniques, such as:
  - quantitative
  - semi-quantitative
  - qualitative analysis
- presenting analysis results in a format suitable for risk evaluation.

Three Distinct Steps

ISO 31000:2018 encourages dividing risk assessment into the following three distinct steps:

1. identify risks
2. analyse risks
3. evaluate risks.

Identify Risks

The primary aim of risk identification is to construct a comprehensive list of risks:

- sources (for example, the operation of a machine)
- events

- causes (for example, the failure to follow a safety procedure)
- consequences (potential or otherwise).

Analyse Risks

The risk assessment stage analyses identified risk exposures to determine their potential likelihood and consequences.

Evaluate Risks

The risk evaluation stage involves determining which risks the organisation can tolerate (risk appetite). For risks the organisation cannot tolerate, the organisation needs to identify appropriate risk treatment options to reduce these risks to a tolerable level.

We will now look at the risk identification process in further detail.

Further Reading

International Organization for Standardization's (ISO) ISO/IEC 31010:2009, *Risk management – Risk assessment techniques* (or ISO/IEC 31010) provides additional guidance on risk assessment techniques that may assist in all three steps of the risk assessment process.

Reduction and Controls

Risk cannot be totally eliminated. In some cases, it is simply not possible, in others it would be prohibitively expensive. Therefore, the aim of risk reduction is to reduce the likelihood and impact of danger and accidents, whether in relation to finances, increased charges or loss of income. It should be remembered that the higher the cost of risk, the more it is necessary to put controls in place.

When reduction measures are effective, potential impacts will be lessened. Risks and reduction measures should be documented and regularly reviewed to ensure they are relevant and effective. Managers responsible for individual risks for which they have documented controls are primarily responsible for ensuring that the controls are in place and operating reliably.

Risk controls can include:

- internal audits that periodically review whether the documented controls exist and are operating;
- periodic management confirmations (or attestations) that the organisation is adhering to the risk plan;
- a risk register that automatically:
  - surveys managers
  - confirms controls are operating
  - notes the field describing the responsible manager
  - generates an email to the responsible individual
- external reviews in key risk areas (such as WHS and treasury).

EXAMPLE

Periodic Management Confirmation

A periodic management confirmation (or testimony) can usually be as simple as a manager stating the following:

I am satisfied we have:

- recorded the material risks in my area of responsibility in the risk system;
- executed the documented controls consistent with the way they have been described.

Other than the following noted issues, we are developing documented control improvement plans according to the agreed schedule.

Other examples that are specific to certain sources of risk are listed in the following table.

Identified Risk	Control
Failure to achieve product growth goals	• Marketing plan • Advertising • Customer surveys
Employee injury	• WHS committee • WHS audits • Training
Printing errors	• Proofreading • Page scanning (including spell check)
Fraud	• Segregation of duties • Reconciliations • System security

Risk Improvement Plans

Risk managers typically monitor risk improvement plans directly to ensure the organisation is executing them. Depending on its sophistication, the organisation can use the risk register as a tool to provide email reminders to responsible managers and schedule formal reviews of the change process.

Hazard Monitoring

Monitoring systems for hazard-type risks are also important and can include:

- workers compensation/accident compensation claims;
- claims by third parties for faulty products;

- property loss reports;
- claims by third parties for bodily injury or property damage;
- motor vehicle accident reports;
- WHS reporting (for example, accident investigation reports);
- operating licence renewals (for example, dangerous goods storage and waste discharge).

Fundamental Information

Recording the following information should form a fundamental part of any monitoring system:

- cause
- time
- place
- amount of losses
- other information the organisation may use for analysing unexpected events/losses.

Risk Financing

Risk financing is concerned with ensuring there is available funding to offset the financial consequences of exposure to risk. Like the other methods of risk sharing, risk financing does not prevent the loss event from occurring. In the long term, any financing arrangement works effectively as long as there is a sharing of the financial consequences of events by spreading the cost over a number of years.

Traditional Risk Financing Options

The following diagram outlines the traditional risk financing options organisations use to fund loss exposures. As highlighted, the most common methods of financing risk are insurance and retention (self-insurance).

Insurance

Traditional insurance is a common method of financing risk whereby an organisation buys insurance cover from one or more commercial insurers. The organisation pays an agreed premium for a specific insurance contract, for a specific period (usually no more than 12 months).

Limited Cover

Insurance contracts do not cover all possible losses or even the total cost of those losses due to a number of factors, including:

- a restricted scope of cover policy wording

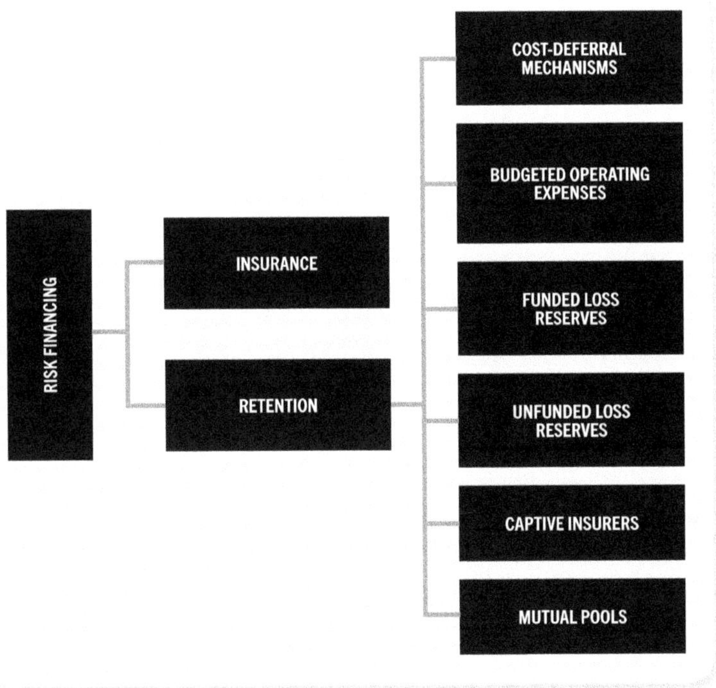

- the cost of premiums over time
- under-insurance
- excesses
- the un-insurability of a particular exposure (such as loss of reputation or nuclear catastrophe).

Catastrophic Losses

Insurance is ideally suited for providing finance for what would be a catastrophic loss. Organisations need to define what they consider to be a catastrophic loss when deciding:

- whether or not to utilise insurance
- what form insurances should take, including the:

  – total amount of cover
  – deductible (or excess) needing to be paid for each claim.

  Each of these factors has a significant impact on cost.

When to Purchase Insurance

If organisations successfully apply the risk management process, they only generally purchase insurance when:

- there is a remote risk of a very large loss (a catastrophe);
- the premium is appropriate;
- the likelihood of the loss is unpredictable but low;
- there is a need to spread the cost of losses over a number of years (thereby spreading the consequences on the organisation's bottom line over a number of years).

It is unlikely for organisations to purchase insurance when:

- the likelihood of the risk exposure is high, but the cost is minor and/or;
- the total amount of loss in any one year would not materially affect the organisation's bottom line or profit.

Loss Stabilisation

A loss stabilisation plan is another form of insurance organisations can use to finance risk. Herein, the insurer agrees to pay the organisation any loss (up to a maximum amount per loss and for the period of the coverage). In exchange, the organisation agrees to pay the insurer a premium equal to the maximum amount payable divided by the period over which the organisation will reimburse the insurer.

Cancellation

The organisation cannot cancel the agreement until the premiums equal payment of:

- the total of any losses
- the insurer's expenses and profits.

The loss stabilisation plan guarantees the insurer a profit. In addition, any surplus monies after an agreed amount of investment income has been taken into account is returned to the organisation or rolled over for a new period of cover.

Considerations

The loss stabilisation plan is one of a variety of risk sharing/alternative risk financing plans now available to organisations. However, these are often quite complex risk financing techniques and take considerable time to establish.

Retention

Every organisation has a certain level of financial resources that, in some instances, may be more secure than those of many insurance underwriters. These organisations have the capacity to fund to some extent their own losses. Furthermore, purchasing insurance cover is always more expensive than retention as the intermediaries, insurer services and stakeholders must be compensated.

How much an organisation is able to self-insure depends on its financial resources and the risks to which it is exposed.

There are two types of retention:

- unplanned
- planned.

Unplanned Retention

Unplanned retention relates to financial exposures organisations fail to identify during the risk identification phase. As a result, the organisation:

- makes no provision to finance losses relating to those exposures;
- must use funds that may have been budgeted for other costs (or as a surplus) to pay for the loss.

Planned Retention

Planned retention relates to financial exposures to risk that an organisation identifies and decides to carry by financing any losses from its business funds.

An organisation is most likely to use retention in the following situations:

- The organisation has no other basis for handling the downside of exposure to risk. For example, many organisations with high losses (such as wood-working and fibre glass industries) find it almost impossible to obtain property insurance.
- Retention offers the cheapest or best method to fund the loss.

Note: The following elements must be present in this situation:

- the number and amount of losses must be predictable over time;
- the organisation must be able to meet the largest single loss;
- the cost of retention should be no higher than the insurance premium/s.

Catastrophic Losses

An organisation must also consider catastrophic losses and their likely effect on the business in addition to withstanding the aggregate losses; that is, an accumulation of small losses. With catastrophic losses, an organisation should only carry losses up to the level that it is able to predict accurately. Above that level, the organisation should arrange insurance or reinsurance.

Administration

When a business decides to self-insure all or some of their risk exposures, they must be willing to undertake the administration of the self-insurance portfolio or outsource this to a provider.

Willingness

An organisation with the ability to finance a loss may not necessarily be willing to do so. An organisation's decision to retain risk is largely dependent on its board's/ management's risk appetite – the level of loss it is willing to accept and its ability to effectively manage losses.

Feedback Mechanisms

There is a need to be specific when using risk management concepts within an organisation as industry terminology is not always understood by stakeholders, both internal and external. Even terms that seem standard may be understood differently by personnel from different departments. Additionally, there tend to be cognitive biases as well as fear and excitement when it comes to dealing with risks.

Feedback is one of these terms as it covers an array of different issues. All risk management professionals who are tasked with providing feedback should make sure they are on the same page as their manager/leader and can deliver on the expectations.

The three main types of feedback are:

- **Feedback loop**

This is part of the 'monitoring and review' step of the risk management process and is designed to ensure that the risk management plan remains relevant and that the execution is efficient.

- **'Post-mortem'**

Any significant event that led to a disruption of normal activities needs to be looked at in detail, including:

– analysing the incident (through butterfly, root cause analysis, etc.)
– evaluating actions taken and what else could have been done
– reviewing lessons learned.

- **Data gathering**

Gathering data assists organisations to develop models and statistical forecasts, which will inform future risk management activities.

Summary

Please keep the following points from this chapter in mind:

- The five major steps of risk assessment are:
  - communicate and consult
  - establish the context
  - assess risk
  - treat risks
  - monitor and review.
- Risk management treatment focuses on deciding which measures will ensure the achievement of objectives.
- The four main options for treating losses are:
  - risk retention
  - risk control by reducing the likelihood and consequence of risk
  - risk sharing
  - risk avoidance.
- Organisations should consider all risk treatment options when determining suitable treatment options.
- Organisations can finance certain residual risks by:
  - conventional insurance methods
  - alternative methods.

Chapter 9

Added Value, Cost and Benefits of Risk Management

Introduction

This chapter outlines the benefits of effective risk management in organisations. It also explores the limitations of risk management and the risks of assuming it is a panacea for all the ills of an organisation.

Learning Outcomes

By the end of this chapter, you should be able to:

- measure the cost of risk;
- describe the benefits of effective risk management;
- describe the limitations of risk management.

Cost of Risk

The review process involves annually measuring the costs saved through risk management. This can be achieved by using cost of risk metrics and measuring the impact of the cost of risk on risk management efforts.

The cost of risk concept involves an organisation ensuring that budgets and objectives for risk costs are properly set, and that variations are monitored, examined and, when required, actioned. The overall progress of applying risk management should also be regularly assessed. The components for a cost of risk measure will vary by the types of risks that the organisation is concerned with and their criteria of assessment. The cost of risk includes any costs associated with the risk impact (if these can be measured in financial terms), the costs of treatment programs and any administrative costs.

Essentials and Assessment of Risk Management, 131–135

Published under exclusive licence by Emerald Publishing Limited
doi:10.1108/978-1-83662-302-120251023

Like traditional metrics used to assess the efficiency of risk management activities within an organisation, the cost of risk consists of four components:

- cost of reduction efforts (motor fleet management costs, medical management/first aid, fire protection, security, quality assurance, etc.);
- cost of retained losses (uninsured losses, including losses that fall below the deductibles);
- cost of insurance premium (including insurance taxes when applicable);
- internal (risk management) administration costs and consultants' fees.

It is worthwhile remembering that once the high initial cost of a physical control measure has been incurred, the organisation generally has the continuing benefit of these measures for little or no extra cost. That is why some include in reduction costs only the recurring costs and the annual depreciation of reduction investments. Conversely, insurance and other risk financing measures often only provide cover for a limited period of time before additional expenditure is required.

Case Study – Just Right Couriers

Just Right Couriers has a fleet of 50 delivery vehicles that range from light trucks to station wagons. This year's insurance premium quote is €50,000. Last year, Just Right Couriers claimed only €20,000 for vehicle accident repair costs so management has decided to self-insure the fleet.

Establishing the self-insurance program will involve determining:

- which areas need to be monitored;
- what types of reports will be required and how frequently;
- who will be responsible for monitoring and reviewing the program.

Self-Help Question 9.1

What factors need to be taken into account when monitoring the efficiency and cost-effectiveness of Just Right's motor vehicle self-insurance program?

Answers to self-help questions are provided at the end of each section.

Benefits of Risk Management

The following are some of the benefits of risk management as detailed in HB 436:2013:

- **Fewer surprises**. Control of adverse events is enhanced by identifying and taking actions to minimise their probability and reduce their effects. Even when such events cannot be prevented, the organisation can achieve a degree of resilience through planning and preparedness.
- **Exploitation of opportunities**. Opportunity-seeking behaviour is enhanced if people have confidence in their understanding of risks and have the capabilities needed to manage them.
- **Improved planning, performance and effectiveness**. Access to strategic information about the organisation, its operations and its environment allows for more sound and effective planning. This in turn enhances the organisation's ability to capitalise on opportunities, mitigate negative outcomes and to achieve better performance.
- **Economy and efficiency**. Benefits in economy and efficiency can be achieved in the targeting of resources, protection of assets and avoidance of costly mistakes.
- **Improved stakeholder relationships**. Risk management encourages an organisation to identify its internal and external stakeholders and to develop a two-way dialog between the stakeholders and the organisation. This communication channel provides the organisation with informed insight into how the stakeholders will respond to new policies, products or decisions, and allows stakeholders to understand why particular actions have been taken.
- **Improved information for decision-making**. Risk management provides more accurate information and analysis in support of strategic decision-making, such as major investments, mergers and acquisitions.
- **Enhanced reputation**. Investors, lenders, insurers, suppliers and clients are increasingly drawn to organisations that are known to have a sound process for managing risk.
- **Director protection**. Sound risk management, facilitates enhanced disclosure to directors and company officers through raising awareness of potential risks, and in demonstrating a proper level of due diligence.
- **Accountability, assurance and governance**. Benefits can be obtained by demonstrating and documenting the management approach adopted, and by focusing each level of the organisation on conformance with requirements and enhanced organisational performance.
- **Personal wellbeing**. Effective risk management of personal risk generally improves the health and wellbeing of self and others.

Source: HB 436:2013 pp. 8–9.

What Risk Management Will Not Do

There is a perception within some organisations that risk management is the solution for everything. While it is an extremely important and a valuable management tool, there are certain things that risk management will not do.

- Risk management will not eliminate risks:

  It is not possible to eliminate all risks but departments which actively identify and manage risks are more likely to be better prepared to respond quickly when things go wrong and to respond to change, in general.
  Source: UK National Audit Office 2000, p. 44.

- Risk management will not manage the organisation.
- Risk management will not stop issues occurring. Not all risks are identifiable – there are always unknown unknowns.

The main thing that organisations need to do is to accept that risk management will not prevent incidents/issues occurring – but that it will reduce the number and/or severity of them if they do occur.

The risk of focusing on risk management above all other strategic management tools and techniques is that other types of exposures will arise. This is why ISO 31000:2018 emphasises that risk management should be integrated into other management processes, rather than suggesting that it become the only process.

Summary

Please keep the following points from this chapter in mind:

- It is important to regularly review the costs that are saved by using risk management.
- This can be done using the cost of risk concept.
- Cost of risk also measures the overall progress of applying risk management.
- There are myriad benefits to effective risk management.
- There are certain things risk management will not do.
- It is important not to expect risk management to solve all problems and remove all issues.

Answers to Self-Help Questions

Self-help question 9.1

The factors that need to be taken into account when monitoring the efficiency and cost-effectiveness of Just Right's motor vehicle self-insurance program are listed as follows.

- Fleet details (year on year):
  - description of vehicles
  - kilometres travelled
  - service regimes
  - warranty claims.
- Driver details (year on year):
  - description of driver, including licence renewals and authorised vehicles to drive by category
  - driver training courses
  - age of driver – for example, incidence of loss under 25
  - male/female split.
- Accident details:
  - type of vehicle
  - time of day
  - location – for example, city/country
  - weather conditions
  - single or multiple vehicle accident
  - police accident investigation reports
  - third party claims
  - total accident costs – for example, vehicle repairs, legal costs, third-party costs
  - management time/costs to administer self-insurance program.
- Cost of risk:
  - the total cost of the self-insurance program must be aggregated and compared with original budgets and what the costs would have been had commercial insurance been purchased.

Chapter 10

Risk and Uncertainty and Their Impact on Strategy

Introduction

This chapter describes the role of the Federation of European Risk Management as Organisations face countless risks daily. Some must be avoided for an organisation to remain solvent, while others must be embraced to maximise profit. Risk management is the discipline that supports organisations to decide which risks are which. Risks that are identified and quantified can be accounted for within an organisation's strategic plan so that all activity is either moving towards or away from risk.

This chapter describes how to assess and quantify risk, how to align risk management with organisational strategy and the elements involved in writing thorough and effective risk policies.

Learning Objectives

By the end of this chapter, you should be able to:

- define risk and risk management;
- describe uncertainty, likelihood and consequence;
- establish a risk rating;
- align risk management with organisational strategy;
- describe the differences between strategic, tactical and operational planning;
- write a risk policy.

Essentials and Assessment of Risk Management, 137–152

Published under exclusive licence by Emerald Publishing Limited
doi:10.1108/978-1-83662-302-120251028

Definitions of Risk and Risk Management

Without risk, there is neither reward nor progress.

We take risks to gain benefits or secure opportunities. To optimise the outcomes from such undertakings, we need to maximise any opportunities that may occur and minimise the downsides of our exposure to risks.

As a discipline, risk management is a multi-faceted process that provides a knowledge base and a logical framework that facilitates effective handling of events that could produce a benefit or cause harm.

Risk Management in Organisations

Business organisations, both large and small, can understand the consequences of their activities in terms of the risks to which they are exposed.

An organisation should grasp opportunities to make a profit and at the same time protect itself from the possibility of financial loss. Because risk taking can be a source of profit and reward for any organisation, the co-ordinated management of all risk exposures plays an important part in the ongoing wellbeing of businesses and organisations as well as for individuals and society as a whole.

This concept is reflected in Head and Herman's (2002) definition of risk management as:

> *[...] using an organisation's resources and activities to counter potential losses and seize potential gains.*

Risk management can help an organisation to avoid crises and to successfully manage consequences should a crisis occur. It can give a company an advantage over its competitors as an organisation that manages its risk will be better prepared for adverse events and therefore able to respond more effectively. By implementing risk management measures and an appropriate business continuity plan, an organisation can ensure it will remain capable of meeting its objectives.

Effective risk management also adds value to a company by maximising possible gains (including profits) while minimising loss and providing cost-effective solutions.

Risk management applies equally to not-for-profit organisations such as churches, charities and government organisations as it does to commercial organisations. All organisations are exposed to a diverse array of risks; therefore, all require a risk management framework. While the objectives of many organisations are to maximise profit, not-for-profit organisations may seek instead to maximise the effectiveness of the services they provide.

Organisations with a fully implemented risk management program will present far less risk.

- They will have identified their risks and implemented risk treatments to reduce them.

- The potential loss estimates will be reduced, and business contingency plans will be in place if required.
- The risk of business interruption will be reduced.

Uncertainty and Likelihood

Effective risk management involves the assessment of inherently uncertain events and circumstances – as explored in the previous chapters, the future can never be totally known and remains in part unpredictable. Assessing this uncertainty requires two dimensions to be addressed: likelihood and consequence.

Likelihood (also referred to as probability) means the number of times an event is likely to occur in a given period of time.

Consequence (also referred to as impact or, when quantified, severity) is the effect the event would have on the business should it occur.

Organisations can analyse risk exposures by combining the information about likelihood and consequence to establish a risk rating, while also taking into account any existing controls associated with the risk exposure.

While unambiguous frameworks can be developed for assessing consequence, assessing likelihood is often less straightforward. This is particularly true for emerging risks where data from past experiences on the likelihood of risks is insufficient, unavailable or irrelevant. When the likelihood assessment appears to be wholly subjective (a guess), the credibility and value of the risk management process are undermined. It is therefore important to be able to assess likelihood with some degree of confidence. This chapter will explore a range of techniques that can be used to assess risk likelihood in an attempt to remove the uncertainty from this vital element of the risk management process.

Uncertainty

Uncertainty is the inability to specify something with precision. Clearly, this can pose a significant problem when making decisions, whether designing an engineering system or planning public policy. In an analytical context, uncertainty can arise about specific quantities, or about the models meant to represent system behaviour.

Uncertainty is not always a negative; the robust, versatile and flexible systems that can mitigate uncertainties can also create additional value for users.

Fundamentally, there are four sources of uncertainty:

- **Incomplete information**, which is when information sources don't have all the information.

- **Disagreement between information sources**, which is when information sources differ, often due to incomplete information or because people make different assumptions or have different perspectives.
- **Linguistic imprecision**, which is when people use imprecise terms and expressions – usually because general conversation does not require precision. When used with others who are not familiar with the intended meanings, or in a setting where exactitude is important, this imprecision may result in uncertainty. This can be exacerbated when dealing with different cultures and using learned languages rather than mother tongues. Linguistic imprecision is extremely common.
- **Variability**, which can also be thought of simply as change. Parameters that change over time (for whatever reason) can give rise to uncertainty. Some of this variability can be due to physics (for example, quantum mechanics), the complex nature of a physical system (for example, solar winds that fluctuate based in part on the internal dynamics of the sun) or human agency (development budgets for new products often change due to changing circumstances and environments).

Many types of uncertainty affect the strategy, tactics and operations of organisations. Mature techniques exist for some classes of uncertainties, such as rolling up component reliabilities to calculate system reliability and mitigating problems with redundancy, while in many other classes, including budget and policy instability and the effects of non-collocated teams during design, techniques are emerging.

Uncertainty and Risk

It is important to note that risk and uncertainty are not synonyms. Uncertainty is neutral, a fact, and can have an upside and a downside. Risk is the effect of uncertainty on a given organisation, and is often equated with the downside of uncertainty, threat, rather than the positive side, opportunity.

The relationship between likelihood and consequence is very important when assessing risk and risk managers need to consider both when determining which risks to focus on.

To assess how risky something is, risk managers should ask:

- How likely is this to happen? (likelihood)

How Bad Would It Be if this did happen? (consequence)

An event that is likely to occur but that would have little or no effect on objectives is not significant whereas an event that is unlikely but that has a high consequence may not occur often, but when it does it could destroy a business.

Therefore, risk managers generally focus on:

- unlikely and likely events with a high consequence (for example, a building fire), because of their potential to disrupt the business;
- likely events with a lower consequence (for example, product warranty claims), because they are almost certain to occur.

Risks that are unlikely with low severity consequences can be left to normal management processes.

Activity | Estimating likelihood and consequence

1. Identify one of the major risk exposures your organisation is likely to face.
2. Estimate the chances of an unexpected event:

   – occurring
   – actually resulting in a loss.

3. Estimate the:

   – consequences of this event
   – loss for the organisation.

Risk management processes often include frameworks for determining the significance of a risk based on both likelihood and consequence, such as the two-dimensional likelihood–consequence approach. The product of multiplying the two dimensions is sometimes called the criticality index and is used to prioritise risks.

In order for risk assessments to be consistent and meaningful, attention must be paid to the way in which likelihood and consequence are assessed. It is relatively simple to assess the consequences of a risk, since this involves defining the situation after the risk has occurred then estimating the possible effect on each objective. Assessing consequence is an exercise in structured imagination: 'If this were to happen, what would the effect be?'

Example – Consequence Descriptions

The following table provides examples of descriptions an organisation may use to assign to the consequences of an unexpected event/loss.

Financial	Regulatory/Legal	Product/Continuity	Human Resources/WHS	Reputation and Image
Extreme (5)				
Over $500,000	Loss of regulatory approval Significant prosecution and fines Very serious litigation (including class action)	Critical service loss for more than one month Key products become obsolete	Unexpected loss of key senior managers Multiple deaths or irreversible injury to more than one person	Major and permanent reputation damage impacting the ability to trade
Major (4)				
$300,000 to $499,999	Major breach of regulation Suspension of right to trade Major litigation	Critical service not back in agreed time Significant changes to products are required	Unexpected loss of senior staff member considered a key dependency Single death or irreversible injury	Serious public outcry
Moderate (3)				
$100,000 to $299,999	Serious breach of regulation with investigation or report to authority with prosecution/ possible moderate fine	Critical service not back in agreed time Moderate adaption to required products	Unexpected loss of several managers Hospitalisation due to a reversible injury	Significant adverse national media/ public attention

Minor (2)				
$20,000 to $99,999	Minor legal issues, non-compliances and breaches of regulation	Local only, service loss for minimum period	Unexpected loss of a senior staff member	Media attention/ heightened local community concern
		Minor product adjustment required	Treatment of a reversible injury with no hospitalisation	
Insignificant (1)				
Less than $20,000	Minor legal, regulatory or internal policy failure	Negligible consequences	Unexpected loss of a single staff member	Minor adverse local public or media attention
		Brief loss of service	Treatment of a minor injury with first aid and no medical treatment required	Complaints
		Change to marketing approach		

The other dimension of risk is less easy to assess. Risk practitioners and project teams alike regularly experience difficulties in assessing the likelihood that a risk might occur. The difficulties largely stem from the fact that risks are possible future events that have not yet occurred, and as such their likelihood of occurrence cannot be measured, only estimated. In a philosophical sense, it can be said that risk does not have a real existence in the present, that only uncertainty is real.

The following table provides example likelihood descriptors an organisation could assign to an unexpected event. The table also provides definitions for each category, which is essential in ensuring key organisational stakeholders use these descriptions consistently across the organisation.

Example Likelihood Descriptions

Likelihood	Descriptor	Description
5	Almost certain	• The event is expected to occur in most circumstances • Risk has more than a 75% chance of occurring • Risk will occur within the next 6 months
4	Likely	• The event will probably occur in most circumstances • Risk has more than a 50–74% chance of occurring • Risk will occur within the next 18 months
3	Possible	• The event should occur in some circumstances • Risk has more than a 25–49% chance of occurring • Risk will occur within the next 36 months
2	Unlikely	• The event could occur in some circumstances • Risk has more than a 25% chance of occurring • Risk will occur within the next 54 months
1	Rare	• The event may occur only in some exceptional circumstances • Not likely to occur in the next five years

Estimation of likelihood also tends to be influenced by a wide range of subjective and unconscious biases, making it even less reliable. Such sources of bias need to be understood and managed if realistic and useful likelihood assessments are to be made. One such bias is cognitive bias, which describes people's predisposition to interpret information through their own subjective experiences, preferences and beliefs. Another is the availability heuristic, which is the tendency to give greater weight to information that is more easily available or recalled.

Uncertainty and Risk Management

A thorough and sound risk assessment is critical to the effectiveness of the risk management process. If the risk likelihood assessment is faulty, risks will not be prioritised accurately, which could lead to a failure to focus on the most significant risks. This in turn could lead to inappropriate responses being selected, meaning risks would not be managed effectively, and this could ultimately lead to a loss of confidence in the risk management process.

Conversely, if the risk likelihood assessment is sound, the resulting understanding of each assessed risk will be more accurate, supporting better decisions in terms of response selection and risk management strategy. The improvement in risk management effectiveness that follows will enhance the credibility of the risk process and will ultimately lead to more reliable achievement of project and business objectives.

In order to ensure the most robust assessment of risk likelihood, a two-part solution is recommended. The first part requires awareness of the issues, including understanding the problems associated with assessing likelihood, the importance of reliable assessment, the effect of psychological influences such as biases, and the various alternative approaches available. The second part involves action to address the concerns, including identifying and managing sources of bias, modifying practice by using different likelihood assessment techniques, monitoring project and risk management performance to determine the accuracy of assessed risk likelihood, and learning lessons to further improve the effectiveness of the likelihood assessment process.

Risk Influenced Strategy

It is essential that the risk management process is considered when making strategic, tactical and operational decisions. This will ensure that the identified risks and their treatments will be incorporated into the broader organisational strategies and plans.

The difference between strategy and tactics is that strategy defines what is to be done and tactics define how. Strategy is all about taking the central idea of an enterprise and making choices as to the future. Tactical management is when tactics are used to implement strategy. This differs from the traditional approach in that traditional management generally dictates that one method is to be used (standard operating procedure, SOP) whereas tactical management allows managers to select any tactic that will best achieve the objective.

Strategic Planning

Strategic planning is an organisation's process of defining its strategy, or direction, and deciding how to allocate resources to achieve this strategy. Generally, strategic planning considers the entire organisation rather than isolated units, and asks at least one of the following key questions:

- What do we do?
- For whom do we do it?
- How do we excel?

Typically, strategic choices apply in the medium term, three to five years, while some extend to long term (up to 20 years). Because of the time periods involved and the nature of the questions dealt with, strategic plans are by nature uncertain and issues that can significantly affect them (e.g. war, geopolitical shocks, catastrophic black-outs) lie out of the control of management. These issues, in conjunction with their potential consequences, are called strategic risks. Untapped opportunities can also be seen as strategic risks.

The timeframe of strategic plans and the level of uncertainty connected with them means these plans are generally less detailed than tactical plans.

Tactical Planning

Tactical planning is short-range planning that emphasises the current operations of various parts of the organisation. Short range is generally defined as a period of time extending about one year or less in the future. Managers use tactical planning to outline what the various parts of the organisation must do for the organisation to be successful at some point in the short-range future. Tactical plans are usually developed for production, marketing, personnel, finance and plant facilities and are detailed in nature.

Because the time period for tactical plans is shorter, the issues that can arise tend to be more within management's control. Concerns like next year's shipping prices and energy consumption are unknown but can be estimated, therefore the uncertainty connected with tactical planning is less (moderate). These issues, in conjunction with their potential consequences, are called tactical risks.

Operational Planning

Operational planning is the process of linking strategic goals and objectives to tactical goals and objectives. It describes milestones and conditions for success and explains how a strategic plan will be put into operation during a given period.

A combination of internal and external factors influences a company's operating situation.

- The internal context includes leadership and staff (competencies and talents), plant and equipment, and the organisation's culture, ethics and values.
- The external context includes clients, suppliers, competition, improvements in technology, laws, government activities, and market, social and economic trends.
- An operational plan addresses four questions:
- Where are we now?
- Where do we want to be?
- How do we get there?
- How do we measure our progress?

Operational risks are those that arise from people, systems and processes and can include classes of risk such as fraud, legal, physical and environmental risks. They result from inadequate or failed internal processes, people and systems, or from external events (man-made or natural hazards). Tailings dam failures, open pit slides, black-outs and processing plant explosions are all operational hazards that generate operational risks.

Plan Implementation

Since upper management generally has a better understanding of the organisation as a whole than lower level managers, upper management generally develops strategic plans. Conversely, because lower level managers generally have a better understanding of day-to-day organisational operations, they generally develop tactical and operational plans.

Despite their differences, strategic, tactical and operational plans are intimately related. Managers need both tactical and strategic planning programs, and these programs must be closely aligned to be successful.

As previously discussed, without risk there is no reward. Risk is therefore inherent in achieving goals, and there is a risk appetite implicit in every strategy. In other words, strategy drives value creation but also entails risk-taking. When strategies change or new initiatives are implemented, new risks may be introduced or existing risks may change. The greater the degree of integration between strategy and risk management, the more likely it is that a company will be able to successfully implement its strategy. Thus, strategic planning is closely connected with ERM.

Risk Management and Strategy

Many strategic objectives are developed under the assumption that effective risk management (including compliance risk management) is in place. However, this is not always the case and the risk officer has a vital role to play in strategy formulation and strategic choices.

Risk management plays two very important roles in relation to strategy:

1. Risk informs strategy by aiding the understanding of the risk that is assumed in the strategy, the nature of that risk, and the level of risk, and how this might change as a result of strategic choices made (and the operating environment).
2. Risk management is essential to the successful execution of strategy.

Strategy must take into account all risks; therefore risk management must be incorporated into the decision-making process. Strategy can then establish a rational process of risk taking that leverages the uncertainties of the future to enhance the present, and so creates real value.

Good risk management practices can not only help to protect established value, they can assist in identifying and capitalising on opportunities to create value. Risk management should influence how the organisation recognises and responds to the uncertainties it confronts. More things can happen than will happen, and risk management provides information and a process to determine how likely it is that something will happen, thereby helping to lessen the uncertainty and consequences of possible events. In other words, it ensures conscious risk taking as part of strategic choice.

Risk officers, in order to influence strategy, ought to ask six fundamental questions about the organisation's strategy and give their advice based around the answers. The six questions relevant to strategy are:

- What is the central idea, or core mission, of the organisation?
- What is uncertain about the organisation's strategy, and how might the uncertainties create opportunities or destroy value?
- What risks are assumed in the organisation's strategy (what is the exposure) and what is the nature of those risks?
- How willing is the organisation to accept those risks?
- Can the risks be managed (does the capability exist within the organisation) and how will they be managed?
- Will the organisation capitalise on the risks (will taking the risk pay off)?

Rather than trying to predict the unpredictable, organisations should look to gain from such events when they do occur. Organisations that account for relevant threats will see opportunities within their context. The key to success is to develop an objective, accurate picture of the risk factors in question, recognise and understand the challenges that exist, and execute the strategy despite these challenges.

The key benefit of incorporating risk management within the strategic process is that it equips the organisation with the confidence to take risk, and to take it responsibly. Ideally, the risk officer will advise the organisation's upper management when and where more risk should be taken in pursuit of upside business value.

Value Creation

With risk management processes well established in many organisations at the tactical or operational levels, executives and boards are increasingly focusing on how to use risk management not only to protect shareholder value but also to enable value creation. To achieve this, risk management needs to be directly aligned to an organisation's strategic decision-making, thus ensuring all significant decisions are supported by a rigorous approach to the identification and evaluation of risk. A critical component of this approach is to develop a common language for the evaluation of risk which is closely aligned with corporate key performance objectives, and an agreed risk tolerance and risk appetite for the organisation.

Risk Policy

Risk policy is the statement of the extent and kinds of risks an organisation is willing to take in pursuing its objectives. It varies from industry to industry and, within an industry, from organisation to organisation according to the organisation's ability to absorb losses and the rate of return it seeks from its operations.

A risk management policy serves two main purposes:

- identify, reduce and prevent undesirable incidents or outcomes;
- review past incidents and implement changes to prevent or reduce future incidents.

For example, a hospital may utilise its risk management policy to continuously analyse and improve its policies and practices to reduce the rate of patients being re-admitted due to hospital-acquired infections.

Knowing how to write a risk management policy is a central part of an organisation's strategic planning and growth.

EXAMPLE

How to Write a Risk Management Policy

The following steps explain how to write a risk management policy.

- Identify the potential risks in the context of the organisation and for all stakeholders.
  - Consider your work within the context of different transactions or processes. Include:
    - long-term strategic objectives and decisions
    - operational or day-to-day activities

- financial management and controls
- intellectual and information technology actions and knowledge
- compliance/regulatory issues and policy decisions.

- Write down all the things that could potentially go wrong and how that might happen. Divide this information into sections to address each individually.

- Analyse all the potential risks that you have identified.
  - Write down how they may occur and potential methods of prevention, additional steps that could be taken to prevent them, and how those risks are evaluated and assessed regularly.
- Assess all the past incidences that your organisation has encountered and how these occurrences were handled.
  - Consult past records to determine how frequently incidents have happened, and how they were handled, including processes that worked and those where there were areas of improvement.
- Estimate the likelihood of each risk re-occurring based on the history of your organisation, best practices and peer experiences.
- Develop a treatment plan for all of the risks that you have identified, prioritising the risks that you have found are more likely to occur.
  - Be sure to outline a step-by-step expectation for how each risk will be avoided, how it will be handled if it does occur, and how it will be recorded.
- Calculate cost estimation for the steps needed to align with the risk management policy recommendations.
  - Provide this information to the internal audience when the policy is proposed.
- Prepare a report for both internal and external stakeholders, sharing what auditing steps are in place to revisit and evaluate the policy.
  - Internal and external stakeholders need different information. Internal stakeholders need to know the greatest risks, who is accountable for what, and how the process will be monitored. External stakeholders need to know risk management is a part of the organisation's culture and how the process and policy have been laid out.

- Create a data tracking system to input all statistics on risk management successes and failures, and train staff to use it.
  - Creating a risk assessment form for use after an incident can be a useful tool to examine whether more precautions should have been taken. This allows all the data to be recorded right after the occurrence, and for the same information to be gathered each time.
- Set up a regular monitoring process to review all risks and evaluate how the treatment plan has been working.
- Revisit the risk management policy every six months to evaluate its effectiveness by comparing incident occurrence rates.

Risk Tactics

Strategy involves the future vision of the business; tactics involve the actual steps needed to achieve that vision.

EXAMPLE

A Motel's Risk Management Strategy

A risk management strategy for a motel might be to develop a business package targeting travel agents that includes an e-commerce solution and assessment of the potential cyber risks.

The motel's tactics might include:

- building a list of local travel agents, and assessing their cyber security programs;
- preparing a business incentive scheme, including penalties if the travel agents contaminate the motel website;
- outlining how the travel agents can use the motel website to make reservations and keep up to date in a cyber-safe manner;
- personally visiting the agents to follow up;
- monitoring the response to determine if the cyber protection target is met.

It should be clear from the example that strategy always comes first, followed by tactics.

However, it should be noted that values and missions come before strategy. For example, a value-based commitment to environmentally responsible hospitality could be reflected strategically by working towards Green Globe certification and tactically by incorporating energy-efficient appliances in the motel retrofit. The values inform the strategy, which then determines appropriate tactics.

Summary

Please keep the following points from this chapter in mind:

- Risk management can help an organisation to avoid crises and to successfully manage consequences should a crisis occur.
- Organisations with a fully implemented risk management program will present far less risk.
- Risk and uncertainty are not synonyms. Uncertainty is neutral and can have an upside and a downside. Risk is the effect of uncertainty on objectives and is often equated with the downside of uncertainty (threat), while the upside (opportunity) is forgotten.
- Assessing uncertainty requires two dimensions to be addressed: likelihood and consequence. Likelihood is also referred to as probability; consequence can be referred to as impact or severity.
- Consequence can quite easily be assessed by considering 'what if' scenarios, but the likelihood is difficult because risks are potential – not certain – future events.
- The risk management process should be considered when making strategic, tactical and operational decisions to ensure that the identified risks and their treatments are incorporated into the broader organisational strategies and plans.
- The difference between strategy and tactics is that strategy defines what is to be done and tactics define how.
- Strategy always comes first, followed by tactics.

Risk policy is the statement of the extent and kinds of risks an organisation is willing to take in pursuing its objectives. It is used to identify, reduce and prevent undesirable incidents or outcomes and to review past incidents and implement changes to prevent or reduce future incidents.

Chapter 11

Risk Identification and Classification

Introduction

Effective risk management requires a thorough understanding of risk, including its classifications, sources and effects.

The previous chapter explored risk management and how it influences organisational strategy with a specific focus on likelihood and consequence. While key elements, they do not provide a broad enough understanding of risk and risk calculations on their own. This chapter will further your understanding of risk by introducing you to different classifications of risk, risk sources, risk exposures and risk diversification.

Learning Objectives

By the end of this chapter, you should be able to:

- classify risk;
- identify and categorise principal risks;
- describe the importance of diversification;
- calculate the expected loss of correlated and uncorrelated risks;
- identify and classify risk exposures.

Risk Classification

Risks can be classified in three main ways, depending on:

- whether they are subject to change (whether they are **dynamic** or **static**);
- how broad their impact would be (whether they are **fundamental** or **particular**);
- whether there is a potential gain (whether they are **pure** or **speculative**).

Essentials and Assessment of Risk Management, 153–172

Published under exclusive licence by Emerald Publishing Limited
doi:10.1108/978-1-83662-302-120251029

Dynamic Risks Versus Static Risks

Dynamic Risks

Dynamic risks arise from the continuous change that is inherent in business and economic environments. For example, changes in price levels, consumer tastes and technology may cause financial losses to businesses and individuals. Dynamic risks are not insurable.

Static Risks

Static risks involve losses that would occur even if there were no changes in the business or economy; for example:

- fire
- accidents
- dishonesty.

In general, static risks are insurable risks.

Fundamental Risks Versus Particular Risks

Fundamental Risks

Fundamental risks are impersonal and involve large sections of the community; for example:

- unemployment
- war
- earthquakes
- flood damage.

Fundamental risks are mainly caused by social, economic and political events; however, they can also result from physical occurrences.

While insurance can handle some fundamental risks, the government usually deals with these (they become a community concern).

Particular Risks

Particular risks are:

- associated with specific individual events (they do not affect the rest of the community);
- personal in origin and consequence;
- usually dealt with by individuals through the use of loss prevention or insurance (for example).

Examples of particular risks include:

- burglary
- theft
- auto accident
- dwelling fires.

Pure Risks Versus Speculative Risks

Pure Risk

Pure risk relates to situations that may involve a loss (but not necessarily) but that involve no gains. For example, if your house burns down, or your car is damaged, there nothing to be gained. Most pure risks are insurable.

Speculative Risk

Speculative risk involves those situations where there is a possibility not only of loss but also of gain. Starting up a business is a good example of speculative risk. Before you start the business, there is no risk. Once you take that step, you can then only win or lose. Most speculative risks are uninsurable.

Inherent and Residual Risk

Risk can also be classified according to whether it exists before and after risk management controls are implemented.

Inherent Risk

Inherent risk is the level of risk before existing risk mitigation strategies and controls are taken into account. Inherent risk is an important concept because it represents the events that could occur if management does not execute those strategies or controls.

Note: Inherent risk is somewhat theoretical as organisations always control their risk (even if in an unstructured manner).

Residual Risk

Residual risk is the level of risk that remains after existing risk mitigation strategies and controls are taken into account. For this reason, when documenting existing risk mitigation strategies and controls, it is essential that the organisation implement them.

Factory example

To further contextualise inherent and residual risk, consider this example of a factory.

Inherent risk

The risk of employee injury is quite high because of the risk factors listed in the first column of the following table. The factory can considerably reduce its inherent risk of employee injury by implementing the related risk controls listed in the second column.

Risk Factor	Risk Control
Forklifts moving around	Designated walking areas
Large machines	Machine guards and operating procedures
Warehouses using high stacks to efficiently use the limited space	Cages around forklifts to protect operators against accidental spills

Residual risk

The factory's residual risk is the level of risk that will remain after the factory implements these risk reduction measures. For example, a factory can designate specific walking areas but that doesn't mean that no one will ever be injured by a moving forklift: accidents happen.

Description and Identification of Principal Risks

Principal risk is the risk of losing the amount invested due to bankruptcy or default. There is always the possibility that through some set of circumstances, invested money will decrease or completely disappear. In this case, principal is lost, not just profits.

A key challenge for any organisation is to identify the principal risks it faces and to develop and monitor appropriate controls. A successful risk management process balances risks and rewards and relies on sound judgement of their likelihood and consequence. An organisation should maintain a key risk register of the principal risks it faces, including the likelihood and consequence of risks and the controls and procedures implemented to mitigate them.

Principal risks can be approached according to their sources (outlined below) but each organisation should develop the taxonomy that assists decision makers at all levels within the organisation.

- **Market and competition**

  Most organisations operate in a highly competitive environment with a broad range of competitors that can quickly evolve due to technological innovation. A failure to develop the organisation's product proposition in line with changing market dynamics and expectations could erode the organisation's competitive position. If great content is central to an organisation's product proposition, increased competition could affect the organisation's ability to acquire content that its customers want on commercially attractive terms.

  Economic conditions have been challenging in recent years and the future remains uncertain. A significant economic decline could impact many organisations' ability to continue to attract and retain customers.

- **Regulatory breach and change**

  Organisations are subject to regulation primarily under their national legislation, major markets and, for most FERMA members, European Union legislation.

  The laws and regulations that apply may be:

  - specific to industry
  - generally applicable, including competition (antitrust), consumer protection, data protection and taxation laws.

  When an organisation is, or might be in the future, subject to proceedings and/or investigation and inquiries from regulatory authorities, its ability to operate or compete effectively could be adversely affected by the outcome of these investigations or by the introduction of new laws, policies or regulations, changes in the interpretation or application of existing laws, policies and regulations, or failure to obtain required regulatory approvals or licences.

- **Customer relations**
  Organisational success relies on building long-term relationships with customers. Failing to meet customer expectations with regard to service could undermine organisations' brand and competitive position.

- **Technology and business interruption**
  The products and services that organisations provide to their customers are sometimes reliant on complex technical infrastructure. A failure in key systems or infrastructure – such as technical platforms, customer management systems or telecommunications networks – could cause a service failure to customers.

- **Supply chain**
  Most organisations rely on a number of third parties and outsourced suppliers, which may be international, to support its supply chain. A significant failure

within the supply chain could adversely affect the organisations' ability to deliver products and service to their customers.

- **Financial**
  The effective management of financial exposures is central to preserving organisational profitability or efficiency. Most organisations are exposed to financial market risks and may be negatively affected by fluctuations in foreign exchange and interest rates. Organisations may also be affected adversely by liquidity and counterparty risks.

- **Security**
  Organisations must protect their customer and corporate data and the safety of their people and infrastructure and should have in place fraud prevention and detection measures. Organisations may also be responsible to third-party intellectual property owners for the security of the content that it uses for its operations. A significant breach of security could reduce the organisation's ability to operate and deliver against its objectives.

- **Projects**
  Organisations invest in and deliver significant capital expenditure projects in order to drive business forward. Failure to deliver key projects effectively and efficiently could result in significantly increased project costs and impede the organisations' ability to execute their strategic plans.

- **Intellectual property protection**
  Organisations, like other service providers, rely on intellectual property and other proprietary rights, including programming content, that may not be adequately protected under current laws or that may be subject to unauthorised use.

- **People**
  In most organisations, staff are critical to their ability to meet the needs of their customers and achieve their business goals. Failure to attract or retain suitable employees across the business could limit organisations' ability to deliver their business plan commitments.

The following table provides another version of what could constitute principal risks and includes potential mitigating efforts.

Principal Risk Source	Potential Consequence	Examples of Mitigating Activity
Sales growth	Delivering sales growth impacted by: • economic conditions • consumer preferences • competitor activity • seasonality • expansion and development of store networks.	• Choice and value-led product offering • Driving market share growth in high headroom product categories • Multi-channel development • Store service standards • Development of delivery proposition • Property pipeline • Mezzanine investment and format enhancement
Profit growth	Increase in product and operating costs including: • cost of raw materials • general level of inflation • property/energy/labour costs.	• Purchasing, sourcing and supply-chain scale leveraging • Forward fixed contractual supply agreements • Cost productivity initiatives
Product supply	Delay or interruptions in the supply of products from third-party suppliers including products sourced overseas.	• Product substitution planning • Management of supplier relationships • Improvements in planning process
Business interruption	Failure or unavailability of operational and IT infrastructure. Delay or interruptions in the services provided by third-party suppliers.	• Business continuity planning • IT shadowing/recovery • Key third-party supplier management
Infrastructure development/ projects	Delay or interruptions in the supply of products from third-party suppliers including products sourced abroad.	• Project management • Board review of status/ progress • Post-implementation project reviews

(*Continued*)

(*Continued*)

Principal Risk Source	Potential Consequence	Examples of Mitigating Activity
People	Reliance on key personnel.	• Succession planning • Competitive remuneration packages • Management development and training programmes
Regulatory environment	• Changes in local and European legislation and regulation. • Changes in local fiscal/ employment policy.	• Engagement with government and regulators directly and through industry representative groups
Currency	Purchase of products in currencies other than national currency, principally the US dollar and the Euro.	• Forecasting currency requirements • Hedging policy

Correlated and Consequential Risks

The concept of correlation is a key one for risk managers.

Generally, correlation is a link or relationship between two things. In statistics, correlation is the link between two random variables (simple correlation) or more than two (multiple correlation) so that their values always vary in either the same direction (positive correlation) or the opposite direction (negative correlation).

Risks are correlated when the variation of one is related to the variation of another.

- Risks are positively correlated if one risk decreases when another decreases and rises when the other rises.
- Risks are negatively correlated if one risk rises when the other decreases.

EXAMPLE

Risk Correlation

Pluie-plus sells umbrellas while Soleil-pro sells sunscreen.

Hillbran invests entirely in Pluie-plus and does very well during the wet winter months but when it becomes sunny, Hillbran's returns decrease.

Marquessa invests entirely in Soleil-pro and does very well in summer but its performance decreases during winter.

Umbrellas and sunscreen are negatively correlated.

In reality, perfect negative correlation as described in the above example is difficult to come by (if not impossible).

When building a portfolio, it is important to select assets that respond to different market forces – this is known as diversification and is often spoken of as the key to reducing investment risk. If there are enough non-correlating assets in a portfolio, the odds that they will all suffer a loss or gain at the same time become very small. It is more likely that one asset will take a loss while another gains. In this way, a well-diversified portfolio can be stable even while individual assets may be rising and falling in value.

A set of non-correlating assets can be assembled into a low-risk portfolio using correlation coefficients.

The correlation coefficient is a measure that indicates the degree to which the movement of two variables is associated (driven by the same market forces). The range of values for the correlation coefficient is −1.0 to 1.0. If a calculated correlation is greater than 1.0 or less than −1.0, a mistake has been made.

A correlation of −1.0 indicates a perfect negative correlation, while a correlation of 1.0 indicates a perfect positive correlation.

For example, above, if sunglasses and sunscreen are 100% correlated (having a coefficient of 1.0), the manufacturers' stock prices would move in the same direction 100% of the time. On the other hand, the sunscreen and umbrellas from our example have a coefficient of −1.0 because their prices always move in opposite directions, which means they move together 0% of the time.

If two assets have a correlation coefficient of 0.0, none of the forces driving their price movements are the same so any corresponding movement will be coincidental. They will be as likely to move in the same direction at any given time as they are to move in the opposite direction, meaning the likelihood of two assets with a correlation coefficient of 0.0 moving together is about 50%. A 0.5 coefficient means they will move in the same direction about 75% of the time.

Related and Correlated Risks

Traditionally, risks and exposures have been studied independently. Since the development of ERM, the need to take a portfolio approach to managing risks has become essential and two concepts have emerged: related risks and correlated risks.

Related risks are risks that are influenced by the presence of another risk. This means they do not exist independently, and they are likely to rise and fall in tandem.

Correlated risks are particular examples of related risk. In practical terms, the term correlated risk refers to the simultaneous occurrence of many losses from a single event, which commonly occurs as a result of catastrophe events. Earthquakes, flood and hurricanes damage and/or destroy multiple buildings in a single area and a single time. This is problematic for insurers if they have insured numerous buildings in that area, as they will suffer multiple losses at once. For example, an insurer would likely avoid providing earthquake coverage mainly to homes in southern France, which is prone to earthquake, and would more wisely diversify across France and even the European Union.

EXAMPLE

Correlated Risks

To illustrate the impact of correlated risks on the distribution of losses, assume that there are two policies sold against a risk where $p= 0.1$, $L= \$100$, where p is the probability of a loss and L is the magnitude of the loss.

The actuarial loss for each policy is $10. If the losses are perfectly correlated, then there will be either two losses with probability of 0.1, or no losses with a probability of 0.9.

On the other hand, if the losses are independent of each other, then the chance of two losses decreases to 0.01 (i.e. 0.1×0.1), with the probability of no losses being 0.81 (i.e. 0.9×0.9).

There is also a 0.18 chance that there will be only one loss (i.e. $0.9 \times 0.1 + 0.1 \times 0.9$). The expected loss for both the correlated and uncorrelated risks is $20.

However, the variance is always higher for correlated than for uncorrelated risks if each has the same expected loss. If a risk-averse insurer faces a highly correlated loss from one event, it will want to set a high enough premium to not only to cover its expected losses but also to protect itself against the higher probability of experiencing catastrophic losses due to the higher variance. Thus, risk-averse insurers will always want to charge a higher premium for correlated risks than uncorrelated risks.

Source: World Finance 2010, www.worldfinance.com/home/risk-encyclopaedia/correlated-risks

EXAMPLE

Correlated Risks in Practice

Another illustration would consider environmental risks and reputation risk, which may be correlated for the following reasons:

- Environmental risks refer to losses resulting from the consumption of resources or the effect of emissions. An environmental risk that affects a sensitive situation (whether human, flora, fauna or other) can cause negative publicity, which can result in reputational damage.
- The two risks, environmental damage and reputational damage, share a cause, meaning they occur together and fall together. They are considered separate risks because losses can be incurred by either or both of the risks.

- Positive correlation: Activities that reduce the environmental risk, such as switching to sustainable resources or through establishing emission control systems, will reduce the likelihood of the environmental risk occurring. This then reduces the likelihood of reputational damage occurring. The opposite therefore also holds true: not paying attention to environmental risks will increase the likelihood of reputational damage.
- Negative correlation: If an organisation borrows money to reduce its environmental emissions, it might reduce its environmental risks but will increase its financial risks. Higher gearing will increase its vulnerability to rising interest rates and put pressure on cash flow. In this case, there is a direct relationship between the environmental risk reducing and the financial risk increasing.

Source: ACCA 2017, *Paper P1: Governance, risk and ethics*,10thedn, BPP Learning Media Ltd, London, available at www.acowtancy.com/

Consequential Loss

Consequential loss is loss of trade as a result of being unable to use business property or equipment. Any loss that directly affects the business's ability to operate and that results indirectly because of damage to physical property or because of an inability to operate resulting from such physical damage may be considered a consequential loss.

Consequential loss is also known as business interruption.

EXAMPLE

Consequential Loss

In June 2015, a tornado destroyed a Goodwill store in Portland, Michigan. The physical structure and the store's inventory were covered under various forms of property insurance but the loss of business revenue from the closure, which lasted until June 2016, was not covered. The revenue losses were consequential and needed separate coverage.

The property insurance paid to replace the physical facility, allowing the business to rebuild at the same location, but the lost revenue was not recovered.

Consequential losses are generally covered under insurance that is known as business interruption or consequential loss insurance, either as part of another policy (common in France) or by separate policy (common in the UK).

Consequential loss insurance means that if property or equipment is damaged, the insured might be reimbursed for the related loss of profits or income, continued overheads (including staff salaries) and additional expenditure, depending on the terms of the policy.

Such insurance also pays for losses incurred even when no damage is incurred. For example, if a supermarket loses stock due to an extended power outage or if a supplier is unable to supply key parts and the business cannot operate, the insured will be compensated.

The risk manager designing an insurance portfolio should be careful to consider what consequential losses the organisation may be susceptible to, and whether insurance would be beneficial.

Classification of Loss Exposure

A **risk exposure** may be an event or incident that has a cause and a consequence; it opens the potential for loss. The consequences of an exposure to risk may be positive or negative.

To appropriately manage risk, risk exposures need to be identified, which can be done by considering the following four characteristics of risk exposures:

- the source of the risk;
- the consequences of the effects of exposure to risk;
- stakeholders affected by the risk;
- current controls in place to treat the risk.

Sources of risk

ISO Guide 73:2009, *Risk management–Vocabulary* defines a **risk source** as an:

> *[…] element which alone or in combination has the intrinsic potential to give rise to risk*

Exposures to risk may arise from a diverse range of sources, as shown in the below table.

Risk Exposure	Example of Source
Management activities/ decisions	• Ill-conceived strategies • Conflicting priorities
Individual activities/decisions	• Negligence
Human behaviour	• Poor attention to process
Commercial	• Unfair competition • Eliminating margins
Legal	• Third party litigation • Legal non-compliance

(Continued)

Risk Exposure	Example of Source
Natural events	• Earthquake • Flood • Fire
Technology	• Systems failure • New products that make current products redundant
Politics	• Drive for greater regulation • Increase in taxes
Economics	• Recession • Changes in the value of the local currency

There are certain situations in which organisations will not be able to directly control their risk exposures – for example, risks related to economic or political circumstances. In other circumstances, even if the effects of such risk exposures are controllable (e.g. insurable), it is essential to know about the different solutions that will mitigate the effects of these exposures.

A risk source can be tangible or intangible and may be categorised (or clustered) in a variety of ways.

The COSO's Enterprise Risk Management Framework suggests these five components are:

1. Governance & Culture
2. Strategy & Objective-Setting
3. Performance
4. Review & Revision Information
5. Information, Communication & Reporting

The following 20 principles are supporting the five components:
Governance & Culture

1. Exercises Board Risk Oversight
2. Establishes Operating Structures
3. Defines Desired Culture
4. Demonstrates Commitment to Core Values
5. Attracts, Develops and Retains Capable Individuals

Strategy & Objective-Setting

6. Analyses Business Context
7. Defines Risk Appetite
8. Evaluates Alternative Strategies

9. Formulates Business Objectives
10. Identifies Risk

Performance

11. Assesses Severity of Risk
12. Prioritises Risks
13. Implements Risk Responses
14. Develops Portfolio View

Review & Revision

15. Assesses Substantial Change
16. Reviews Risk and Performance
17. Pursues Improvement in Enterprise Risk Management

Information, Communication & Reporting

18. Leverages Information and Technology
19. Communicates Risk Information
20. Reports on Risk, Culture and Performance

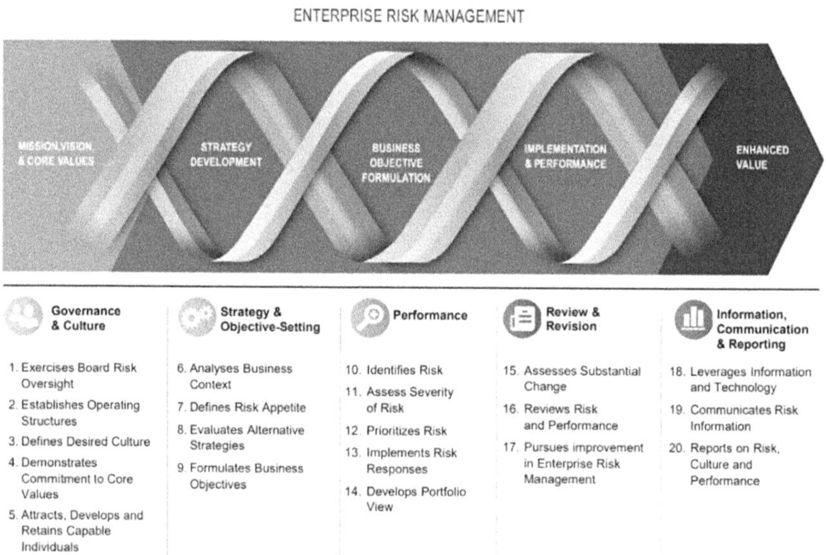

Also, as shown in the diagram below, sources can be divided into **global** and **organisational**, then into various subcategories.

The Risk Spectrum

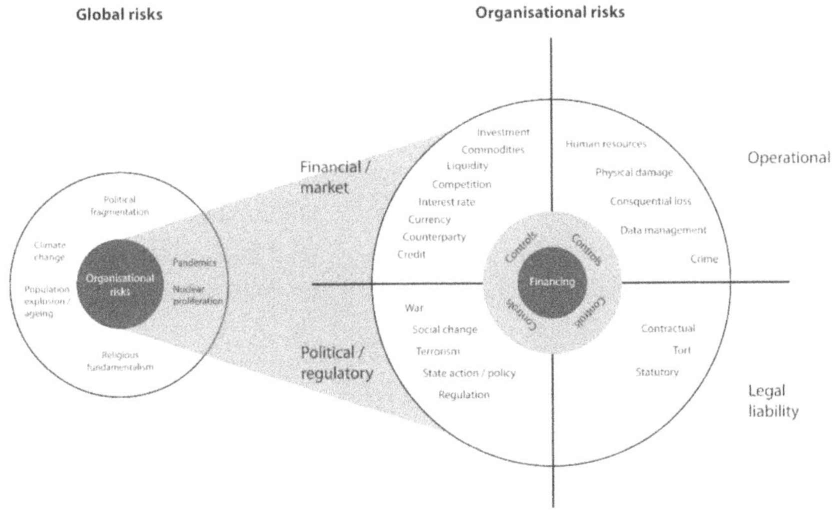

> **Activity | Risk sources in your organisation**
>
> Take note of examples of the different sources of risks that your organisation is exposed to and determine whether they would be categorised as global or organisational sources of risk.

Self-Help Question 11.1

Consider each of the following situations and match them with the type of risk source that they represent. For each situation, please select what you believe to be the most appropriate source of risk.

Situation	Risk source
1 Change in import tariffs	A Financial/market
2 Overthrow of governments	B Data management
3 Damage to plant equipment by a forklift	C Legal liability

→

Situation		Risk source
4 Severe Acute Respiratory Syndrome (SARS) epidemic	D	Political and regulatory
5 Compliance of computer system with date recognition	E	Political fragmentation
6 Unconscious error in processing advice	F	Pandemic
7 Sustained losses on the stock exchange	G	Currency
8 Change to health and safety laws	H	Physical damage
9 Foreign exchange rate fluctuation	I	State action/policy

Answers to self-help questions are provided at the end of each section.

The Economist Intelligence Unit and the FERMA risk management model divide risks into four broad categories:

- **Hazard risk** is related to natural hazards, accidents and fire and arises from property, liability or personnel loss exposures that can be insured.
- **Financial risk** has to do with volatility in interest rates, exchange rates, stock markets and commodity markets, defaults on loans, assets, and liability mismatch. It includes such risks as market risk, credit risk, liquidity risk and price risk.
- **Operational risk** is associated with systems, processes and people and deals with issues such as succession planning, human resources, information technology, control systems and compliance with regulations.
- **Strategic risk** stems from trends in the economy and society, including changes in the economic, political and competitive environments, as well as from demographic shifts, customer priorities, competitive conditions and geopolitical developments. Risks result from an organisation's inability to adjust to these changes in the environment in which it operates.

Hazard and operational risks are classified as pure risks, and financial and strategic risks are classified as speculative risks.

The focus of the risk quadrants is different from other risk classifications that risk management may have considered. Whereas the classifications of risk focus on some aspect of the risk itself, the four quadrants of risk focus on the risk source and who traditionally manages it. For example, the chief financial officer traditionally manages financial risk, and the risk manager traditionally manages hazard risk. Just as a particular risk can fall into more than one classification, a risk can also fall into multiple risk quadrants. For example, embezzlement of funds by an employee can be considered both a hazard risk, because it is an insurable pure risk, and an operational risk, because it involves a failure of controls.

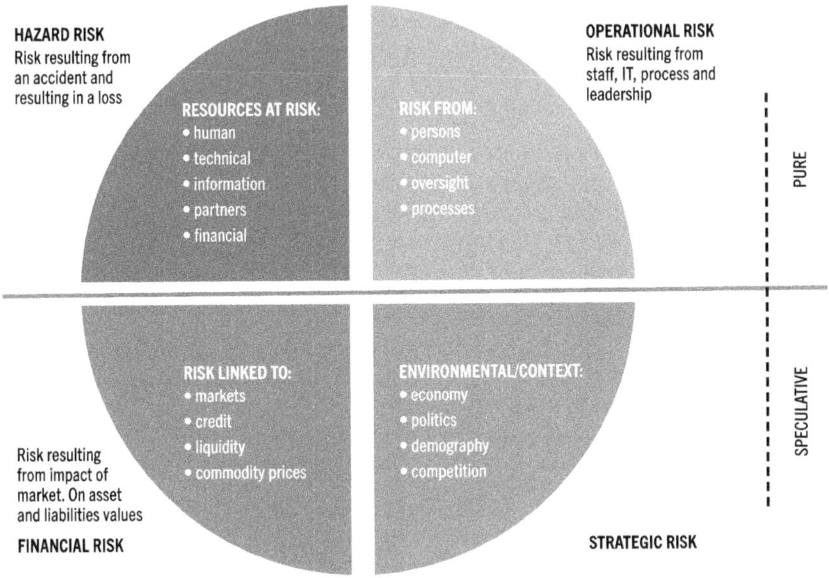

Organisations define types of risk differently. Some organisations consider legal risks as operational risk, and some may characterise certain hazard risks as operational risks. Financial institutions generally use the categories of market, credit and operational risk (which includes all other risks, including hazard risk). Each organisation should select categories that align with its objectives and processes.

The method used to classify risks is not as important as understanding and analysing risks. Indeed, the uncertainty inherent in risk means that it is difficult to identify all risks, let alone classify them. Organisations should carefully examine their value chains and come up with their own ways of categorising risk before quantifying them as much as possible. They can then decide which risks to hold and which to transfer.

EXAMPLE

Risk Categories at Deutsche Bank

Credit risk	This risk arises from all transactions that give rise to actual, contingent or potential claims against any counterparty. The bank distinguishes between three kinds of credit risk: default risk, country risk and settlement risk.

Market risk	This risk arises from uncertainty due to changes in interest rates, equity prices, foreign exchange rates and commodity prices.
Liquidity risk	This is the possibility of being unable to meet payment obligations when they are due or having to pay them at very high costs.
Operational risk	This is the possibility of suffering losses in relation to employees, contractual specifications and documentation, technology, infrastructure failure and disasters, projects, external influences and customer relationships. This definition includes legal and regulatory risk but excludes business and reputational risk.
Reputational risk	This is the risk that publicity concerning a transaction, counterparty or business practice involving a client will have a negative impact on the public's trust in the bank.
Business risk	This is the risk arising out of potential changes in general business conditions, such as the market environment, client behaviour and technological changes.

Consequences of the Effects of Exposure to Risk

Managing a risk exposure's effect on an organisation and its objectives is the primary purpose of risk management. Identifying the consequence of a risk involves:

- identifying which organisational objectives may be affected;
- establishing what the likely effects on the objectives might be;
- determining where, when, why and how the risks are most likely to occur.

A risk exposure may have potential identified sources of risk with the consequences for property, reputation and image, people, income, legal liability and environment.

The measure that is used to record the financial consequences of a potential exposure to risk will largely depend on the organisation's objectives – for example, if the organisation's objective is growth, then the risk exposure would be measured in market share rather than in dollar terms.

Risk Stakeholders

After figuring out what might happen and what its eventuation might entail, it is necessary to work out who would be affected by the risk/incident/event occurring.

The stakeholders affected by any given risk exposure should be identified. To this end, the step of **stakeholder identification** and **analysis** performed as a part of the **communication and consultation** activities should provide a firm basis, although some risks may not affect all of an organisation's stakeholders. In this particular stage, it is important to identify the persons, organisations or any other entities that are exposed to potential benefit or loss by the identified risk.

Current Controls in Place to Treat the Risk

After a risk has been identified and described in terms of its source, potential impacts and the stakeholders which it may affect, it remains to document what controls, if any, are already in place to treat the risk.

This is a key aspect of identifying individual risk exposures and detailed coverage of risk treatment methods and evaluations will be presented in Blocks 03 and 04.

Summary

Please keep the following points from this chapter in mind:

- Risks can be classified as dynamic or static, fundamental or particular, or pure or speculative.
- Principal risk is the risk of losing the amount invested due to bankruptcy or default.
- Risks are positively correlated if one risk decreases when another decreases and rises when the other rises. Risks are negatively correlated if one rises when the other decreases.
- The correlation coefficient is a measure that determines the degree to which two variables' movements are associated.
- A consequential loss is the amount of loss incurred as a result of being unable to use business property or equipment. It is insured under certain insurance policies only.
- A risk exposure is an event or incident that has a cause and a consequence; it opens the potential for loss.
- Managing a risk exposure's effect on an organisation and its objectives is the primary purpose of risk management.

Answers to Self-Help Questions

Self-help question 11.1

Situation		Risk Source
1 Change in import tariffs	I	State action/policy
2 Overthrow of governments	E	Political fragmentation
3 Damage to plant equipment by a forklift	H	Physical damage
4 Severe Acute Respiratory Syndrome (SARS) epidemic	F	Pandemic
5 Compliance of computer system with date recognition	B	Data management
6 Unconscious error in processing advice	C	Legal liability
7 Sustained losses on the stock exchange	A	Financial/market
8 Change to health and safety laws	D	Political and regulatory
9 Foreign exchange rate fluctuation	G	Currency

Chapter 12

Risk Identification Techniques

Introduction

According to ISO 31000:2018, after channels of communication and consultation have been opened and the context established, the next step in managing risk is risk assessment. The aims of risk assessment are predominantly to understand and measure the characteristics of an organisation's risk exposures to inform decision-making and actions.

Risk assessment involves three steps:

1. identification
2. analysis
3. evaluation.

The primary aim of **risk identification** is to put together a comprehensive list of risk sources, events, their causes and their potential consequences. These elements were explored in the previous two chapters.

IEC 31010:2009, **Risk management – Risk assessment techniques** provides additional guidance on risk assessment techniques that may assist in all three steps of the risk assessment process.

Learning Objectives

By the end of this chapter, you should be able to:

- identify risks;
- select the most appropriate tool or technique for identifying risks;
- select the best sources of information for identifying risks;
- describe other methods of identifying risks.

Methods of Identifying Risks and Loss Exposures

Risk identification is the systematic identification of all material exposures to risk, whether under the organisation's control or not. It is all about identifying

Essentials and Assessment of Risk Management, 173–192

Published under exclusive licence by Emerald Publishing Limited
doi:10.1108/978-1-83662-302-120251032

what can happen to the organisation, how and why it might happen, and when and where it is likely to happen.

As defined in Section 3.5.1 of ISO/Guide 73:2009 Risk management – Vocabulary, **risk identification** is the:

> *[...] process of finding, recognizing and describing risks*
>
> NOTE 1: Risk identification involves the identification of risk sources, events, their causes and their potential consequences.
>
> NOTE 2: Risk identification can involve historical data, theoretical analysis, informed and expert opinions, and stakeholder's needs.

Organisations must always ask the following two questions to identify their risks:

- What could go wrong?
- What must go right?

When identifying risk exposures, an organisation should carefully consider all possible causes and scenarios. The organisation cannot construct a systematic plan for managing the effects of risk exposures until it determines:

- what can happen to the organisation;
- how and why it might happen;
- when and where it is likely to happen.

This risk identification step aims to produce a descriptive, all inclusive list of an organisation's material risks.

It is important to remember that organisations need to identify both:

- downside risks
- risks that will threaten the achievement of organisational strategies.

Only after all of an organisation's material risk exposures have been identified can the best methods to handle them can be determined.

A risk exposure is an event or incident which has a cause and a consequence. The consequences of an exposure to risk may be positive or negative.

EXAMPLE

GPG's risk consequences

The consequences of GPG's exposure to risk may be:

- positive – GPG could aim to grow its newsletter business by 15% in the next 12 months (the risk being that this goal will not be achieved); or
- negative – GPG employees or visitors could be stealing office supplies, such as paper.

Risk Identification

The process of identifying risks to be managed is best undertaken by breaking down the subject of the risk assessment into key parts or topics.

Before undertaking the risk identification process, it is important to gather information pertaining to historical incidents and emerging issues affecting the subject of the risk assessment activity. This may include data specific to the organisation and general information relevant to the subject under assessment. This information may be gathered using a range of sources including, but not limited to, internal incident data, results from audits, staff interviews or group discussions, questionnaires and open source data.

The process adopted for identifying a comprehensive list of risks will be dictated by time and budget constraints. Where the risk assessment activity requires consideration of a broad range of risks, a staged approach may be appropriate. A high-level assessment may be undertaken to identify and assign priorities to focus detailed analysis on areas of the highest priority.

The risk identification process is most effective when key stakeholders are involved in structured brainstorming workshops. Each key part or topic is reviewed one by one and the following factors identified:

- **What are the sources of risk or threat?** What has the inherent potential to harm or facilitate harm?
- **What could happen?** Events or incidents that could occur whereby that would affect the achievement of objectives.
- **Where?** The physical locations/assets where the event could occur or where the direct or indirect consequences may be experienced.
- **When?** Specific times or time periods when the event is likely to occur and/or the consequences realised.
- **How?** The manner or method in which the risk event or incident could occur.
- **Causes:** What are the direct and indirect factors that create the source of risk or threat?
- **Business consequences:** What would the effect on objectives be if the risk were realised?
- **Business areas/stakeholders affected:** What parts of the organisation and what stakeholders might be involved or affected?

A preliminary review (a detailed review is completed during the risk analysis process) of existing controls should also be undertaken to identify the:

- controls that currently exist to minimise the likelihood and consequences of each risk;
- vulnerabilities that exist that could undermine the effectiveness of the controls.

When each part or key component has been reviewed and a list of all risks established, consideration is given to whether the list is comprehensive, the objectives and scope of the risk assessment activity have been adequately covered and the information relied upon is valid and credible.

Risk Identification Techniques

A number of techniques are commonly used to identify risk exposures and to determine potential consequences. The risk identification methods used by an organisation should be determined by its context and the organisational activities that are to be included in the risk management process. The quality, relevance and reliability of the obtained information are pivotal to the entire risk management process.

Note 2 of Section 3.5.1 of ISO/Guide 73:2009 *Risk management – Vocabulary* states that risk identification may involve:

- historical data
- theoretical analysis
- informed and expert opinions
- stakeholder needs.

The tools and techniques for risk identification at the disposal of an organisation may include, but are not limited to:

Risk Identification Data	Risk Identification Technique
Historical data	• Examining financial statements • Reviewing statistical records • Performing or reviewing site inspections • Reviewing legislative acts and business codes of practice • Analysing flow charts and organisational activities
Theoretical analysis	• Using scenario analysis • Analysing client contracts
Informed and expert opinions/ stakeholder needs	• Consulting risk owners, management, operational staff and experts • Using questionnaires/surveys/checklists • Conducting risk identification workshops • Reviewing strategies and plans

Several of the above-mentioned risk identification techniques may involve a team of people. This team should include people closely connected with the particular activity under review as well as others who are not closely involved. Some team members who are not closely involved need to be included in the risk identification process because those who are close to an activity or operation can sometimes fail to recognise a problem or risk. In order to ensure that the team adopts a wide perspective in identifying potential problems, the team should come from various areas of the organisation; for example, production, security, health and safety, finance or management.

Historical Data

Examining Financial Statements

Examining the financial statements of an organisation will provide a broad outline of the possible financial exposures that an organisation may face. Those financial statements may offer clues as to what the major sources of the organisation's income and profit may be or what the likely loss events may be and the exposures against which the organisation needs protection.

Common financial statements that can assist with risk identification for an organisation include:

- balance sheets
- profit and loss (P&L) statements
- cash budgets/cash flow records.

Valuable risk information may also be gleaned from:

- asset register and valuations
- sources and application of funds statement
- operating statements
- revenue and expenditure statements.

Balance Sheet

The balance sheet lists an organisation's current assets, liabilities and its net worth, providing an overview of a business at a specific date. When reviewing exposures to risk from a balance sheet, the risk management specialist needs to ensure that the figures are the latest available. Costing values that are required for accounting purposes are not necessarily those needed for risk management.

From the balance sheet, both assets and liabilities provide clues to potential loss exposures. An asset review needs to identify those assets which may reduce in value through loss. Similarly, the liability section of the balance sheet needs to identify future/contingent liabilities.

If accurate replacement values (as opposed to book values) are required to assess the maximum possible loss potential of a business, the risk specialist may need to seek additional input from financial staff and/or external specialists such as valuers.

In addition, the balance sheet and P&L statement of an organisation provide a means of determining both the organisation's financial strength and the potential maximum loss that the organisation could withstand.

Activity | Balance sheet

1. Review your own organisation's balance sheet.
2. Identify your organisation's:
   - net assets
   - annual surplus or profit.
3. Consider the relative size of current and non-current assets and liabilities.
4. Using this information, estimate the maximum amount your organisation could lose before becoming insolvent.

Profit and Loss Statements

P&L statements provide the details of revenue, expenses and profits for a specific accounting period. Like the balance sheet, P&L statements are related to past performance and past activities. However, they can still help identify the effects of exposure to risk. It is important to analyse each income or expense item to determine the possible upside and downside associated with the exposure. If a major loss occurs, well-prepared cash budget or cash flow analysis can help the risk management specialist understand the expected post-loss liquidity levels of the business. P&L statements are also useful in analysing business interruption exposures.

The following table provides examples of P&L statement-related exposures.

Risk Exposure	Effects of Risk Exposure
Sales	• Loss of customers
	• Redundancy of product
Wages	• Strikes
	• Unfair wage claims
	• Inadequate resources
	• Unplanned staff turnover

Cash Budgets/Cash Flow Records

A well-prepared cash budget will provide information on the anticipated outcomes of an organisation in terms of liquidity. Changes in net working capital are revealed in cash flow records and indicate changes in operations during the period of reporting. Each change in the source and application of funds may reflect a significant change in the organisation's exposure to risk.

Reviewing statistical records

Organisations gather statistics on numerous activities, procedures and processes. The statistical records kept by organisations which may be relevant to the risk identification process include:

- sales/marketing reports
- staffing, employee and attendance records
- production output reports
- incidents/near misses
- outages/strikes
- previous losses (often the claims history)
- customer complaints
- other reports.

All of these records can assist with the identification of exposures to risk and the likely effects of these exposures.

Using claims histories, past occurrences can be noted, particularly past near misses or incidents that could happen again. The potential for loss increases if steps are not taken to reduce or eliminate the specific risk. An organisation's past loss history can also be used to project future trends and identify areas of poor housekeeping or supervision. It is important that both insured and uninsured losses are considered.

Information about possible exposures to risk can also be gleaned from numerous other sources, including (but not limited to):

- government records and statistics
- competitors
- industry associations
- external statistics for the particular industry
- insurance company records
- water authority maps
- weather bureau data
- electricity authorities.

Performing or Reviewing Site Inspections

Site inspections allow a first-hand look at exposures, thereby providing the immediate identification of obvious potential risk exposures. Site inspections can reveal much about the processes and procedures used by an organisation. They can also reveal much about the likely risks to which the organisation is exposed from outside the boundaries of the organisation's own site; that is, the area surrounding the actual physical site. It is suggested that a site inspection should follow the same process regardless of the site. For example, a process used for fire surveys is to start the inspection by walking around the boundary of the site looking outwards at the surroundings, before continuing to walk around the site and gradually working towards the centre. This entails looking not only at all of the buildings but also at the site's plant and processes, as well as other contents associated with the site.

Site inspections also provide an opportunity to clarify observations by obtaining information from staff members. Employees are often a valuable source of information regarding machinery reliability, maintenance schedules and spare parts availability as well as exposures to risk.

Site inspections can assist in identifying the occupational health and safety and housekeeping standards of an organisation and its operating effectiveness. A site inspection also helps to identify exposures to risk in the surrounding environment. For example, a factory may be situated in a flood plain near a river, or on an earthquake fault line, or next to a munition's depot or fireworks factory.

Following a site inspection, the risk management specialist (or whoever has conducted the inspection) should debrief site management on their findings before leaving the site and should then produce a survey report that can be used to assess the likely effects of the organisation's exposures to risk. The survey report is often also used by underwriters to assess risks and determine the premium, terms and conditions of insurance contracts.

For example, a site inspection of a factory situated in a flood plain near a river should show the steps the organisation and/or authorities have taken to minimise flood damage and should investigate the history of flooding.

Reviewing Legislative Acts and Business Codes of Practice

Legal risk management specialists need to review the relevant legislation of the country in which they are operating to ensure that the organisation is aware of and complies with relevant statutes. Laws and regulations that should be reviewed are workplace or occupational health and safety Acts, dangerous or hazardous goods regulations and trade legislation. An organisation should be aware that if it does not comply with relevant laws and regulations that there are potential criminal penalties.

Legal risk management specialists must understand the ramifications and penalties related to legislation and regulations, and industry codes of practice, to ensure that an organisation complies with all requirements.

In some organisations, a compliance system exists that makes it easy to identify key legislation. In others, a legal risk management specialist needs to identify the key obligations. Developing a risk matrix that identifies the legislation or regulation, the overall risk level (e.g. low or high) and the key risks can be useful.

Analysing Flowcharts and Organisational Activities

Organisational activities and processes can be illustrated through flowcharts and diagrams. They can provide an overview of the operations of an organisation. Flowcharts should include all areas of the organisation for review. For example, a typical organisational flowchart of a manufacturer would indicate the path of raw materials from the supplier to their arrival at the organisation, through the various processes undertaken to become a final product (including key operations and equipment), to storage of the product, and finally the process for despatch to the customer. Flowcharts would also include the finance, marketing and maintenance pathways of an organisation. The larger an organisation, the more likely that flowcharts will have sectioned areas/departments/processes.

Flowcharts are particularly useful for identifying key operations upon which an entire production process may depend – bottlenecks – thus identifying the vulnerability of a particular process to possible interruption. Flowcharts also help identify organisational interdependencies. They will show key operations and equipment and perhaps provide additional information on the services that the company and its dependencies undertake for certain suppliers or customers.

EXAMPLE

Motor Manufacturer

A motor manufacturer that uses just-in-time techniques for stock management is highly exposed to delivery risk by parts suppliers – if the parts suppliers fail to deliver, only limited stock is available to enable production to continue.

It is important that flowcharts are considered in conjunction with other risk identification methods. Flowchart analysis tends to highlight physical risks and does not take into account the potential losses that may arise from non-visible activities, for example, design and technology.

Theoretical Analysis

Using Scenario Analysis

Essentially, scenarios are stories that describe the possibilities for a given set of conditions. Scenario analysis is the technique of depicting alternative futures and analysing how various strategic decisions might lead to different outcomes.

Scenario analysis was first used in the work on the atom bomb in the 1940s and has developed since then into a well-established methodology for estimating the likelihood or frequency of the occurrence of unexpected or unwanted events.

Scenario analysis involves the following steps to determine the likelihood of an event occurring:

1. identify the unexpected or unwanted event;
2. describe the circumstances to be investigated;
3. identify the critical control points;
4. develop an event tree or scenario tree;
5. quantify and evaluate the nodes of the event/scenario tree.

Analysing Client Contracts

All contracts an organisation makes with customers, suppliers and contractors should be reviewed to check the proposed activity envisaged by the contract and the indemnities granted by either party. These indemnities may alter the normal common law position between the parties to the contract. This could result in additional exposures being accepted by the organisation. It could also affect the current insurance policies and therefore place a greater financial burden on a business overall. Whilst such contracts do have a considerable benefit, this analysis usually focuses on the downside exposures associated with the contract.

Utilising Systems Engineering Techniques

Systems engineering is a branch of engineering concerned with the development of large and complex systems where the system is an assembly or a combination of interrelated elements or parts that are working together towards a common objective.

Systems engineering focuses on:

- the real-world goals for services provided by, and constraints on, such systems;
- the precise specification of system structure and behaviour, and the implementation of these specifications;
- the activities required in order to develop an assurance that the specifications and real-world goals have been met;
- the evolution of such systems over time and across system families.

It is also concerned with the processes, methods and tools for the development of systems in an economic and timely manner.

Informed and Expert Opinions/Stakeholder Needs

Communicating and consulting with others is vital when working through the process of identifying exposures to risk. Potential exposures to risk should be discussed with as wide a range of people as possible to gain their professional opinions and to gauge their concerns.

Such a collaborative approach allows stakeholders to contribute to and understand the decision-making process and reasoning behind risk management activities.

Consulting Risk Owners

Risk owners, who are accountable for managing risk (with a corporate/legal liability for their decisions or lack thereof) are the most important source of information regarding risk in an organisation. As such, risk owners are likely to understand the risks that risk management specialists need to capture.

Consulting with Management

Managers, particularly those with extensive experience of an activity or long-term employment with an organisation are well placed to identify exposures to risk and the likely effects. The only danger is that by qualification they may focus on particular exposures to risk, such as production, while missing other exposures to risk, such as strategic issues. A good example is power utilities, which usually employ a number of engineers who are good at identifying generation and distribution risks but may have little experience or ability in identifying financial risks.

Departmental managers can provide guidance and direction on identifying exposures to risk (and likely effects) in their particular department because they are intimately involved in the operations of the department. Depending on the activity, it may also be prudent to involve key operators and other staff in this process to ensure that all exposures are identified.

In addition to consulting management, operational staff members often know the most about problems, hazards and risks associated with particular areas of operation within an organisation. These people are a valuable source of information when identifying the risk exposures that an organisation faces and providing information about the most appropriate risk treatment measures for these risk exposures.

Consulting with Experts

Some experts outside an organisation may be familiar enough with the organisation (or the type of organisation, or the particular type of activity) to contribute valuable information to the risk identification process.

External experts and consultants useful in identifying risks may include:

- practitioners in law
- finance experts
- statisticians
- accountants
- auditors
- strategic planning consultants.

Using Questionnaires/Surveys/Checklists

There is a wide range of questionnaires, surveys and checklists available for risk identification purposes; for example, surveys used to identify asset, liability, revenue/expense, reputation and image, and workplace health and safety risk exposures. The aim of all these information-gathering documents is to identify the exposures to risk by listing specific opportunities or hazards to which the organisation could be exposed and then to seek information about them from relevant personnel. It is important that surveys, checklists and questionnaires from a range of personnel are examined to ensure the most comprehensive identification of possible effects from the exposures to risk.

Many risk management consultants, insurers and brokers produce standardised questionnaires, checklists and surveys that can often be adapted for a particular industry and/or organisation. However, these standardised forms may not adequately highlight relevant exposures for a particular organisation's needs, so it is important to adapt the forms accordingly.

Standardised questionnaires, surveys and checklists have further strengths and weaknesses. Their strengths are that, when properly drafted, they can be issued and answered by people with little risk management expertise. They can also be used for multiple sites. However, their weaknesses are that they do not encourage people to provide more than a limited set of answers or to 'think outside the box'. Respondents are often not motivated to consider all of the possible ramifications or to provide their thoughts and ideas about a particular risk exposure. However, these weaknesses can sometimes be overcome by using forms that include a combination of open and closed questions to obtain both facts and opinions. In general, questionnaires, surveys and checklists should be used in conjunction with other risk identification and assessment methods. Standard questionnaires, surveys and checklists do not normally cater for specialised exposures to risk which require more defined analysis.

Considerable time and care need to be applied to the design and wording of surveys, checklists and questionnaires to ensure they capture the required information about risk exposures.

Activity | Risk identification questionnaires

Refer to **Appendix 1 – Example: Risk identification questionnaire** for examples of the types of questions used to determine occupational health and safety risks.

Look at the questionnaires, surveys and checklists used by your organisation to identify and assess exposures to risk. Discuss with colleagues or your supervisor whether any of these documents have needed to be modified for specific circumstances or situations.

Risk Identification Workshops

Risk identification workshops are the most commonly used risk identification technique as they assist in identifying risks and sharing risk issues with those attending the workshop.

Risk identification workshops are essentially brainstorming. Brainstorming is a good starting point for risk identification and involves a group of staff (5–8 people is generally the optimum size for a group) identifying an organisation's exposures to risk. Specific types of staff are often more aware of particular exposures to risk and so may have a personal interest in solving the management problems of a particular type of risk exposure; for example, financial, operational, human resource and legal.

Where possible, the use of a slice group provides an excellent means of utilising the corporate memory and knowledge of the organisation or business unit. A slice group brings together senior managers, supervisors and staff from across the organisation rather than across a specific department or business unit, which may be swayed by a strong manager.

Brainstorming also allows for in-depth interaction between the different team participants. The technique works best when group participants use their imaginations and avoid placing an excessive emphasis on detail. A risk identification workshop attempts to identify and document, under a number of risk category headings, the likely effects on the organisation of its exposure to risk. The workshop can focus on a particular element or activity within the organisation (e.g. a process or operational risks) or a particular department (e.g. risks faced by the IT department) or it can explore the full range of exposures facing an organisation – from potentially catastrophic to minor events. For example, a catastrophic event may be an oil tanker hitting the factory's LPG tanks or a scandal that is broadcast by the national media, while a minor event may be a broken window or a staff resignation.

A schedule of keywords covering many areas of risk may trigger participants' recognition of potential exposures to risk, while other tools such as a risk identification table may help to bring out and clarify the results of brainstorming.

Example Risk Identification Table

Reviewing Strategies and Plans

Business strategies, plans and projects are significant sources of risk for organisations. Besides the risk that the organisation will not successfully execute these initiatives, there are a number of risks specific to each item.

Reviewing strategies and plans is an area of risk management that can be very attractive for managers who are looking for techniques to assist them to successfully deliver on their goals.

Essentially, reviewing strategies and plans is a desktop exercise, which means sitting at a desk and working through the factors that could threaten the required outcomes. This exercise should be supplemented with management interviews to ensure the risks are fully understood and well-articulated.

Activity | Risk identification techniques

Select a client and imagine that you are reviewing their exposures to risk. Identify the types of information you would hope to obtain by examining each of the following:

- information gathered from management interviews
- flowcharts
- annual accounts
- current insurance policies
- site inspection report
- risk questionnaires/checklists/surveys
- loss/claims histories
- contracts and agreements with customers, suppliers, contractors
- organisational charts
- health and safety procedures
- information gathered from a risk identification workshop
- business plans.

Types of Exposure to Risk				Area of Impact				
	Assets	Revenue	Cost	People	Performance	Timing & Schedules	Environment	Intangibles
Property								
Financial								
Liability —personal								
Liability – general								
Health and safety								
Production								
Marketing								
Environmental								
Security								
Political								
Key personnel								

Notes: The types of exposure to risk and the areas of impact presented in the table above should not be regarded as either prescriptive or exhaustive. Risk identification classifications and tables should be customised to suit each individual organisation.

Self-Help Question 12.1

Patrice Kisnorbo works in a remote area across town that is poorly serviced by public transport. After some time, Patrice decides to purchase a car to facilitate an easier daily commute.

She purchases a practical vehicle, taking out a loan for 75% of the purchase price.

Identify any unexpected events that may occur as a result of Patrice's ownership and operation of the car.

Answers to self-help questions are provided at the end of each section.

Sources of Information

The most comprehensive and best available sources of information should be used when analysing an organisation's risk exposures and evaluating the consequences and likelihood of potential losses.

The most common method of arriving at measurement, analyses and forecasts is a review of each identified risk exposure by management, and relevant specialists, using an agreed set of factors and a standard methodology.

The main sources of information for risk analysis may include:

- information obtained from the risk identification process
- industry practice, experience and benchmarks
- industry literature
- market research
- expert industry opinion
- personal knowledge and expertise
- financial, process or systems modelling.

Information from the Risk Identification Process

Data on an organisation's operations can be obtained from various sources, as outlined above.

The information entered into the risk register during the risk identification step should provide a firm basis for analysis, but it will rarely encapsulate all that is required to comprehensively assess a risk.

Industry Practice, Experience and Benchmarks

A valuable source of information for analysing risks is the practice, experience and benchmarks of the industry in which the organisation operates. Utilising industry practice, experience and benchmarks enables comparison of the exposures to risk of the company in question with other companies in the industry.

Industry Literature

Published articles, books and other printed material regarding the industry in which the organisation operates is a valuable source of information on industry practice, experience, techniques and processes.

Market Research

Market research may also provide valuable insights into the requirements of customers, problems associated with suppliers and the public image and reputation of the organisation in question. Market research may be conducted by or on behalf of the organisation, or may be accessible from other pre-existing sources.

Internet Search Engines

Internet searches can be a valuable source of risk identification.

For example, an organisation manufacturing a particular machine may do a search to see if any liability issues have arisen in similar machines.

Expert Industry Opinion

Experts in the industry in which the organisation operates can often provide valuable insights into the various problems experienced by the industry and possible solutions to these problems.

Personal Knowledge and Expertise

Every person undertaking analysis of exposures to risk and their likely effects has considerable knowledge and expertise that can often greatly assist in the risk analysis process.

Financial, Process or Systems Modelling

Finally, financial, process or systems modelling can be used to test a wide range of scenarios. Using modelling techniques (such as '@ Risk') on the available financial, process and systems data can help accelerate the risk analysis process.

Other Methods

The methods of identifying risk outlined above are the most standard across organisations. However, there are a few other methods available to risk professionals.

Cindynics

Cindynics is the science of risk analysis, or the science of hazards. The term was coined from the Greek word **kindunos**, meaning hazard.

The beginnings of cindynics can be traced back to the 1755 earthquake in Lisbon, which prompted the famous polemic battle between Voltaire and Rousseau that concluded that mankind could refuse fate. This is reflected in Bernstein's comment, 'Risk is not a fate but a choice'. In a way, this can be considered the first public episode of what is essential in managing risks: a clear refusal to passively accept fate and a desire to actively shape the future through reducing probabilities, thus reducing uncertainty.

The scientific approach to assessing perils and hazards began in December 1987 during the UNESCO Palace congress organised by Association de Cadres Dirigeants de l'Industrie (ACADI). The purpose of the congress was to discuss emerging technological risks and the work of the congress participants provided the basis for cindynics as a discipline. Since then, cindynics has continued to grow.

Basic Concepts of Cindynics

The basic theory of cindynics is that every person involved in managing a given situation will have a different perspective on the hazard. Cindynics establishes a five-dimensional approach to risk identification, arguing that this method allows more complexity than the two-dimensional likelihood–consequence approach.

The first is the concept of a cindynic situation, which requires a formal definition. This can be understood only in the light of what constitutes a peril and hazards study. According to the modern theory of description, a hazardous situation (cindynic situation) can be defined only if:

- it is perceived by the observer studying the system
- the field of the hazards study is clearly identified by:
  - limits in time (life span)
  - limits in space (boundaries)
  - limits in the actors' networks involved.

The second concept is the hyperspace of danger specific to each actor. The five dimensions of this hyperspace are:

- **First dimension: Memory, history and statistics(statistical)**

This consists of all the information held in data banks of organisations that have sought feedback from their experiences (such as flight incidents, monitored forest fires and insurance claims data).

- **Second dimension: Representations and models drawn from the facts(epistemology)**

This is the scientific body of knowledge that enables computation of possible effects using physics, chemical principles, material resistance, propagation, contagion, explosion and geo-cindynic principles (for example, flood, volcanic eruptions, earthquake, landslide, tornadoes and hurricanes).

- **Third dimension: goals and objectives (teleological)**

Goals and objectives must be clearly defined, as without clearly defined goal sit is easy for organisations to go too far. For example, two common objectives for risk management – survival and continuity of customer (public) service – lead to fundamentally different cindynic attitudes therefore organisations need to harmonise these two conflicting goals to progress successfully.

- **Fourth dimension: Norms, laws, rules, standards, deontology, compulsory or voluntary controls, etc. (deontological)**

Normative sets make life possible in society. For example, the need for legislation to organise road traffic was felt as soon as there were enough automobiles to make it impossible to rely on courtesy of each individual driver. Having a compulsory code makes driving on the road reasonably safe and predictable. Therefore, rules for behaving in society are designed to reduce the risk of injuring others.

It is useful to consider whether rules can be defined if objectives are not clearly defined beforehand, and whether personal safety should always outweigh freedom of experimentation.

- **Fifth dimension: Value systems (axiological)**

This is the set of fundamental objectives and values shared by a group of individuals or other collective actors involved in a cindynic situation.

These five dimensions, or spaces, can be represented on a five-axis diagram and the resulting diagram is a representation of the hyperspace of danger.

In combining these five dimensions in different ways, some traditional fields of research, both theoretical and applied, can be identified.

- Combining facts, statistics and models gives the feedback loop so crucial to most risk managers in large organisations.
- Combining objectives, norms and values leads to practical ethics. Social workers have identified authority functions in this domain. These functions are founded on the values that underpin the objectives and define the norms that will be enforced hereafter. If there is no authority figure to enforce the norms, daily minor breaches will soon lead to major breaches.

This extended framework provides a broader picture that allows risk managers to visualise the limitations of actions. The hazard study for a given situation aims at comparing and contrasting the different actors' hyperspace thus providing the risk management professional, or any decision-making person, with a list of the fault lines in a complex system. Hazard studies represent potential adverse events, especially in the area of human factors. It is efficient only if extended to all the actors and networks involved in the situation and if its analysis covers all five dimensions mentioned above.

Dysfunctions

The first stage of establishing a diagnostic tool as described above consists in identifying the networks and their state in the five dimensions of the cindynic model. The next stage is to recognise the dissonances (incoherencies) between two or more networks of actors involved in a given situation. These dissonances must be analysed from the point of view of each actor, and in each dimension and between the dimensions.

This prevention framework aims to reduce the level of hazard in any situation.

Analysing the actors' networks according to the five dimensions can facilitate the identification of deficits specific to an organisation's exposures. The gaps between what is and what should be can provide insight into the changes a prevention campaign should bring about. These deficits can be:

- total absence of one or more dimensions (no data available);
- inadequate coverage of a dimension;
- degeneration, most often disorder, of a dimension (mafia model in Russia);
- impediments in a plan combining two dimensions;
- lack of feedback from experience (dimensions, statistics and models);
- ethical impediment whereby authorities responsible for ensuring that rules are respected in the social field cannot operate as they should (dimensions, norms and values);
- isolation or lack of cohesiveness between the dimensions.

These deficits always appear in reports commissioned to investigate catastrophes, and often the conclusions of these reports are essentially the same.

Situations with dissonances and deficits will naturally intensify unless they are changed under the leadership of an executive commissioned to close the gaps between actors, i.e. reduce or suppress the dissonances and deficits identified.

Catastrophes can influence change by forcing a violent and sudden revision of the content of the five dimensions, which are usually modified, with revised facts, models, goals, rules and values being determined. However, it is preferable that the deficits and dissonances be reduced through planned negotiation and mediation. This diminishes the cindynic potential and aims to reach a level that is unlikely to trigger major disturbances or chaos in the situation.

See the example case study in Appendix 5 for more information on cindynics.

Summary

Please keep the following points from this chapter in mind:

- Risk identification is the systematic identification of all material exposures to risk, whether under the organisation's control or not.
- As defined in Section 3.5.1 of ISO/Guide 73:2009 Risk management–Vocabulary, risk identification is the:

  […] process of finding, recognizing and describing risks

- This risk identification step aims to produce a descriptive, all inclusive list of an organisation's material risks.
- A risk exposure is an event or incident which has a cause and a consequence.
- The process of identifying risks to be managed is best undertaken by breaking down the subject of the risk assessment into key parts or topics.
- The risk identification methods used by an organisation should be determined by its context and the organisational activities that are to be included in the risk management process.

- The quality, relevance and reliability of the obtained information is pivotal to the entire risk management process.
- The most comprehensive and best available sources of information should be used when analysing an organisation's risk exposures so as to provide the necessary data for evaluating the consequences and likelihood of potential losses.
- Cindynics is the science of risk analysis, or the science of hazards.

Answers to Self-Help Questions

Self-help question 12.1

Unexpected events that may occur as a result of Patrice's ownership and operation of the car are listed in the following table.

Opportunities	Risks
Independence from the limitations of public transport and freedom to travel whenever and wherever you please	• Inability to service the loan if you lose your job • Mechanical or electrical • Loss or damage from an accident • Loss or damage to property in the vehicle due to theft or involvement in an accident
Possible savings in travel time	• Loss or damage to a third party's property • A third party's injury or death if there is a car accident • Your or another passenger's injury or death if there is a car accident • Possibility of incurring a traffic infringement notice (for example, a speeding or parking fine)

Chapter 13

Risk Analysis Tools and Techniques

Introduction

This section describes the tools and techniques commonly used to analyse risks, a process designed to identify significant risks that pose a material threat to the organisation. The three main risk analysis techniques are described, along with the tools that support their use.

Learning Objectives

When you have completed this section, you should be able to:

- recall some of the key sources of information for risk analysis.
- distinguish between the following three main risk analysis techniques:

  – qualitative
  – semi-quantitative
  – quantitative.

Analysing Risks – An Overview

Once an organisation identifies its risk exposures, it needs to analyse and quantify the effect and extent (size) of their potential consequences.

Risk analysis is the analysis of individual risk exposures in terms of their likelihood and consequence. Section 3.6.1 of ISO/Guide 73:2009 Risk management – Vocabulary defines risk analysis as a:

> *[…] process to comprehend the nature of risk and to determine the level of risk*

Essentials and Assessment of Risk Management, 193–208

Published under exclusive licence by Emerald Publishing Limited
doi:10.1108/978-1-83662-302-120251034

NOTE 1: Risk analysis provides the basis for risk evaluation and decisions about risk treatment NOTE 2: Risk analysis includes risk estimation.

In summary, risk analysis is about quantifying each identified exposure. Analysing risk exposures distinguishes minor tolerable risk exposures from major exposures, which means less time is spent on minor risks and more time is spent focusing on the significant risks that could have material consequences on the organisation.

Risk analysis is not an exact science as its evaluation depends on the organisation's subjective judgement regarding potential future events.

Once an organisation's risk exposures have been identified, the effect and extent of their potential consequences need to be analysed.

Understanding the Risks

The more an organisation understands its risk (the extent, the likelihood and how it is controlled), the better its analysis. An organisation must be able to:

- identify existing control measures for identified risk exposures;
- determine planned future strategies;
- locate historical and operational data.

To most effectively analyse risk exposures, an organisation should ideally use a combination of the following three risk analysis techniques:

- qualitative
- semi-quantitative
- quantitative.

However, organisations should be aware that some risks can only be analysed using one technique (e.g. quantitative analysis for financial risks).

EXAMPLE

The cost of losing a building in a fire can be quite precisely measured as the total loss can be quantitatively calculated.

The risk of reputational damage because of poor product performance is more aligned to being qualitatively measured.

Past Versus Future

Regardless of the selected method/s of analysis, it is important to recognise that the past does not always accurately reflect the future in terms of loss likelihood and consequences.

Monitoring the context and the changing environment is important to ensure the organisation's assumptions about risks are well founded.

Qualitative Methods

Qualitative analysis may be described as a method that uses words, descriptions and scales to describe the extent of the probable consequences and likelihood that a particular incident/event will occur.

Using qualitative analysis in the first instance provides a general indication of the risk level and is by far the most popular choice for organisations because it is easier, more cost-effective and less time consuming than other methods. However, such techniques do not provide statistically valid numerical data and estimates upon which risk exposures can be ranked.

Note: The organisation can conduct more specific, in-depth quantitative analysis, which is a numeric analysis, if the qualitative analysis reveals this need. The most effective analysis of risk exposure comes from a combination of techniques.

Uses

Organisations generally use qualitative analysis:

- to identify exposures to risk requiring further analysis;
- in situations where the level of risk does not require further analysis;
- when there is inadequate information available to conduct quantitative analysis.

Qualitative risk analysis should utilise any available factual data and information.

Qualitative Risk Analysis Tools

Qualitative analysis is often conducted using descriptive scales.

The descriptive scales used for qualitative analysis are usually adjusted or altered to reflect the circumstances of the particular organisation and the risk being considered. The type of scale used to measure the consequence and likelihood of risk exposures generally depends on the nature and range of both the consequence and likelihoods being investigated.

Scales can be designed using either descriptive terms or numerals. Scales that use numerals may appear to be quantitative, but they cannot be arithmetically manipulated therefore care should be taken when designing and interpreting them.

EXAMPLE

Qualitative Tools and Tables

The following are examples of qualitative measurements for likelihood and consequence of loss resulting from exposure to risk. It is essential that tables like this are tailored to the specific circumstances of an organisation, because, for example, a financial consequence that is extreme for one organisation may be moderate for another.

Qualitative measures of likelihood

Level	Descriptor	Description
A	Almost certain	The event will occur on an annual basis
B	Likely	The event has occurred several times or more
C	Possible	The event might occur once in your career
D	Unlikely	The event does occur somewhere from time to time
E	Rare	Heard of something like this occurring elsewhere
F	Very rare	Have never heard of this happening

Qualitative measures of consequence

Level	Descriptor	Description
IV	Catastrophic	Most objectives cannot be achieved
III	Major	Some important objectives cannot be achieved
II	Moderate	Some objectives affected
I	Minor	Minor effects that are easily remedied

Qualitative consequence descriptions

Financial	Regulatory/ Legal	Description	Human Resources/WHS	Reputation and Image
Extreme (5)				
Over $500,000	• Loss of regulatory approval • Significant prosecution and fines • Very serious litigation (including class action)	• Critical service loss for more than one month • Key products become obsolete	• Unexpected loss of key senior managers • Multiple deaths or irreversible injury to more than one person	• Major and permanent reputation damage impacting the ability to trade

The following table is an example of a broad organisational assessment about risk likelihood and consequence of fire in particular workplaces.

Qualitative measures of likelihood

Occupancy	Likelihood	Consequence
Dairy farm	Low	Medium
Metal assembly factory	Low	Medium
Cement plant	Medium	High
Library	Low	High
Office	Low	High
Shopping centre	Medium	High
Printing	Medium	Medium
Foam rubber manufacturer	High	High
Parking garage	Low	Low

Qualitative Risk Analysis Techniques

Qualitative risk analysis techniques may be carried out according to any number of established methods.

Some of the common methods are outlined in the following table.

Note: Some of the techniques outlined require significant training and understanding of systems and activities to be effectively used as part of the risk analysis process. They are largely undertaken by experienced risk management specialists.

Technique	Common Applications	Features
'What if?' scenarios	• Primarily for systems review • Can be used in all industries	• Lists hazards/safety issues • Identifies: – possible accident scenarios – contingency planning – compliance verification • Unsuitable for complex processes • Incapable of identifying organisational interdependencies • Very user-friendly • Inexpensive

(Continued)

(*Continued*)

Technique	Common Applications	Features
Hazard and operability studies (HAZOP)	• Can be used in all industries • Most appropriate in chemical and process-driven industries	• Lists process hazards • Identifies the consequences of deviations • Can assess adequacy of hazard controls and pinpoint appropriate controls
Failure mode and effect analysis (FMEA) and failure mode and effect and criticality analysis (FMECA)	• Generally used for reliability analysis of single components and for accident investigation	• Lists: – components failures – causes – consequences – criticality • Useful for identifying single-point failures • Time-consuming • Expensive

Semi-Quantitative Methods

Qualitative analysis techniques using descriptors and the like have their limits as they provide relatively imprecise estimates. In addition, descriptors cannot be easily converted for use in software programs for modelling purposes, as number values are required to perform calculations.

To facilitate calculations and modelling, organisations can assign numbers to codify descriptive terms in qualitative risk analysis methods. This is described as a semi-quantitative method of analysis, as numbers are used to express qualitative descriptors.

Semi-quantitative risk analysis uses expanded qualitative scales (words and descriptors) to produce a more detailed, numerical ranking scale.

Semi-Quantitative Measures of Likelihood

Level	Descriptor	Indicative Frequency (Expected to Occur)
A	Almost certain	Once a year or more frequently
B	Likely	Once every 3 years in your career
C	Possible	Once every 10 years
D	Unlikely	Once every 30 years
E	Rare	Once every 100 years

It should be noted that the numeric ranking employed in semi-quantitative analysis is not indicative of the high degree of precision that a fully quantitative model might produce. Despite their limitations, semi-quantitative methods do provide crude mathematical estimates to assist analyses.

EXAMPLE

Semi-Quantitative Analysis in Practice

Using a scale based on qualitative descriptors, survey respondents estimated the likelihood of the following two risk exposures: an aeroplane crash and a power failure.

The arrows in the following diagram represent the average respondent's estimation of those likelihoods.

Semi-quantitative analysis in practice

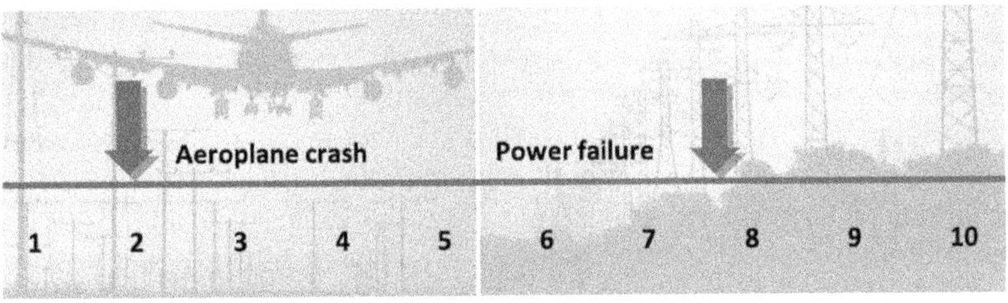

Note: Researchers ascribed numbers to the descriptive terms (very rare to certain) and the space between those terms to facilitate the calculation of the risk exposures. However, this is not necessarily a precise analysis of the data as an event rated 8 is not twice as likely to occur as an event rated as 4.

Quantitative Methods

Quantitative analysis may be described as using numerical values for both consequences and likelihood using data from a variety of sources. With the ability to precisely define event likelihoods and consequences in terms of actual numerical values, an organisation can use relatively straightforward statistical methods of risk analysis to generate more precise measures.

Organisations tend to only use quantitative analysis for significant and core business risks as it can be costly; the use of quantitative analysis can rarely be justified, nor is it always possible, across an entire risk portfolio.

Risk quantification can be conducted to varying degrees, depending upon the information and data an organisation has available about their exposures to risk. For some risk exposures, more precise values for likelihood and consequences can be determined and used for more detailed analysis. The likelihood of events sometimes can be calculated through detailed analysis of past losses providing more accurate probabilities for future events. For consequences, for example, total values of financial losses or actual duration of lost time can be identified through analysis and can provide more precise calculations to determine the level of risk.

Quantitative risk analysis techniques provide numerical data for ranking risk exposures. However, these techniques require a disciplined and long-term approach to recording and interpreting data to provide accurate and valid inputs. The quality of the analysis is dependent on the accuracy and statistical validity of the data and models used, as well as the skill of the person undertaking the analysis. It should always be remembered that there are usually assumptions which underpin the assignment of quantitative amounts.

With the ability to precisely define event likelihoods and consequences in terms of actual numerical values, an organisation can use relatively straightforward statistical methods of risk analysis to generate more precise measures.

EXAMPLE

Quantitative Analysis in Practice

Returning to the example risk exposures of an aeroplane crash and a power failure, it might be possible to accurately determine the statistical probability of those events. The likelihood of a business in a metropolitan area experiencing a power failure could perhaps be established based on information from the power company and the business records. Aviation experts might be able to calculate the probability of an aeroplane crashing into the metropolitan area.

Using these quantified probability values, you could calculate actual likelihoods as part of the risk analysis. In the table below, 0 represents the absolute impossibility of an occurrence in a given time frame, whereas 1 represents its absolute inevitability in that same time frame. All those values between 0 and 1 represent a mathematically relative ratio of such likelihood.

The values between 0 and 1 represent a mathematically relative ratio of such likelihood.

Semi-Quantitative Analysis in Practice

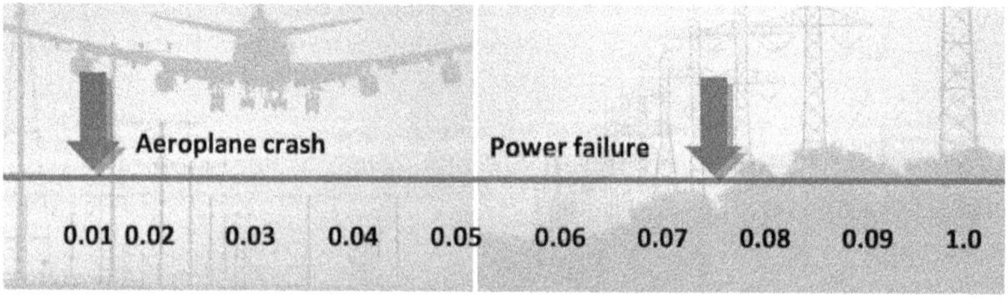

Note: Researchers ascribed numbers to the descriptive terms (very rare to certain) and the space between those terms to facilitate the calculation of the risk exposures. However, this is not necessarily a precise analysis of the data as an event rated 8 is not twice as likely to occur as an event rated as 4.

Statistical Methods

Statistics is a method of mathematical analysis that takes a given set of data (most often quantitative data) and uses models, representations and summaries to gather, review, analyse and draw conclusions from it. It interprets data in mathematical ways that enable meaningful conclusions to be drawn.

There are many types of statistics, but two common ones that are often used together are descriptive and inferential statistics.

Descriptive

Descriptive or summary statistics describe or summarise data sets. They are useful because they break down large amounts of raw data into small, easily understood summaries, thereby providing an overview of the results.

There are two main measures of descriptive statistics:

- Measures of central tendency, which show common patterns and central distribution points of a data set. The most common and well-known types are the mean, median and mode, which show the average, the half-way point and the most common result respectively.
- Measures of variability, also known as measures of spread, which show how spread out the data distribution is. Common types are range, quartiles, absolute deviation and variance.

Descriptive statistics can be presented using tables, graphs or discussions of the results, ideally in combination.

Inferential Statistics

Inferential statistics project potential properties from data sets. Inferential statistics apply when the group to be studied is too large to be investigated and a sample set is used to represent the larger set, for example in demographic research. Inferential statistics use the sample data set to develop and test hypotheses and make estimates about the properties of the broader population.

The key differences between descriptive and inferential statistics are that descriptive statistics describe the properties of the immediate data set only while inferential statistics assume the data set is a sample and infers the properties that would exist in a larger set.

Quantitative Risk Analysis Techniques

Quantitative risk analysis techniques may be performed using any number of established methods, some of which are outlined in the following table.

Note: Many of the techniques outlined in the following tables require significant training and understanding of systems and/or activities in order to be effectively utilised as part of the risk analysis process. They are largely undertaken by experienced risk management specialists.

Technique	Common Applications	Features
Human error analysis (HEA)	• Generally used for analysis of safety critical tasks • Can be used in all industries • Mainly used in aerospace and nuclear industries	• Evaluates: – human error and associated hazards – consequences • potential steps for mitigation of 'human error'
Reliability block diagrams	• Generally used as a reliability prediction tool • Suitable for mechanical systems • Can be used in all industries • Most appropriate in the aviation industry	• Uses process and failure data to determine system reliability
Fault free analysis (FTA)	• Can be used in all industries • Mainly used in aerospace and nuclear industries • Used for accident investigation purposes • Used throughout all stages of operations, but particularly relevant in the design stage	• Systematic review to identify events that lead to a hazard (event sitting at the top of the 'tree') • Identifies and quantifies failures leading to an unwanted event • Achieves best results using modelling and quantification software • Good for complex systems where combinations of events and interdependencies exist
Event tree analysis (ETA)	• Used to model dependencies and escalation of events • Mainly used in process- driven sectors	• Involves systematic mapping of realistic event scenarios • Good technique for modelling catastrophic events

(*Continued*)

Technique	Common Applications	Features
First order reliability methods (FORM)	• Used to predict sensitivities and likely failure regime • Can be used in all industries • Mainly used in structural engineering	• Very systematic • Provides a numerical estimate of the likelihood of failure for variable inputs
Monte Carlo methods	• Can be used in all industries • Mainly used in the finance sector	• Used to model uncertainty of investment decisions • Provides a range of outcomes • Enhances the estimation of risk • Difficult to apply due to the need to create a mathematical model

Source: Adapted from Rasche, T 'Risk analysis methods – a brief review'.

Further Reading

Risk assessment techniques

Organisations should utilise the most relevant, comprehensive and best available techniques when analysing risks. IEC 31010:2009 Risk management – Risk assessment techniques is a useful starting point for available techniques.

While a detailed knowledge of IEC 31010:2009 is not necessary to successfully complete this learning module, interested readers may choose to purchase it from www.iso.org.

Risk Analysis Software

The specific risk analysis methods used by an organisation will depend upon the activities undertaken by the organisation and the resources available for the risk management process.

Exposures to risk can be analysed using a number of software packages that are specifically designed to record and analyse incidents and losses, undertake predictive modelling and analyse risk exposures. The software collects and analyses information to highlight specific areas of concern requiring further evaluation, for example, the statistics may identify an increased employee accident rate within a section of an organisation, or statistics may reveal an increased rejection rate from a manufacturing process. An investigation could then be conducted to determine whether the increased rate is due to poor training, inadequate supervision, poor use of protective clothing, malfunctioning machinery or some other factor. From there the appropriate action can be taken to minimise the effects of the exposure.

Larger Organisations

Larger organisations generally use software-based technologies to record and analyse risk exposures.

The marketplace also has a large array of general risk recording and analysis products including:

- methodware™
- Risk Wizard
- Riskware.

The following people and organisations commonly use these software packages:

- risk management specialists and consultants
- large organisations
- banks
- finance and insurance companies
- large broking organisations.

Smaller Organisations

For smaller organisations, a well-structured Microsoft® Excel™ spreadsheet could be a viable solution.

Risk Modelling

Risk modelling has been used for years in industries for which taking calculated risk is integral to the business, specifically the financial services, insurance and energy industries. Since the beginning of the century, organisations in both the public and private sectors have developed a wide array of risk models and simulations to address all types of risk, including strategic, tactical, operational, compliance and geopolitical. The development of large databases (big data) and the advancement of cognitive sciences and IT capabilities allow for a more practical approach to risk modelling while the increasing complexity and volatility of the economic environment make modelling more necessary as a value creation tool.

A risk model is an attempt to represent a real system through a set of mathematical relationships and equations that use probability distributions. Building a model requires access not only to sufficient reliable and relevant historical data but also to experts who can understand the likelihood of a given event occurring and its potential consequence (this approaches uses Bayesian networks, as it combines new information into old information). Financing or gathering enough relevant data is one of the two greatest challenges of any effort in risk modelling; the other one is to make decision-makers comfortable with the models and to support them to make the best use of them during their decision-making processes.

Quantifying risk is at the heart of risk modelling. Quantifying credit risk, that is, potential losses due to the inability of debtors to reimburse loans, is at the heart of lending institutions' mission. For investment funds, it is essential to assess market risks, which are potential losses due to negative fluctuations of a portfolio's market value. When it comes to operational risk, quantifying potential losses resulting from failing processes is a relevant issue for all organisations, private and public.

For risk modelling in a complex system to be efficient, particular attention must be paid to systemic risk, which is the risk that an entire system or process will collapse. It is therefore essential to consider process interdependencies at the operational level.

Risk Modelling in Practice

At the beginning of the 21st century, a number of significant episodes took place that illustrated the ability of modelling scenarios to predict actual events. The models predicted that certain incidents could trigger catastrophic breakdowns in complex systems built on interacting processes and this effect was seen in the large-scale blackout that affected central Canada and America's north-east in August 2003, and the major blackouts that occurred in London, eastern Denmark, southern Sweden and Italy in September that same year.

Another major blackout took place on the evening of 4 November 2006, in parts of Germany, France, Belgium, Austria, Italy and northern Spain. This provides an even better illustration of the main features of phase transitions in operational risk: the blackout appears to have been caused when a 380-kV power line stretching across the river Ems was switched off to allow the Norwegian Pearl to enter the North Sea.

The blackout snowballed only half an hour after the line had been cut, which was in line with the expectations derived from expert analysis: cutting the line would have shifted major regions of the grid closer to intrinsic instability so that the probable fluctuations that might be expected to occur within a few hours, rather than several years, could cause the actual large-scale breakdown of the grid itself.

Emerging Developments

The development of Big Data and the introduction of dynamic data visualisation tools have raised new prospects for the use of data analytics to address risk.

However, data analytics has its limitations, and the major issue is that the use of historical data is backward-looking. The underlying assumption is that the future will mimic the past, and correlations in the past behaviour of the system are sought in order to infer root causes, or chain of causations.

However, extrapolating past results into future ones is not predictive as the internal and external contexts in which organisations operate are always changing; therefore, the past is not necessarily a good predictor of the future. This is where modelling can be more useful than data analytics and other statistical techniques.

Risk models are powerful decision-making tools for strategic purposes. They can be used to assess many types of risk, including understanding the uncertainties – both threats and opportunities – of developing and achieving strategic objectives and shedding some light on very specific questions. The issues at stake can be varied, and can include threats to the supply network, the geopolitical risks involved in entering an emerging market and how a hacker or a terrorist might come after the organisation. Once developed, risk models can be used not only to assess how a system behaves under normal operating conditions but also under different levels of disturbances resulting from 'what if' scenarios. In this case, the model informs decision-makers considering the organisation's level of risk tolerance or risk appetite and therefore is instrumental in enhancing an organisation's resiliency so that it is able to withstand destabilising events.

Too often, managers and decision-makers assume that risk models are very expensive to develop and/or configure and that they require many months or even years to be operational. Nowadays, many tools and accelerators are readily available that help in creating or adapting even complex models relatively quickly, in a number of weeks or few months.

Risk models are not restricted to corporate use and can be deployed throughout an organisation. Companies with a mature ERM program need to have assigned key risks to risk owners and set up a governance structure. Governance is needed to monitor and oversee the quality of the assumptions made by the various models, and to ensure coherence when competing models are offering divergent outputs.

Organisations that wish to use risk models need to understand that models are only one component of the overall process of gathering and using information about risks to make informed decisions. A tactic that is gaining momentum calls for the organisations to put in place a risk analytics sharing centre, which is a hub where risk information is stored. This centre is linked to primary data sets and other types of business intelligence to provide a dynamic view of the organisation's risks and how they're evolving and/or emerging. Risk models and other dynamic forms of risk sensing and data analytics can be used to present this view. More mature organisations are even fully integrating risk intelligence with business intelligence.

Simulation

A model can be used to simulate a system such as business or production process, or even a balance sheet. Simulation consists of looking at how a system will behave under different sets of conditions or assumptions. These simulations help guide decision-making and provide insights into the underlying system or process so that it can be made more efficient, stable, resilient or secure – depending on what is desired. The model itself is not frozen or static and can be adjusted and strengthened as the underlying conditions or assumptions change, as new results are gathered (allowing for a feedback loop) or based on the outcomes of the simulation.

In risk management, simulation can be used not only to quantify risks but also to guide decisions and actions to enhance opportunities and curb threats, and to monitor risk management efforts over time. Modelling and simulation are the two sides of the same coin and help reduce the complexity when making pivotal business decisions or investments in two ways:

1. Creating a model inherently involves stripping away unnecessary or non-essential information so that only the key elements remain, thus reducing a multidimensional problem to a more manageable form.
2. Using simulation to see how underlying systems behave in certain conditions or scenarios lends a measure of comfort in making decisions as surprises are reduced or avoided. It also increases the level of control in decision-making as adjustments can be made to the system or process to drive it in a preferred direction.

Limitations

Models and simulations should not be used to replace business acumen or common sense. Modelling and simulation take into account mostly the 'known unknowns' and offer results in terms of the probability of a given outcome occurring but they do not remove all uncertainty. The best they can really do is to reduce it to a comfortable level.

Various recent crises – whether financial, geopolitical or natural – have proven that long-held, widespread assumptions are simply not relevant anymore. Simulations can be a very powerful tool to test assumptions – realistic, probable, possible or even impossible – to see their impact on the model and, in turn, understand how assumptions affect decisions about how to run a business. Models and simulations must be seen as a compass to guide decision- making, rather than an autopilot that makes decisions.

Encompassing both past data gathering and experts' opinion collecting (including using Bayesian networks), risk modelling provides decision-makers with a refined view of the future, thus limiting the span of possible evolutions and limiting the impact of uncertainty, that is, the range of possible outcomes.

Continuously reviewing and improving the model through experience feedback will ensure that implementation is kept relevant and applicable for optimal performance and strengthened resilience when disturbances occur.

Summary

Please keep the following points from this chapter in mind:

- Risk analysis involves evaluating and quantifying individual risk exposures in terms of their likelihood and consequence.
- Risk analysis is not an exact science – it depends on subjective judgement regarding potential future events.
- The more an organisation understands its risk, the better its analysis.
- An organisation should ideally use a combination of qualitative, semi-quantitative and quantitative analysis techniques.
- The past does not always accurately reflect the future in terms of loss likelihood and consequences.
- Qualitative analysis uses words to describe the magnitude of potential consequences and the likelihood that those consequences will occur.
- Qualitative analysis techniques using descriptors and the like have their limits as they provide relatively imprecise estimates.
- Semi-quantitative risk analysis uses expanded qualitative scales (words and descriptors) to produce a more detailed, numerical ranking scale.
- Quantitative analysis may be described as using the use of numerical values for both consequences and likelihood using data from a variety of sources.
- Organisations tend to only use quantitative analysis for significant and core business risks as it can be costly.
- A risk model is an attempt to represent a real system through a set of mathematical relationships and equations that use probability distributions.

Chapter 14

Financial Models for Risk Management

Introduction

At the end of the previous chapter, risk modelling was introduced as part of the discussion of risk analysis tools. This section explores the specific use of risk models within the financial decision-making universe and describes the uses and limitations of each.

Learning Objectives

By the end of this chapter, you should be able to:

- describe the benefits and limitations of each financial model;
- outline the differences between KRIs and KPIs.

Capital Asset Pricing Model (CAPM)

Although risk has always been a factor in financial decision making, it was primarily based on business acumen, or rules of thumb, until 1951, when a young academic proposed using as a proxy for risk in a given asset the volatility of the probability distribution of possible future outcomes or return. Harry Markowitz, who later won a Nobel Prize in Economic Sciences, chose to measure the volatility by the standard deviation (σ) or variance (σ^2) of the probability distribution, reflecting an asset's possible outcome.

The CAPM is derived from Markowitz's discussion on risk premium and provides an equation to model the relationship between the level of systematic risk, which is risk inherent to markets, and the expected return of assets, particularly stocks and shares. It is the model used most widely by financial institutions and fund managers to optimise the risk/return arbitrage.

Essentials and Assessment of Risk Management, 209–216

Published under exclusive licence by Emerald Publishing Limited
doi:10.1108/978-1-83662-302-120251036

CAPM aims to assess the return of a proposed investment for a given level of risk, stating that the return on an investment is acceptable when it is equal to its cost of capital. When the return is optimised for a given level of risk, the only way to earn a higher return is to accept more risk. If the expected return is not equal to or greater than the required return, the investment should not be made. Thus, CAPM is a tool that enables investors to assess the profitability of proposed investments.

CAPM is based on limited inputs and is true in the case of a normal distribution but not for other probability distributions where other elements, such as skewness, need to be considered. Furthermore, the model assumes no transaction costs (assets that are bought and sold without any fee).

When the restricting conditions set above are taken into account, CAPM concludes that the cost of equity capital (i.e. the capital owned by shareholders measured as the current market value of all of the company's assets minus the total of all its liabilities) is determined only by the riskiness of an asset compared to overall market risk, which is quantified by a measure traditionally represented by the Greek letter beta (β). Beta is linked to the comparative volatility of the asset and the market and takes into account the correlation between the two.

Although more sophisticated models have been developed to address the issues of asset pricing and portfolio selection, such as the Sharpe diagonal model, CAPM is still commonly used as it is simple and can be used in many different situations. Financial institutions use CAPM to price risky securities and provide expected returns for assets based on the level of risk estimated for those assets, thus computing capital.

The formula for calculating the expected return of an asset given its risk is as follows:

$$\overline{r}_a = \overline{r}_f + \beta_a(\overline{r}_m - r_f)$$

where:

r^f= risk-free rate
β_a = volatility of the security
$\overline{r}_m$ = expected market return

The theory underlying CAPM is that investors need to be remunerated both for time value of money (which is the principle that money is worth more in the present than in the future because of potential interest and investment earnings) and the risk they bear. The time value of money appears in the equation as the risk-free rate (r_f) and compensates the investors for delayed consumption. The risk-free rate is usually assumed to be the yield of government bonds (e.g. US Treasuries) of the same maturity.

The CAPM equation also provides an assessment of the level of compensation (premium) an investor will want for taking on the risk involved. The premium is calculated by comparing the asset's returns to the market's return over a period of time and to the market premium ($r_m - r_f$). Thus, the risk premium is the return of the market in excess of the risk-free rate.

International CAPM

The international CAPM is based on the same concept but extends to international markets. While CAPM calculates the return investors expect for a given level of local risk, the international CAPM incorporates international risks, including foreign exchange risks. This is useful for portfolios dealing with several currencies, which implies adding a foreign currency risk premium.

Risk and Diversification

For a portfolio of assets, or securities, there is both systematic risk, also known as market risk and undiversifiable risk, and unsystematic risk, also known as diversifiable risk.

Systematic risk is shared by all securities and is undiversifiable because it is inherent to the market itself. Unsystematic risk is the risk linked with individual assets, and therefore can be reduced by diversification, which involves including more assets or securities in a portfolio. Diversification depends on the specific context of local financial markets, and in developed markets such as the UK or US a portfolio comprising 30–40 securities will be sufficient to diversify the portfolio so that risk exposure is limited to systematic risk only. In less mature financial markets, a larger number will be necessary as assets are more volatile.

According to CAPM, rational investors should not accept unsystematic risks as they are not rewarded for them, they are only rewarded for systematic risks. Therefore, returns must be linked to an asset's contribution to the portfolio's overall riskiness rather than an asset's inherent riskiness. In CAPM, the beta (volatility) of the portfolio is the factor that determines the reward for the systematic exposure accepted by an investor.

Efficient Frontier

The CAPM assumes that the risk-return profile of a portfolio can be optimised, which means it will display the lowest possible level of risk for its level of return. Additionally, since each additional asset introduced into a portfolio further diversifies the portfolio, each asset in a portfolio must be value-weighted to achieve the best possible level of return for its level of risk (assuming that all assets are infinitely divisible). Such optimal portfolios make up the efficient frontier.

Because the unsystematic risk is diversifiable, the total risk of a portfolio can be viewed as beta.

Economic Capital

Economic capital (EC) is a term mostly used in financial services to refer to the amount of capital an organisation needs to ensure it can stay solvent even in worst-case scenarios. It is calculated by an organisation's finance department and represents the amount of capital that the organisation needs to have to support any risks that it takes with a minimal chance of bankruptcy.

To calculate EC, organisations can use internally developed models or commercial software. Some examples of such software are *Portfolio Manager* by Moody's Analytics, Strategic Analytics, *Credit risk+* by Credit Suisse and *Credit Metrics* by JP Morgan.

Quantifying EC involves assessing the amount of capital that is required to support a given risk. The calculations are based on the organisation's financial strength, or credit rating, and expected losses. Financial strength is the likelihood that the organisation will not become insolvent over the measurement period and is the confidence level in the statistical calculation. Most banks, per Basel III, use a confidence level between 99.96% and 99.98%, which is the insolvency rate expected for an organisation with an AA or Aa credit rating. The organisation's expected loss is the anticipated average loss over the measurement period, and represents the cost of doing business. Expected losses are usually absorbed by operating profits.

EC is used for measuring and reporting market and operational risks across a financial organisation. It measures risk using economic realities rather than accounting and regulatory rules, thus offering a more reliable account of the situation. It is therefore considered to provide a more realistic measure of an organisation's solvency. For a bank, computing the EC and using it in risk/reward ratios shows which lines of business it should pursue to maximise the risk-reward trade-off.

Since EC is a bank-specific or internal measure of available capital, there is no common global definition of it. However, there are some elements that many banks have in common when defining EC. EC estimates can be covered by elements of Tier 1, Tier 2, and Tier 3 (see below), definitions used by rating agencies and other types of capital, such as planned earnings, unrealised profit or implicit government guarantee.

EC is relevant because it primarily aims to support business decisions and therefore can provide answers to key business decisions and when evaluating different business units.

Performance Measures

Performance measures that use EC include return on risk adjusted capital (RORAC), risk adjusted return on capital (RAROC) and economic value added (EVA). Business units that outperform the others according to these performance indicators are allocated more capital in order to optimise risk. Value-at-risk (VaR) and similar measures are also based on EC and are used by financial institutions for risk management purposes.

While a financial institution's or a holding company's EC figure is partly driven by its risk appetite, its RC requirement is driven by supervisory metrics set out in the regulatory guidance and rule books. Moreover, by contrast with regulatory capital (RC) models under Basel II, such as the advanced internal rating based (AIRB) model for credit risk, banks can make their own choices on how to model EC. For example, banks can choose the functional form and the parameter settings of their model. Therefore, EC modelling may adjust or ignore assumptions of AIRB for credit risk.

AIRB assumes that a loan portfolio is large and homogeneous, that longer term assets are more risky, as reflected in the so-called maturity adjustment capped at five years, and that higher quality ratings have higher correlation to reflect systemic risk. It also evaluates risk by rating classes and assumes perfect correlation between rating classes and diversification within a rating class.

Risk Management and Economic Capital

Banks and financial institutions have long-term uncertainties that they must account for. The Basel Accords were developed in this context, with the objective of enhancing risk management programs in banks and financial institutions. Basel III stipulates the minimum amount of capital that banks should hold against their risks. It also sets out regulations for modelling RC and encourages organisations to use EC models.

Regulatory Capital

While EC is the amount of risk capital that an organisation estimates is necessary to remain solvent, RC reflects the minimum amount of capital needed to meet all risks dictated by regulations and legislation. From a regulatory perspective, the minimum amount of capital is part of a bank's eligible capital. Total eligible capital according to Basel II is provided by the following three tiers of capital:

- Tier 1 (core) capital includes common stock, qualifying preferred stock, and surplus and retained earnings.
- Tier 2 (supplementary) capital includes general loan loss reserves, certain forms of preferred stock, term subordinated debt, perpetual debt, and other hybrid debt and equity instruments.
- Tier 3 capital includes short-term subordinated debt and net trading book profits that have not been externally verified.

These tiers may be constituted in various ways according to legal and accounting regimes in Bank for International Settlement (BIS) member countries. Additionally, the tiers absorb losses differently with Tier 1 being best able to absorb losses. Banks need to calculate their minimum capital requirements for credit, operational, market and other risks to establish how much Tier 1, Tier 2 and Tier 3 capital is available.

EC Versus RC

Since the development of the Basel Accords, EC has become an important measure for banks and financial institutions. It provides a useful supplementary instrument to RC for business-based decisions. Organisations are increasingly using EC frameworks, and this growth is likely to continue. It is interesting to consider whether EC could one day supersede RC

Key Risk Indicators

Key risk indicators (KRIs) are used by management to indicate how risky an activity is as they are designed to provide early warning of any increase in risk exposure in the organisation. KRIs are becoming a fundamental aspect of ERM as they complement key performance indicators (KPIs) so well. KRIs differ from KPIs as KRIs indicate whether there may be a future adverse consequence to an activity while KPIs measure how well something is being done.

As with likelihood and consequence criteria, organisations should develop their own KRIs according to their own specific size and context. When developing KRIs, organisations should ensure that:

- they have a proper business context;
- they are measurable;
- someone is assigned responsibility for each;
- there is buy-in from the team;
- they relate to the risk management portfolio.

Developing KRIs

The theory behind KRIs is that there is always evidence of a developing risk. For example, a piece of plant has a coloured pressure gauge that uses yellow to show when the pressure is at the upper ranges of the safety threshold and red to show when the pressure has exceeded the safety threshold. There is also an alarm that will sound when the pressure reaches the red. If the dial hits the yellow zone, this is evidence that a problem could be developing. The aim of KRIs is to identify and document the potential warning signs, then quantify the consequences and develop actions to be taken when the warning signs appear.

The information sources and risk identification techniques described in Chapter 3 should be used to set KRIs. Previous experience is also useful, as failures or poor performance indicate areas of risk and the related consequences.

KRIs should be developed according to the following steps:

1. identify key risks;
2. identify the root causes of these risks – be sure to identify the actual cause of the risk, not a side effect;
3. define the measurements;
4. design ways to capture the data, report on it and address it;
5. identify trigger levels – these are the levels at which action must be taken. In the example above, the dial reaching the yellow could be the call to action;
6. establish monitoring and review programs, communication channels and escalation procedures.

It is important to note that the risk management process involves identifying risks, their likelihood and consequence, and implementing measures to reduce or avoid the consequences. Generally, a single KRI cannot account for all of these steps. Therefore, KRIs should be developed to separately measure likelihood, effects and actions.

EXAMPLE

Poorly Mentoring Employees

GPG identifies that poorly mentoring employees is a KRI. It has found that employees who are mentored well stay longer, are more productive and are happier in the workplace.

GPG needs to consider how likely it is that employees will be managed poorly, what the consequences are and how it can address the issue. It comes up with the following KRIs:

- time spent on mentoring (hours per week). GPG decides that the less time is spent on mentoring, the more likely it is that the risk will arise;
- employee engagement. GPG decides to develop an index to map the amount of communication against engagement levels;
- improve mentoring processes. GPG decides to develop training for all employees responsible for mentoring others to ensure that all relevant staff are aware of the requirement and have strategies to help them mentor well.

Benefits of KRIs

There are a number of benefits to organisations that effectively develop and measure their KRIs.

Clearly defining KRIs demonstrates an organisation's commitment to risk management, facilitates timely and accurate reporting, allows meaningful comparisons of risk, enables effective monitoring of risk and supports the development of a framework for dealing with risk. Also, because KRIs provide early warning signals, organisations are able to deal with risk situations before they escalate into significant or serious events.

As with all risk management measures, KRIs should be monitored and regularly reviewed to ensure they are relevant and effective. How often each KRI is reviewed will depend on the KRI.

Limitations of KRIs

If KRIs are not properly established from the outset, numerous problems can arise.

Dangers when setting KRIs include:

- setting too many, which makes them hard to manage;
- not taking risk appetite into account;
- misunderstanding the underlying cause of risk;

- setting KRIs that only offer vague or generalised information;
- not establishing communication channels and escalation procedures to come into effect if an issue is identified – channels and procedures will vary depending on the KRI;
- not aligning KRIs with KPIs;
- not setting appropriate trigger levels.

In addition, KRIs may already exist in an organisation's risk management framework, albeit under a different name. It is important to review the framework thoroughly before investing in significant KRI development.

Summary

Please keep the following points from this chapter in mind:

- The CAPM aims to assess the risks and returns of a proposed investment, stating that the return on an investment is optimal when it is equal to its cost of capital.
- CAPM is a tool that enables investors to assess the profitability of proposed investments.
- EC refers to the amount of capital an organisation needs to ensure it can stay solvent even in worst-case scenarios.
- EC is used to measure and report market and operational risks across a financial organisation. It measures risk using economic realities rather than accounting and regulatory rules, thus offering a reliable account of the situation.
- RC refers to the minimum amount of capital an organisation needs according to regulations and legislation.
- EC and RC can be used together to make sound business decisions.
- KRIs indicate how risky an activity is by providing early warnings of any increase in risk exposure in the organisation.
- KRIs should be monitored and regularly reviewed to ensure they are relevant and effective.

Chapter 15

Risk Register, Risk Matrix, Risk Profile, Risk Map

Introduction

The importance of documenting risk management framework activities and outcomes has been discussed throughout a number of chapters in this book.

This chapter will explore the tools and techniques that are available to risk managers for documenting these processes.

Learning Objectives

By the end of this chapter, you should be able to:

- document the risk identification process;
- complete a risk register;
- complete a risk matrix;
- complete a risk profile;
- complete a risk map.

Documenting the Risk Identification Process

Organisations should document the risk identification techniques and process they've used so that their purpose, method of execution and results are all well recorded.

The documentation should capture the approach, method or technique used for risk identification, the scope of the risk identification process, the participants who took part in the process and the information sources consulted to gather the relevant information.

Essentials and Assessment of Risk Management, 217–233

Published under exclusive licence by Emerald Publishing Limited
doi:10.1108/978-1-83662-302-120251038

Risk Register

Perhaps the most important document that should be generated as a result of the risk identification process is a risk register.

A risk register is a core risk management document that contains detailed information about each identified risk exposure.

During the risk identification stage, information the organisation records in the risk register includes:

- a detailed description of each risk exposure:
  - what can happen
  - how it could happen
  - its source
  - its potential consequences
- the likelihood of a risk actually occurring;
- people responsible for managing the risk (clear accountability is crucial);
- any existing treatment measures or controls to mitigate the exposure.

EXAMPLE

Risk Register with Consequence Table

Function/ activity

Completed by .... Date:................

The risk (what can happen)

The risk (what can happen)

Source of risk

Risk rating

Likelihood code	Consequence code		Moderate	Major	Catastrophic
	Insignificant	Minor			
Almost certain	Medium	High	High	Catastrophic	Catastrophic
Likely	Low	Medium	High	High	Catastrophic
Possible	Low	Medium	High	High	Catastrophic
Unlikely	Low	Low	Medium	High	High
Rare	Low	Low	Medium	Medium	High

Existing controls and adequacy

Risk accepted

Once established, the risk register is the core tool the organisation uses to record, control, report and monitor ongoing risk management activities.

Once established, the risk register is the core tool the organisation uses to record, control, report and monitor ongoing risk management activities. It can be referred and added to while the risk assessment activities are undertaken as well as serve as a resource for all future risk management reviews and projects.

The risk register should be customised by each organisation to reflect their specific structure and activities.

The example risk register contains fields for recording:

- consequence ratings
- likelihood ratings
- level of risk
- risk priority in terms of treatment requirements.

These aspects of a risk register are important but this information is often not immediately available during the risk identification step. The fields may instead be completed during risk assessment, analysis and evaluation.

A Central Repository

The risk register is an important tool because it is the central repository of identified risks. As a central repository of identified risks, the risk register facilitates:

- the reporting of risk profiles and action plan progress;
- the risk manager's ongoing liaison with the executive management team regarding the management of risk;
- ongoing workshops and interviews, as it requires regular updating to ensure risk data is current;
- the review and documentation of risks for which risk managers are responsible, including the progress of risk management activities.

Practicality

The risk register must be practical, meaning it should:

- only record material risks for the organisation:
  - an organisation manages minor risks as part of the ongoing management process (no need for a risk management overlay)
  - risk registers that include a large volume of inconsequential risk data become very difficult and uneconomic to manage

- contain concise risk descriptions to allow easy navigation of the data
- be sensibly structured

  – organisations can maintain small risk registers in a spreadsheet but may need to use software for larger and more complex data.

Use

As a minimum, the risk register should be capable of:

- being maintained in a secure manner (to assure data integrity)
- sorting the data by:

  – risk size
  – risk owner
  – department
  – action deadlines
  – risk category

- providing meaningful reports to upper management and the board.

  It is also useful if the risk register can:

- provide reminders to risk owners so they can update progress on risk improvement plans;
- allow read access to all risk owners with write access only for their specific risks;
- provide an audit trail of changes so the risk manager can monitor progress;
- report movements in the risk profile (boards often inquire about what happens to specific risks).

Reporting Inconsistencies

One of the most common problems with risk registers is that risk owners do not describe risks in a consistent way. This reporting inconsistency means the organisation may misunderstand information and reporting can be confusing.

The following table lists some of the common errors in describing risk.

Error	Description
Being inconsistent in the description of risk	For example, sometimes describing cause and sometimes describing consequences
Long, complicated descriptions	• Descriptions that are too long and complicated make it difficult for management to navigate around the risk profile • A separate field in the risk register should be used to describe the risk in further detail

Describing the cause of risk rather than the risk itself	• The risk register should focus on how the risk impacts the organisation. For example, a flood is an issue only if it affects the organisation, which could mean damage to and the inability to operate out of buildings • This risk could have a number of causes each of which would require different mitigation plans. It is best practice in this case to follow the description of the risk with cause (for example, damage to buildings by fire).
Poor risk description	The risk register needs to be specific about risks. For example, the risk register should not describe the loss of customers in general terms such as 'poor market conditions'.

Self-Help Question 15.1

In developing their risk management program, GPG develops a risk identification information report based on:

- inspections
- interviews
- collated key documents.

Contents of the report

GPG's risk identification report includes the following sections:

- general risk information
- a flow chart of operational activities
- a detailed site plan of GPG's premises
- financial information
- business environment commentary
- the organisational structure.

Possible risk exposures

Review the materials in Appendix 2, which summarises sections of GPG's risk identification information report.
1 Extract a list of as many possible risk exposures as you can.

Answers to self-help questions are provided at the end of each section.

The Risk Matrix

The analysis and evaluation stages of the risk management process produce a series of risk ratings as set out in the following table. These ratings describe the level of risk remaining after taking into consideration the effectiveness of the current control environment.

Likelihood	**Consequence**				
	Insignificant (1)	Minor (2)	Serious (3)	Major (4)	Catastrophic (5)
Almost certain (5)	Medium	High	High	Extreme	Extreme
Likely (4)	Medium	Medium	High	High	Extreme
Possible (3)	Low	Medium	Medium	High	High
Unlikely (2)	Low	Low	Medium	Medium	High
Rare (1)	Low	Low	Low	Medium	Medium

The risk levels shown in this matrix reflect the organisation's risk tolerance and act as a guide to the risk escalation process.

Example – Risk Escalation

GPG Risk Rating Definitions

Risk Rating	Level of Required Management Attention
Extreme	To reduce the risk rating to high or lower (if possible), take immediate action to modify the: • threat • frequency; or • consequence Executive management group to closely monitor status from month to month
High	• Review the risks and reduce by additional mitigation measures • Executive management group to review status quarterly
Medium	• Modify the threat, frequency or consequence to reduce the risk as far as practicable • Executive responsibility to ensure no major changes in the external or internal environment on a quarterly basis
Low	Manage by routine processes and reassess at next annual review

Self-Help Question 15.2

Note: This self-help question requires you to use your imagination as there is no right or wrong answer. Use the following matrix to document the controls GPG should implement for six of the risks you identified in the previous self-help question.

GPG simplified risk register template

Ref	Risk exposure	Controls
1		
2		
3		
4		
5		
6		

Answers to self-help questions are provided at the end of each section.

Activity | Rating GPG's risk exposures

Now that GPG has a list of their risk exposures, they need to decide which ones present the most significant threats to the organisation. Marjorie Crawford, their finance manager, suggests they determine:

- the likelihood of each of the loss exposures occurring
- what the consequences each of these exposures are.

1. Using the knowledge from your review of **Appendix 2**, estimate the likelihood of each of the six risk exposures you identified in the previous activity by assigning one of the following descriptors:

   – almost certain
   – likely
   – possible
   – unlikely
   – rare.

2. Refer to the GPG classifications and codes table in **Appendix 3**.
3. Enter the alphabetical code associated with the selected likelihood descriptor into the likelihood column of the risk rating template.
4. Estimate the extent of the consequences for each of your identified exposures as:

   – insignificant
   – minor
   – moderate
   – major
   – extreme.

5. Refer to the classifications and codes table in **Appendix 3**. Enter the numerical code associated with the selected descriptor into the consequence column of the risk rating template.
6. Refer to the GPG risk analysis matrix in **Appendix 3**. Using your estimates of likelihood and consequence, determine a risk rating for each of the identified exposures.
7. Refer to the classifications and codes table and enter the appropriate codes into the risk rating column to complete the risk rating template.

GPG simplified risk rating template

Ref	Risk Exposure	Likelihood	Consequence	Risk Rating
1				
2				
3				
4				
5				
6				

The Risk Profile

One of the main areas for the organisation to monitor is changes to the risk profile, as this drives much of risk management activity.

Changes to the following context elements are key indicators of changes to the risk profile:

- organisational objectives
- operating environments (for example, changes to systems, disposals and acquisitions)

- legislative changes
- business plans and strategies
- major projects
- external factors (for example, economic and market conditions)
- stakeholders.

These factors often point to changes in the risk profile that an organisation needs to identify, assess, treat and report.

The status of risk profiles for project activity should also be included in the review process to ensure they are up to date and incorporated in the overall risk register.

Monitoring Changes

The risk profile should be monitored using both informal and formal monitoring and review processes.

Informal Monitoring

Informal monitoring occurs on a daily basis and can include:

- discussions with staff
- reading reports
- inspecting the site
- making general inquiries.

Examples of informal monitoring systems include:

- log analysis – some businesses typically compile logs in areas such as:
  - security
  - visitors
  - breakdowns
  - phone calls.
- staff meetings, where employees raise and discuss incidents
- customer complaints.

Formal monitoring

Formal monitoring includes:

- scheduled reviews
- establishing reporting systems (for example, assessment of risk profile)
- an audit program
- treatment action logs.

These programs are generally dictated by the organisation's structure, activities and markets. For example, the organisation probably needs to supply a quarterly risk report if the board meets quarterly.

Many organisations establish management risk committees to monitor the risk. Alternatively, the board may monitor risk directly.

A common formal technique to update an organisation's risk profile is for executives to review the organisation's risk profile in a workshop setting. As the executive group is the first to know if the risk profile (and all associated actions) are on track, a formal half-yearly or annual workshop (depending on the size of the organisation) ensures a regular, structured review. These executive workshops can also provide executive input into the risk management program and how the organisation can adapt and improve its risk management program.

Other Risk Profiling Techniques

Other risk profiling techniques include:

- meetings with key executives from across the organisation;
- periodically sending risk profiles to risk owners for their review or update/s (if the organisation structures the risk register well, this reporting is easily generated and can be tailored to the needs of the organisation);
- questionnaires;
- desktop reviews using information gathered in the initial risk identification process.

Risk Mapping

Risk mapping is a decision-making tool that provides a visual perspective of an organisation's risks and their priority ranking. Basic risk maps provide a matrix of the likelihood and consequences of risks identified on an organisation's risk register. Risk mapping leads to a representation called a risk matrix (see section above) or heat map.

Variations of these maps can add other dimensions or aspects of risk like degree of control and velocity.

These maps can also be used to categorise risk in relation to an organisation's risk appetite, which is 'the amount and type of risk an organisation is willing to pursue or retain' (3.7.1.2 of ISO/Guide 73:2009 Risk management – Vocabulary). The categorisation of risk relative to risk appetite will help determine the appropriate level of risk management.

The goal of risk maps is to improve an organisation's understanding of its risk profile, risk appetite and the nature and impact of its risks exposures, thus improving its risk assessment models.

Basic Risk Map

A basic risk map translates the risks identified in the risk register into a risk matrix. This matrix can be used to analyse the risks that are within or outside an organisation's risk appetite and therefore serves as a basis to prioritise risk management and treatment for the risks that are outside the risk appetite. The term impact is used to convey the concept that the outcome can be either positive or negative. Different colours are often used to represent the different levels of impact and likelihood combined. This technique is sometimes referred to as heat mapping.

Risk Map Variations

Risk management professionals can use variations of the risk map to bring in different dimensions, such as time. Risk managers can use risk maps to identify the time-based urgency for each risk. Time dimension risk maps can be used with the basic risk map to set monthly, quarterly or annual priorities. These maps can be used to assist in the design and implementation of the risk management process as well as for follow-up in existing programs.

Risk management professionals can also use risk mapping to identify inherent, residual (current) and optimum levels of risk. Inherent risk is important because the difference between inherent and residual risk provides a measure of the necessity and the effectiveness of the current risk treatment. If the difference between inherent and residual risk is small, either the risk does not need to be treated or the treatment is ineffective. The difference between the residual (current) level of risk and the optimum risk represents the risk treatment opportunity to further reduce the risk. A risk map can be used to depict the effects of the current risk treatment techniques on the likelihood and impact of risks. It can also show opportunities to improve risk treatment. Catastrophe plans can also help reduce the likelihood as well as the consequences of risk. Note that property insurance, extent and limits, should be reviewed and aligned with the amount of cash needed to finance the catastrophe plans.

Risk Map in Project Mode

When assessing project and program risk, the most commonly used approach is to assess the likelihood and consequence for each potential risk event and draw a risk map as shown below.

This is a good way to visualise the project risks that have been identified for deeper analysis and review. By multiplying likelihood and consequence, it is possible to come up with a risk rating that can be used to compare and prioritise different types of risks for the development of mitigation plans.

The challenge with this approach is that the categorisation of both the risk likelihood and consequence are estimations based on currently available information and knowledge. The situation will change over the lifetime of the project as more information is gained.

It is good practice to repeat the assessment at regular intervals throughout the duration of the project to update the mitigation actions and define new ones.

Summary

Please keep the following points from this chapter in mind:

- Organisations should document the risk identification techniques and processes they've used so that their purpose, method of execution and results are all well recorded.
- A risk register is a core risk management document that contains detailed information about each identified risk exposure.
- The risk matrix enables organisations to produce risk ratings that describe the level of risk remaining after taking into consideration the effectiveness of the current control environment.
- One of the main areas for the organisation to monitor is changes to the risk profile, as this drives much of risk management activity.
- Risk mapping is a decision-making tool that provides a visual perspective of an organisation's risks and their priority ranking.

Answers to Self-Help Questions

Self-help question 15.1

Ref	GPG's Risk Exposure	Ramifications
1	Raw materials are stored largely in one area	Leave GPG's stocks vulnerable to: • fire • water damage • other damage
2	GPG's document management system (DMS) stores master copies of clients' work	If GPG's DMS was damaged or destroyed, clients: • would not be able to access master copies of important documents • could take legal action against GPG
3	Hydraulic trolleys/ forklifts transport raw materials from the storage area to the printing plant	This business process would be interrupted if the forklift/trolley is damaged or stolen
4	One single printing machine	There is a significant reliance on the single printing machine because print production cannot continue if the printer breaks down

→

Ref	GPG's Risk Exposure	Ramifications
5	Folding machinery	A breakdown of folding machinery could interrupt regular business operations
6	The collation and binding operations reliance on key pieces of machinery	The collation and binding operations depend on key pieces of machinery that may be difficult to source/ replace quickly if damaged or destroyed
7	Reliance on one particular supplier	Reliance on one particular supplier could endanger production
8	Reliance on one particular distributor	Reliance on one particular distributor could endanger distribution
9	The doorways between building one and building two are permanently open	This presents an increased level of risk if there is a fire at the premises
10	There is no sprinkler system in building one	The building is only protected by: • fire hose reels • extinguishers
11	GPG's premises are bounded by a river on one side	This could present a significant risk if the river is susceptible to flooding
12	LPG, oil and diesel storage tanks	The LPG, oil and diesel storage tanks present a risk of fire/explosion
13	• The LPG, oil and diesel storage tanks are unfenced • There is easy access to the tanks from the scrubland	This presents a significant risk to GPG if one tampers with any of the tanks
14	Staff parking their cars on the bitumen at the side of the access roadway near the main plant operations	• Creates traffic congestion • Could cause an accident which: – damages GPG's premises – results in staff/public injury
15	• An absence of gatekeepers • Gates being left open after hours	Leaves GPG vulnerable to theft

→

Ref	GPG's Risk Exposure	Ramifications
16	Miscellaneous equipment and parts: • around the waste skip area • inside the buildings	• Indicates poor housekeeping standards • Could cause an accident as the skip is adjacent to: – finished products – the flammable liquid store
17	The computer back-up is stored onsite in a fireproof cupboard	Although the back-up is stored in a fireproof cupboard, one could damage or steal the data
18	Building valuations are outdated	• Current insurances are likely to be inadequate • If a loss occurs, GPG could incur considerable costs because they are underinsured
19	• The staff lunchroom is situated next to the materials storage area and the recharger facility • There is evidence that staff smoke cigarettes in the lunchroom	This situation poses a significant fire hazard
20	There is a fireworks manufacturer situated next to GPG's premises	The adjacent fireworks manufacturer presents a significant risk in terms of fire and explosion
21	Contracts with Commonwealth Government departments	GPG may lose a significant portion of its revenue stream if it is not successful in renewing its contracts
22	Reliance on only one operator for specialty machinery such as: • printers • binders	• Reliance on only one operator could mean deadlines are jeopardised • Clients could take legal action against GPG for delays in production or delivery

→

Ref	GPG's Risk Exposure	Ramifications
23	Government policy change	Government policy change which allows entities to source printing from the private sector exposes GPG to the following negative outcomes through price competition: • lost clients • reduced margins
24	Machinery purchased from China (a new supply source)	GPG has not used this supply source before and the machinery may be: • unreliable; or • not sourced according to schedule
25	Existing client pressure	Existing clients may pressure GPG to: • cut costs • defer • cancel print jobs they would traditionally order
26	Alternate overseas suppliers	• May be unreliable • Product quality may impact on the quality of print jobs
27	A tense union environment	Could result in heated industrial action
28	Failure to successfully penetrate the private sector market	Lost revenue and opportunities

Self-help question 15.2

GPG can control almost all of its identified risk exposures and the following table lists some examples of these risk exposures and controls.

Ref	Risk Exposure	Controls
1	Raw materials stored in one area	• Multiple storage points • Investigate offsite storage
2	Damage, destruction or theft of DMS	• Storage of DMS back-up offsite • Alert clients to security measures taken to protect DMS

Ref	Risk Exposure	Controls
3	Theft of, or damage to, hydraulic trolley or forklift	• Driver education course for forklift driver/s and trolley operators • Secure after-hours lock-up
4	Breakdown of machinery	• Have back-up machinery or parts available with a contractor • High priority maintenance agreement
5	Reliance on one supplier	Spread supply acquisition across a number of suppliers
6	Reliance on one distributor	Spread distribution services across more than one distributor
7	Doorways between buildings always open	Ensure doorways between buildings are closed after hours
8	No sprinkler system in building one	Install sprinkler system
9	Flood (GPG bounded by a river)	Move operations to another site or install flood barriers
10	Tampering with storage tanks	Install security fencing around tanks
11	Explosion of storage tanks	• Ensure all WHS/housekeeping standards are met • Monitor tanks regularly
12	Parking/traffic congestion outside premises	Enforce policy that cars are only to be parked within designated parking areas
13	Theft due to poor security	• Employ security to man gates • Ensure gates are locked after hours
14	Equipment and parts left around waste skip and inside buildings	Enforce stringent housekeeping procedures
15	Computer back-up stored onsite only	Store computer back-up offsite
16	Outdated building valuations	• Update valuations • Seek appropriate level of cover
17	Staff smoking in staff/ lunch room	Strict enforcement of no-smoking policy

→

Ref	Risk Exposure	Controls
18	Increased fire risk exposure due to neighbouring fireworks manufacturer	• Minimise storage of combustible material between GPG and fireworks manufacturer • Install drencher system on exposed wall and roof
19	Revenue: Renewal of government department contracts	Undertake early renewal program, offering a discount for early renewal
20	Reliance on one operator for specialist machinery	Train/hire other staff to operate machinery
21	Lost clients and reduced margins through private sector competition	• Client management plan • Lock in clients to longer term contracts • Review production costs to achieve benchmark efficiency
22	New machinery sourced from China unreliable or delivered late	• Undertake a detailed evaluation of supplier and product reliability • Include penalties for late delivery in purchase agreement • Obtain satisfactory warranty terms and repair service standards
23	Existing clients cut or defer jobs	Include scheduling arrangements in contracts
24	New material suppliers unreliable or poor quality	• Perform analyses of potential suppliers and obtain references • Initial rollout to include a mix of existing and new supplies
25	Industrial action	• Continued liaison with unions • Staff satisfaction surveys • Staff remuneration benchmarking
26	Failure to penetrate private sector market	• Detailed marketing plan with milestones and accountabilities • Engage marketing specialists

References and Recommended Reading

Standards and Handbooks

- International Organization for Standardization, ISO 31000:2018, *Risk management—Guidelines*, International Organization for Standardization (ISO), Geneva.
- International Organization for Standardization, ISO Guide 73:2009, *Risk management—Vocabulary*, International Organization for Standardization (ISO), Geneva.
- International Electrotechnical Commission, IEC 31010:2009, *Risk management—Risk assessment techniques*, International Electrotechnical Commission (IEC), Geneva.
- The Committee of Sponsoring Organizations of the Treadway Commission 2004, *Enterprise Risk Management—Integrated Framework*, The Committee of Sponsoring Organizations of the Treadway Commission.

Print Material

- Bracker, J 1980, 'The Historical Development of the Strategic Management Concept', *Academy of Management Review*, 5(2), pp. 219–224.
- Bernstein, P 1998, *Against the gods: The remarkable story of risk*, John Wiley & Sons, Australia.
- Hanson, D et al. 2013, *Strategic management: Competitiveness and globalisation*, 5th edn, Cengage Learning, South Melbourne.
- Head, G and Herman, M 2002, *Enlightened risk taking: A guide to strategic risk management for nonprofits*, 3rd edn, Nonprofit Risk Management Center, Washington, DC.
- Head, G and Herman, M 2002, *Enlightened risk taking: A strategic risk management guide for non-profits*, Non-profit Risk Management Centre, Washington.
- ©2011, *Risk appetite and tolerance guidance paper*, Institute of Risk Management (IRM), London.
- Keetelaar, D 2006, Fiserv Solutions Australia Risk Management Framework (internal document), Australia.
- Louisot, J and Ketcham, C 2014, *ERM—Enterprise risk management: Issues and cases*, 1st edn, Wiley, Melbourne.
- Rasche, T 2001, 'Risk analysis methods—a brief review', Minerals Industry Safety and Health Centre (MISHC), The University of Queensland.

Online Material

- aCOWtancy 2017: provides access to approved practice and revision kits for ACCA exams, www.acowtancy.com/exam-centre/acca-p1/ab45f117-a084-c232-f701-201378fa5555/answer (site accessed 25 May 2017).
- Deutsche Bank, *Annual report*, 2008. https://annualreport.deutsche-bank.com/2008 (site accessed 7 June 2017).
- Kloman, H F 1998, 'The risk spectrum', *Risk Management Reports*, March 1998, www.riskinfo.com (site accessed 25 May 2017).
- Rajgarhia, A 2011, 'LML Piaggio Case', Legal Service India, http://www.legalservicesindia.com/article/article/lml-piaggio-case-702-1.html (site accessed 20 April 2017).
- Swiss Re 2011, 'Spotlight on emerging risks', www.swissre.com/rethinking/emerging_risks/QA_Reto_Schneider.html (site accessed 20 April 2017, 2012).
- World Economic Forum 2010, 'Global risks report', http://www3.weforum.org/docs/WEF_GlobalRisks_Report_2010.pdf (site accessed 20 April 2017).
- World Finance 2010, www.worldfinance.com/home/risk-encyclopaedia/correlated risks (site accessed 25 May 2017).
- https://fr.scribd.com/doc/24343421/Portfolio-Theory-Sharpe-Index-Model
- www.columbia.edu/~ks20/FE-Notes/4700-07-Notes-CAPM.pdf
- www.investinganswers.com/financial-dictionary/stock-valuation/capital-assetpricing-model-capm-1125
- www.investopedia.com/terms/m/modernportfoliotheory.asp
- www.investopedia.com/terms/s/sharperatio.asp
- www.math.chalmers.se/~rootzen/finrisk/gr1_HannesMarling_SaraEmanuelsson_MPT.pdf
- www.prudentnetwork.com/prudent-perspective/correlation-and-risk-management
- www.ways2wealth.com/investing/PostId/18/modern-portfolio-theory

Appendices

Appendix 1

Example: Risk Identification Questionnaire

1.1 General details		
Employee numbers		
Health and safety individuals		
1.2 Management information	Yes	No
Is there a health and safety agenda item at management meetings?	☐	☐
Is the health and safety policy issued and known?	☐	☐
Does management review all health and safety problems and solutions?	☐	☐
Are managers and supervisors held accountable for corrective measures?	☐	☐
If managers and supervisors are held accountable for corrective measures, how are they held accountable?		
Is safety incorporated into general work practice?	☐	☐
Is there a health and safety budget?	☐	☐
Are regular supervisor/employee discussions held?	☐	☐

1.3 Health and safety rules and procedures		
Poor ☐ Fair ☐ Good ☐ Excellent ☐		
	Yes	No
Are there general and specific health and safety rules?	☐	☐
Are they written and distributed to employees?	☐	☐
Are rules enforced?	☐	☐
Are rules reviewed annually?	☐	☐
Are safe operating procedures posted at job locations?	☐	☐
1.4 Pre-placement health assessments		
Poor ☐ Fair ☐ Good ☐ Excellent ☐		
What is the company policy?		
	Yes	No
Are all employees medically examined prior to employment?	☐	☐
Is a specialist medical check carried out if required?	☐	☐
Are reference checks carried out (for example, safety record and workers compensation)?	☐	☐
1.5 Induction procedures		
Poor ☐ Fair ☐ Good ☐ Excellent ☐		
	Yes	No
Is there a full formal induction regarding safety and general employment conditions (for example)?	☐	☐
Are there written handouts?	☐	☐
Is the job induction carried out by a supervisor?	☐	☐
Is the employee reviewed regularly, utilising a checklist?	☐	☐
Is all information kept on an employee's file?	☐	☐
Are procedures reviewed annually?	☐	☐

1.6 Self-inspections		
Poor ☐ Fair ☐ Good ☐ Excellent ☐		
	Yes	No
Is there a formal self-inspection program?	☐	☐
Are all departments included on the program?	☐	☐
Are guidelines and a checklist used?	☐	☐
Do managers and supervisors conduct inspections?	☐	☐
Is follow-up action on hazards and priorities assigned?	☐	☐
Is the checklist/inspection system reviewed regularly?	☐	☐
Is there a hazard rectification system?	☐	☐
1.7 Equipment/process audits		
Poor ☐ Fair ☐ Good ☐ Excellent ☐		
	Yes	No
Are new and existing hazardous equipment/processes audited? (use of checklists)	☐	☐
Is there liaison with statutory bodies?	☐	☐
Is ventilation considered and periodically checked?	☐	☐
Is effectiveness of guarding analysed?	☐	☐
Are operator training requirements assessed?	☐	☐
Are procedures regularly reviewed?	☐	☐
1.8 Training		
Poor Fair Good Excellent		
	Yes	No
Are all training needs assessed?	☐	☐
Is there basic health and safety training for all levels?	☐	☐

1.9 Safety publicity/promotion		
Poor ☐ Fair ☐ Good ☐ Excellent ☐		
	Yes	No
Are safety signs and posters used?	☐	☐
Are safety signs and posters maintained/changed regularly?	☐	☐
Is personal protective equipment used?	☐	☐
Are safety committee minutes posted and distributed?	☐	☐
Are films, talks and safety demonstrations held?	☐	☐
Are targets set and displayed?	☐	☐
1.10 Statutory requirements		
Poor ☐ Fair ☐ Good ☐ Excellent ☐		
	Yes	No
Is there knowledge of all health and safety requirements?	☐	☐
Are accidents reported on time?	☐	☐
Is there liaison with statutory authorities?	☐	☐
Is there a central chemical hazard file?	☐	☐
Are chemical data sheets posted at the workplace?	☐	☐
1.11 Use of specialist resources		
Poor ☐ Fair ☐ Good ☐ Excellent ☐		
	Yes	No
Is use made of internal specialist resources to assist with identification and rectification?	☐	☐
Is use made of external specialist resources?	☐	☐
When a problem is identified, are specialists called in?	☐	☐
Are specialists used to identify problems?	☐	☐

1.12 Ergonomics		
Poor ☐ Fair ☐ Good ☐ Excellent ☐		
Is there ergonomic input into:	Yes	No
work tasks?	☐	☐
work stations?	☐	☐
new equipment/machinery?	☐	☐
potential problems elsewhere?	☐	☐
injuries after they have occurred?	☐	☐
1.13 Effective care		
Poor ☐ Fair ☐ Good ☐ Excellent ☐		
	Yes	No
Are there adequately trained personnel?	☐	☐
Are there adequate numbers?	☐	☐
Are there adequate facilities and maintenance of the facilities?	☐	☐
Is there basic first aid for supervisors?	☐	☐
Is there basic first aid for employees?	☐	☐
Are there regular first aid drills?	☐	☐
Is there adequate medical care through a nurse/doctor?	☐	☐
1.14 Rehabilitation		
Poor ☐ Fair ☐ Good ☐ Excellent ☐		
	Yes	No
Is it practised?	☐	☐
Are there policies and procedures?	☐	☐
Is there supervisory input?	☐	☐
Are all activities documented?	☐	☐
Are there alternative duties available?	☐	☐
Are specialist services available?	☐	☐
1.15 Accident investigation		
Poor ☐ Fair ☐ Good ☐ Excellent ☐		
What accidents are investigated?	☐	☐

What follow-up action is taken and by whom?	☐	☐
If forms are completed, who fills these in?	☐	☐
	Yes	No
Is there a form available?	☐	☐
Are forms fully completed?	☐	☐
Is there costing of each accident?	☐	☐
Are investigators trained?	☐	☐
1.16 Work injury register		
Poor ☐ Fair ☐ Good ☐ Excellent ☐		
What action is taken on problems highlighted and by whom?		
	Yes	No
Is a register kept?	☐	☐
Are incidents recorded in a register?	☐	☐
Is there an analysis of the register?	☐	☐
Is there costing of injuries?	☐	☐
1.17 Claims control		
Poor ☐ Fair ☐ Good ☐ Excellent ☐		
	Yes	No
Are personnel allocated?	☐	☐
Are claims reported to an insurance company?	☐	☐
Is there regular contact with insurers?	☐	☐
Are claims reports prepared quarterly?	☐	☐
Does management receive and review reports?	☐	☐
Does management take action on reports?	☐	☐
Are cost controls established?	☐	☐
1.18 Regular management reports		
Poor ☐ Fair ☐ Good ☐ Excellent ☐		
Does the monthly management report detail:	Yes	No
accident numbers?	☐	☐

claim numbers?	☐	☐
action taken on accidents?	☐	☐
analysis of injuries and action?	☐	☐
responsibilities assigned?	☐	☐
safety/injury trends and targets?		
comments on level of safety activities?		
1.19 WHS summary		
Poor ☐ Fair ☐	Good ☐	Excellent ☐
Overall score		

Pre-accident	**Score**
1.1 General (non-measurable)	
1.2 Management involvement	
1.3 Health and safety rules and procedures	
1.4 Pre-placement health assessments	
1.5 Induction procedures	
1.6 Self-inspections	
1.7 Equipment/process audits	
1.8 Training	
1.9 Safety publicity/promotion	
1.10 Statutory requirements	
1.11 Use of specialist resources	
1.12 Ergonomics	
Post-accident	**Score**
1.13 Effective care	
1.14 Rehabilitation	
1.15 Accident investigation	
1.16 Work injury register	
1.17 Claims control	
1.18 Regular management reports	
Total	

Appendix 2

GPG Background Information

The Site

The site at which GPG is situated has two buildings required for GPG's operations, which are referred to as:

- Building one
- Building two.

Building Construction

Both buildings are constructed:

- of brick
- on concrete slabs
- as single storeys
- with metal decking on steel frame roofs.

Building One (South)

Building one:

- houses the entire printing plant
- stores:
    - paper
    - inks
    - machine parts
    - finished products.

The finished product store occupies approximately 22% of the total building area.

Firefighting facilities for Building one are limited to fire hose reels and fire extinguishers.

Building Two (North)

Two permanently open doorways join building two internally, which:

- is used as the general store;
- includes receiving and dispatch.

Employees also use the lunchroom area in this building.
Automatic fire sprinklers protect Building two.

Building and Plant Replacement Value

According to a note accompanying the accounts, the buildings at the plant have been valued at a historical cost (15 years old).

Current replacement values are approximately 3.5 times higher than the values used for current insurance cover.

The west, north and east

A two-metre high chain link wire fence binds the west, north and eastern sides of the site.

Chain Link Wire Fence

The South

A wide, slow-flowing river binds the site on the southern side. The ground slopes away gently to the river.

Storage Tanks

Near the river's edge, there are unbunded and unfenced storage tanks containing:

- liquid petroleum gas (LPG)
- diesel
- oil.

Car Parking

While there is adequate car parking space for employees on a gravel carpark at the western side of the main buildings, employees prefer to park their cars on the bitumen at the side of the access roadway nearer to the main plant operations. This appears to lead to considerable congestion.

Gates

There are no gatekeepers at either of the gates and no regulated traffic flow has been observed. It has also been observed that both gates were still open at 6.00 p.m. even though the day operators finished work at 4.30 p.m. and only about 5% of the 80 employees were still onsite.

Housekeeping

There was a considerable amount of miscellaneous equipment and parts around the waste skip area and some inside the building.

Data/records

The plant manager has advised that raw material and finished product stock records are kept on a small computer in the office area. Backups are produced on a weekly basis and stored in a fireproof cupboard adjacent to the safe in the front office.

Smoking

Despite prominent 'no smoking' signs, there is considerable evidence of smoking:

- in the lunch area;
- adjacent to the recharger facility in the production building.

GPG's Projected Output

With GPG winning the tenders for printing materials for two government departments, it is expected its output will increase by approximately 60% over the next two years, if there is no loss of other business.

Required Equipment

It is most likely that the 60% output increase will require an additional printing machine, which needs to be housed in a separate building. These machines are sourced from Germany, although China has been touted as an alternative supplier of machines at a lower cost.

Contracts

In addition, the contracts for the government departments will be required (as a governance requirement) to be formally retendered every three years.

GPG's Operational Activities

The following flowchart (shown below) summarises GPG's operational activities.

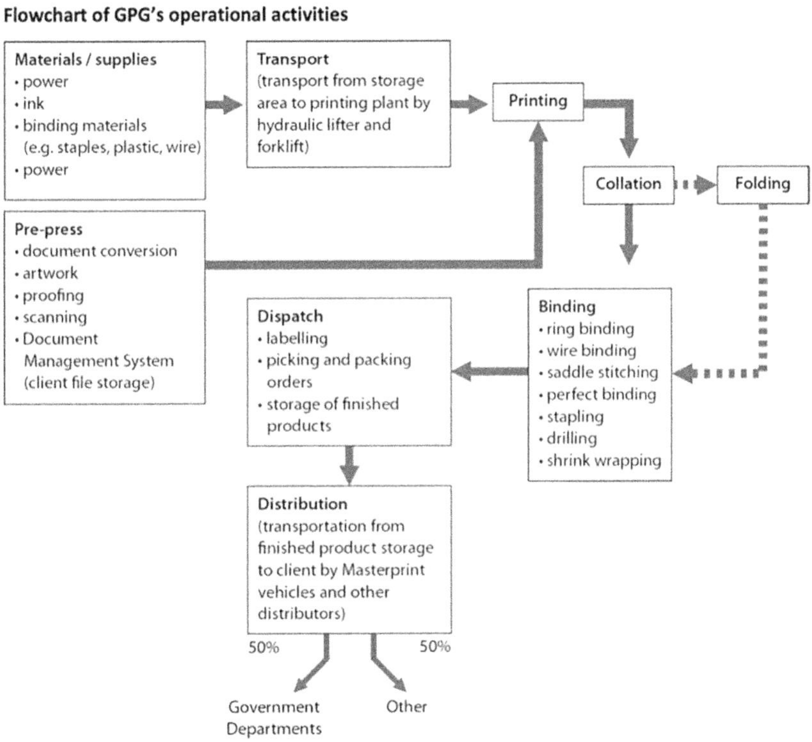

Site Layout

The following diagram is the site layout for GPG.

Business Environment

GPG has been successful for many years mainly because it is the government's 'preferred' printing supplier. Unfortunately, the government has recently

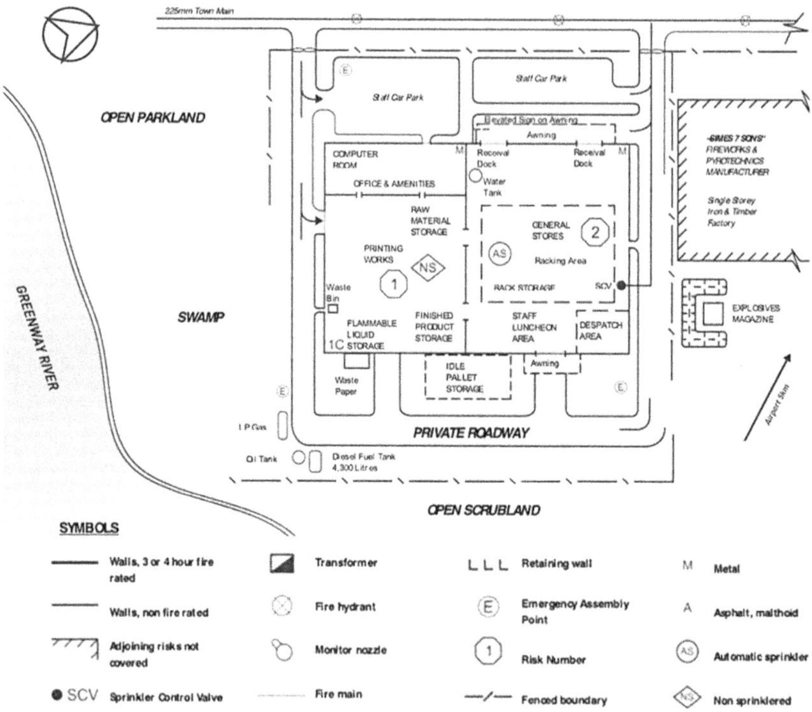

announced its desire to allow tenders from other suppliers to ensure more efficient business outcomes.

GPG is unsure about the impact of this government announcement on their business as it has not conducted any pricing benchmarking against the private sector for many years. However, GPG expects there will be considerable price competition as other printing suppliers seek to increase their market share.

Cost Cutting

The government has also been undertaking cost-cutting initiatives, which have resulted in departmental and government agency (which rely on annual funding) budget reductions. GPG is unsure of the business impacts involved with government agencies determining how to achieve their required savings.

Alternative Supply Sources

To prepare itself for the impending competition, GPG has been examining alternative supply sources. To date, GPG has sourced all supplies from local companies. GPG has been aware for some time that importing materials would yield considerable savings (as they are considerably cheaper) but has little experience in importing key raw materials.

Capital	$10,000,000
Net assets	$15,000,000
Trade debtors	$1,300,000
Cash and investments	$3,500,000
Trade creditors	$1,105,000
Annual profit	$800,000
Shareholders	N/A (government-owned)
Annual sales	$20,000,000
Margin on product sold	45%
Staff	80
Annual revenue growth	5% (past 12 months)
Location/s	Richmond, Melbourne (inner city factory)
Vehicles	• 3 delivery trucks and 14 cars • (incl. sales/executive staff vehicles) • 5 forklift trucks
Business	Printer of fine quality: • brochures • magazines • leaflets • annual reports • newsletters

Unions

The union has also communicated its concerns about how GPG will respond to its new challenges. Specifically, the union:

- believes GPG should conduct business as usual;
- has indicated it will fight any staff reductions.

Private Sector Customers

Despite having earned a reputation for being a high-quality printer, GPG has never supplied products to non-government organisations. In line with GPG's revised business plan, management has begun to:

- investigate the possibility of seeking new private sector customers;
- develop a marketing plan to potentially deliver that outcome.

Other Details

The following table summarises other pertinent GPG business details.

Organisational Structure

The following diagram outlines GPG's organisational structure. The organisation has been very stable in recent years. All executives have been with the organisation for a minimum of five years.

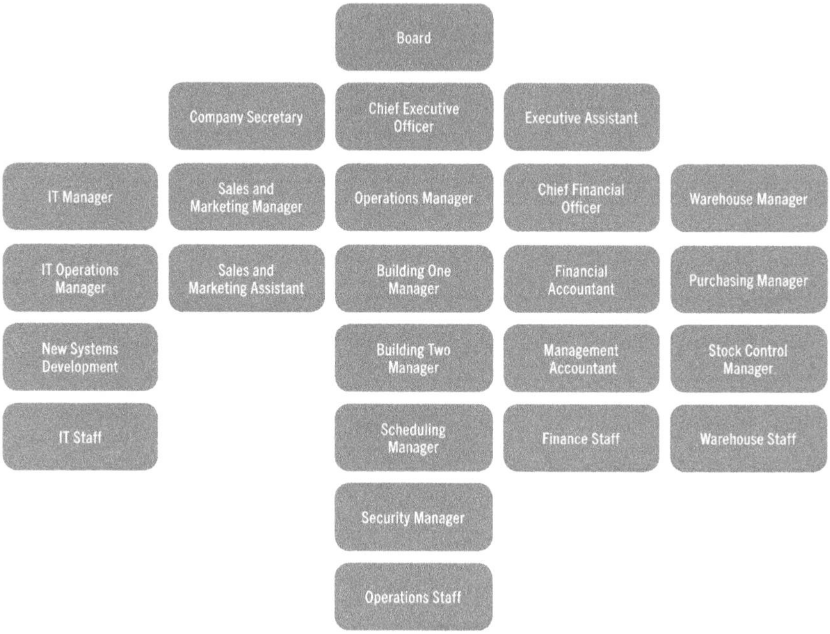

Appendix 3

GPG's Risk Assessment Reference Tables

Descriptors and Classification Codes

The following table provides descriptors and classification codes for:

- likelihood
- consequence
- risk rating.

Descriptors and Classification Codes

Likelihood				
Descriptor	Almost certain	Likely	Possible	Unlikely
Code	A	B	C	D
Consequence				
Descriptor	Minor	Moderate	Major	Severe
Code	I	II	III	IV
Likelihood				
Descriptor	Almost certain	Likely	Possible	Unlikely
Code	A	B	C	D
Likelihood				
Descriptor	Low	Medium	High	Catastrophic
Code	L	M	H	C

GPG Classifications and Codes Tables

GPG Risk Analysis Matrix

	Consequence code				
Likelihood code		I	II	III	IV
	A	High	High	Catastrophic	Catastrophic
	B	Medium	High	High	Catastrophic
	C	Medium	High	High	High
	D	Low	Medium	Medium	High

The following table defines the risk ratings derived from the risk analysis matrix.

GPG Risk Rating Definitions

Risk Rating	**Level of Required Management Attention**
Catastrophic	• Immediate action required • Senior executive management/board accountable
High	• Senior executive management attention needed • Management accountability and responsibility specified
Medium	• Manage by specific monitoring or response procedures by accountable line managers
Low	• Manage by routine procedures • Unlikely to need specific application of resources

Appendix 4

Example: Risk Register

Risk Category	Business Unit	What Is the Issue/Risk That May Occur?	Commentary (e.g. Circumstance and Sources)	Existing Mitigation Actions or Controls	Likelihood	Consequence	Overall Rating	Control Rating	Actions We Need to Take	Who	When	Status
Reputation / moral	XYZ	Visitor injury/death/ illness due to poor asset management/ maintenance	The current site is now quite old and there are issues with the quality of: – paved areas – balcony deterioration	– Site by site review program for all assets (underway) – Site manager review of evident risks	Low	Large	A: Significant	Requires improvement	10-year asset management plans are to be produced across all sites with remedial actions identified and rectified			A national asset maintenance manager has been appointed with a key focus on remedial capital expenditure and asset maintenance plans with particular focus on older assets
Compliance	ABC	Non-compliance with fire regulations	A fire approximately four years ago highlighted compliance issues with respect to the facility Engineers are working with management to achieve compliance via the installation of fire sprinklers and hydrants A project management group has been established to ensure this project stays on track but is impacted by the responsiveness of regulators	– Full-time staff member – Security patrols – Smoke detection system and emergency warning and intercommunications system (EWIS) installed – Implemented fire warden and escape plan – Project management group	Low	Large	A: Significant	Adequate	Acceleration compliance works			– The contractor has been selected and the process is in the final stages of procurement. – The physical work is expected to be completed in June 2018 so the issue is very close to being resolved

Risk Category	Business Unit	What Is the Issue/Risk That May Occur?	Commentary (e.g. Circumstance and Sources)	Existing Mitigation Actions or Controls	Likelihood	Consequence	Overall Rating	Control Rating	Actions We Need to Take	Who	When	Status
Strategic	XYZ	Failure to successfully market the new product	Given the decline of our current product line in recent years, the success of the BBB product is crucial to the long-term prosperity of the business	– Project plan with clear timelines	Medium	High	A: Significant	Adequate	– No further risk mitigation required			
			Our competitors have similar issues therefore being first to market will have considerable benefit to our business	– Consumer group tests to assess acceptance – Marketing plan covering multiple media options – Internet sales channel under development					– Constant monitoring of progress by the executive and the board is required			

Appendix 5

Example: Case Study

The Group was founded in 1863 in a major French merchant harbour with dual-core business maritime shipping and founding products trading. It took its name in 1898 from the name of the new owner. Since then it has diversified to all transportation means, logistics, the aerospace industry, and purchasing as opportunities for investment arose.

The Group has 3,000 total staff, of which 1,700 are in transport. The site it occupies is 400,000 m^2, of which a third is devoted to transport.

Annual turnover is experiencing regular growth as evidenced by the three-year numbers:

- 2014: €300 million
- 2015: €350 million
- 2016: €400 million

The Group has set three strategic objectives:

- Objective 1: optimise working capital;
- Objective 2: enhance productivity;
- Objective 3: offer optimal security to customers.

Smithson Inc.

Smithson Inc., the subsidiary, is focused on air freight and is headquartered in the freight zone at CDG Airport. Its activity comprises 80% of military goods and equipment with clients both in the public sector (Ministry of Defence and its industrial affiliates) and the private sector (Dassault, Thalès, EADS, etc.) and destinations include countries like Taiwan, Spain, Pakistan and Jordan.

Due to the type of shipments, Smithson has two main obligations: confidentiality and national interest, for which it works with the intelligence and counter-intelligence agencies.

Compliance is a key issue, including the Warsaw Convention, the International Air Regulation (IATA) and the ADR (Accord for Dangerous Goods by Road), to name but a few. Furthermore, the company has chosen to be certified ISO 14000 and ISO 9001:2015.

One of its main competitive advantages is to be able to charter very wide bodied aircraft including the Antonov 124. It can also boast the completion of difficult projects like the evacuation of equipment for an international automobile rally (2,000 metric tons moved in 60 hours).

Risk Management Audit

1. Traditional Risk Centres Approach – Risk Owners

A consulting firm is brought in to audit the current situation of Smithson Inc. in terms of risk management at the Group's initiative.

The managing director (MD) of Smithson Inc. proved highly motivated and a sound source of information regarding the risk management in his division. Although the Group does not yet have a fully-fledged ERM program throughout its divisions, due to the specificity of the activity of Smithson and its involvement in military equipment, the managing director has a keen sense of risks and security for its customers.

The diagnostic developed here does not aim at exhaustiveness but rather at identifying major exposures that would prevent the company from reaching the goals/performance expected by the Group's leadership.

Therefore, the interview with the MD is centred on the key question: What resources are needed for what objectives?

The key of risk management is enhancing the chances of reaching the goals whatever the uncertainties that may bear on the organisation.

The MD translation of the Group objectives at the level of Smithson is the following:

- Economic efficiency (turnover growth and working capital optimisation);
- Citizenship and ethics, that is, CSR (compliance – certification, regulation – safety and security for the customers)

The first model for establishing a systematic diagnostic of exposures (risk assessment) is based on the taxonomy of the organisation's resources grouped into five classes of resources:

- **Human:** Losing the necessary talents and competencies, increase in workers' benefit programs: the central question is how to attract and retain talents and maintain a safe and productive work environment? Other key questions are: Are fire drills and training organised regularly? How are dangerous materials stored?
- **Technical:** Damage to plant and equipment, and industrial processes. The question could be: Are sprinklers efficient whatever the circumstances (sensitivity, content type)?
- **Information:** Loss of information, brand image, reputation: How are data stored? Where is sensitive information? Who has access? What do social media say about the company and its services? Also what about cybersecurity? Finally, is the Russian involvement in the main large-bodied aircraft (Antonov) a source of risk to reputation and trust of the customers?
- **Partners:** Clients and suppliers/subcontractors: Are the partners selected according to the organisation's main objectives? Are the contractual relations rigorously organised? Are the partners followed and controlled regularly?
- **Financial:** Loss of revenues: losses resulting from the preceding events and external ones such as strike, political unrest and economical downturn.

Exhibit 1 below provides an illustration of the Smithson's major exposures that could result from a fire or a theft (including cybercrime). It represents exposures

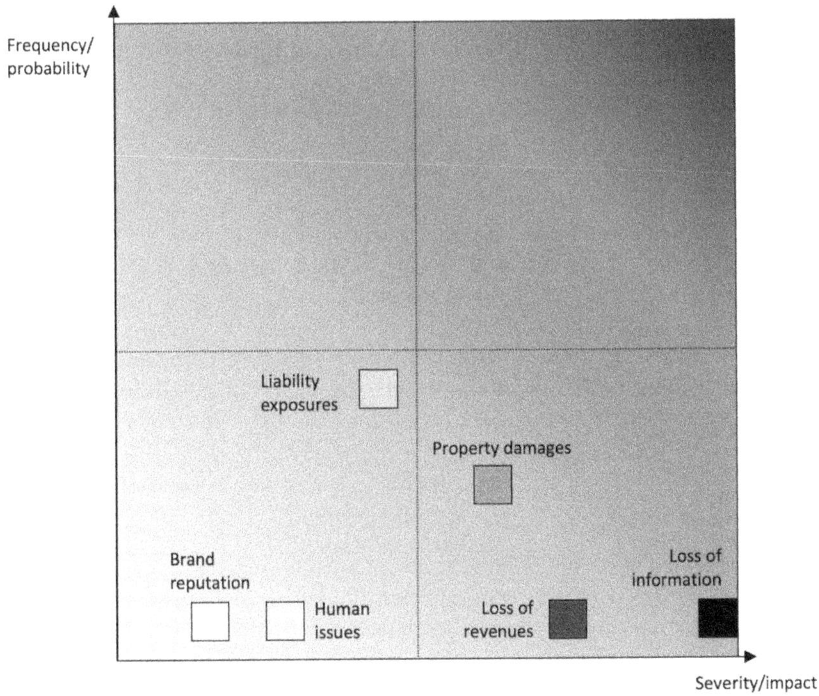

Exhibit 1 Risk Matrix

as a combination of likelihood and consequence but does not show prioritisation as a systematic quantification has not been conducted. A loss of information might have strategic consequences for the company as it is at the core of the company's mission for its customers in highly sensitive goods.

Loss of information is a real possibility in the current cyber climate, though still of low probability. However, the direct impact combined with the potential damage to reputation makes it a high priority for the company aligned with the stated objectives.

As service providers are used and sensitive information is shared with major subcontractors, the risk of loss of information can be generated off-site and any risk management effort must be shared with all involved. A trust analysis must be conducted for all partners, included those within the Group.

Treating this risk will rely on both sets of tools, risk reduction and risk financing, but in the end it is essential that the risk treatment effort aims primarily at reducing the probability of this happening (risk prevention). Crisis/continuity plans should be developed to limit the damage should it occur (loss protection). Risk financing could be considered to smooth out the impact on working capital (one of the Group's objectives).

Recommendations

The financial situation of the Group and its subsidiary allows it to improve its risk situation whereas the computer equipment replacement in case of a fire is really secondary. However, some improvement is possible through:

- physical protection of data in the company premises;
- overall IT system auditing, in the company and at its major partners;
- auditing of protection at the major service providers;
- training to raise awareness of staff concerning IT security, but also the handling of hazardous substances and materials.

If Smithson does develop an ERM program it should be at the initiative of the Group, but Smithson's MD could volunteer to be a test centre should the decision be taken at the board level to launch the initiative and test the system in a limited scope.

2. Cindynic Approach

When confronted by a potentially hazardous situation, each actor has his/her own vision and his/her own representation of danger and this will impact the overall situation and specifically the prioritisation of the sources of hazards.

It might seem simplistic to reduce the complex situation to a five-dimensional hyperspace as a tool to develop a global analysis. However, a complex system can even be less apprehended in a two-dimensional matrix where only likelihood and consequence are represented.

Introduction to the Cindynic Approach. The cindynic approach is based on the definition of a situation in terms of time and space. It applies to a limited number of actors' networks involved in the situation and who may modify its context through their actions and interactions.

The vision of each actor is based on five dimensions that define his/her perception of hazards: three constitute the space of reality/quantification (cindyno-metrics) and the others constitute the space of ethics in action. The two spaces are linked with a common dimension, the bridge for objectives or goals.

The five dimensions are (for more detail see the section on cindynics):

- dimension of historical facts and statistics (statistical);
- dimension of representations and models based on facts (epistemology);
- dimension of goals and objectives (teleological);
- dimension of norms, laws, regulations, standards, and codes (deontological);
- dimension of systems values (axiological).

The hyperspace of danger is illustrated here:

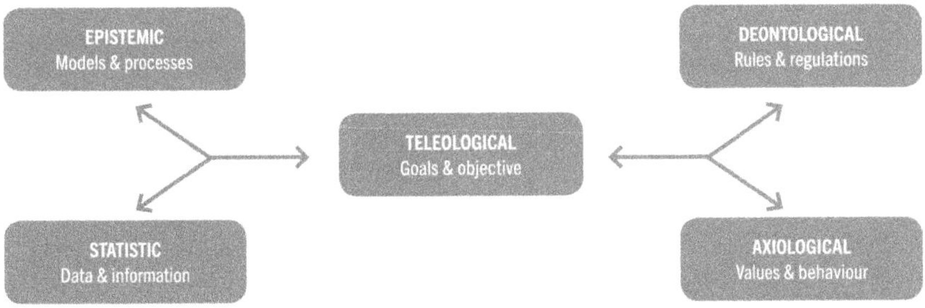

Thus, the five axes of the hyperspace of danger define six plans:

- cindyno-metrics plan: statistics and epistemic axis;
- ethics plan: deontological and axiological axis;
- political plan: teleological and deontological axis;
- ecological plan: teleological and ethical axis;
- practical plan: teleological and epistemic axis;
- programmatic plan: teleological and statistic axis.

Cindynic System Analysis. All the actors have their own objectives and they are conditioned by their understanding of the situation and their own ethics and regulations. Based on the five dimensions, a description of the situation may be developed on the main actors as is proposed here (see next page).

Identification of Major SCD at Smithson. The description allows establishing an inventory of the main points of friction that generates risks in the situation. They are called systemic cindygenic deficits (SCD); the numbering refers to G-Y Kervern's description:

- SCD 3: Lack of communication

Information does not flow or has interferences between actors, and specifically between the Group and its subsidiary.

- SCD 4: Lack of vigilance with external context and stakeholders

Insufficient consideration of shipment's sensitivity and the possibility of malicious activity.

- SCD 5: Insufficient interest for safety and security

Due to the specificity of cargo, and information retained by the organisation especially among its upstream partners (suppliers, service providers, subcontractors, etc.)

- SCD 7: Lack of experience feedback

Actors	Epistemic	Deontological	Teleological	Statistic	Axiological
Group	The processes and models are developed and conducted	– Comply with all air regulations – Follow up on certification	– Performance guarantee – Appropriate answer to complex requests – Turnover – Optimise working capital – CSR	Group historical data and business data	Represent the Group in all dimensions and experts' relevance in all of the Group's trades
Airport	Crisis management and experience feedback	Different regulations may apply depending on the activity and the ministry involved	– Encourage different activities – Profitability – Ensure the security of aerial transport of goods and people	Based on own historical data and from international airport and IATA	Ensure that all activities on site go smoothly for passenger wellbeing
Ministry of Defence	Military strategy and visions	Set by the government policies and the President's guidance	Protect French interests inside and outside the territory	Confidential information hard to obtain (classified)	Military rules and regulations
Service provider: IT	Database management systems	Contractual responsibilities and national and European legislation on the protection of personal data	Protect third party goods	Need to have discussion with provider and the professional organisation	Confidentiality and data protection
External partners: customers	Economic models	– Contractual obligations – Market situation – Compliance with deadlines	– Optimise good relations (reputation profitability). – Global economies – The best link between quality and price	Need to have discussion with partners and the professional organisation	Commercial values Reliability of delivery Look at proposals from subcontractors

It should be extended to events in similar organisations that might be repeated in the organisation's own activities.

- SCD 10: Lack of rigorous and systematic preparation for a crisis

The sensitivity of the cargo handled and the need for utmost confidentiality lead to the possibility of a crisis in which the partners' trust is at risk. This requires being ready to handle any disturbance and prevent it to generate a crisis.

Conclusion of the Cindynic Analysis. *The identification of the SCD indicates fault lines in a complex system and remedies can be developed and implemented without waiting for any event or near miss, and in the absence of any prior data. Therefore, the cindynic methodology is ideal to take into account human factors and anticipate potential 'human breakdown' and adopt a pro-active approach to enhance the system resilience. It is like a root cause analysis where human factors are at the forefront of the issues.*

When it comes to Smithson Inc., the solutions might be the following:

- Set up a system of intranet and a whistle blower channel and policy to ensure that communication flows both top–down and bottom–up.
- Reinforce the efforts in economic intelligence and ask commercial team members to be closer to clients' concerns.
- Develop training and actions to raise staff awareness of safety issues for themselves and their co-workers as well and as a competitive advantage for the company.
- Implement systematic feedback exercises whenever an incident is detected internally or externally and develop a non-blame culture to ensure that all participate in the effort without fear.
- Identify the major sources of disturbance and develop continuity planning and a way to function in crisis mode so as to preserve the company's reputation in all circumstances, including specific communication channels and content for the economic partners entrusted to their usual contacts (commercial team for customers, purchasing for suppliers and sub-contractors, IT for specific providers, etc.).

Attachment – Minutes of the Interview with Smithson's MD

- Goals and objectives

- **Activities:** Freight, logistics and purchasing
- **BU mission:** Offer solutions in all types of national and international transports, managing specialised transport equipment.

- Resources

- **Organisation of premises, staff, plant and equipment:** An office building, and a warehouse for the storage of cargo. The warehouse is equipped with a scanner.

- **Origin of products, equipment and information:** Freight is 80% military goods and equipment.
- **Markets**: International and national, with customers both public (state and governments) and private.
- **Means – technical resources:** The structure is dedicated to clients in the aerospace industry and military goods and equipment to provide solutions to their specific needs thanks to a team of experts in different areas. A network and an example unique in Europe with the various qualifications (JAR – joint aviation requirements *145 – Approved Maintenance Organisations, 21 —Certification Procedures for Aircraft and Related Products and Parts*, confidential defence and NATO). Due to the aeronautical culture, new hires are sensitive to turn-around time. And there is a strong will for tracking and tracing parts with a permanent attention on keeping the client informed on the whereabouts of the equipment expected.
- **Know-how:** Transport of dangerous and sensitive equipment, aeronautical and military equipment, air freight: charter, grouping, AOG shipments (aircraft on the ground).

• Specific questions

- **Have you identified probable/possible adverse events?**

No risk has been identified as probable, in spite of the rise in cyber-attacks that should raise questions.

- **Have you elaborated event/disturbance scenario?**

No scenario has been developed.

- **What type of staff training do you have in place?**

Staffs working in the warehouse who are daily in contact with sensitive material, have no specific training. However, they seem to follow the rules that are supplied by the customers regarding storage, handling, etc.

- **Do you organise evacuation drills?**

No drill is regularly organised either at the warehouse of the office building. Note that the offices are on the ground floor of the building.

- **Where is data/information stored?**

The company's data are stored in a host service provider based in Normandy and also on the computer hard drive.

- **What are the fire reduction measures?**

Warehouses are equipped with sprinklers systems, not the office building only equipped with smoke detectors. The usual excuse being that sprinklers would destroy the computers.

- **What is your level of trust and confidence with economic partners (upstream and downstream?**

The Group enjoys a strong reputation and has been an actor in the aeronautical business for a long time. As far as the subsidiary is concerned, it works for top-tier partners known for excellence around the world, which implies a strong confidence and loyalty from the customers.

– **Who is responsible for the management of risks?**
The MD is at the head of the transport division of the Group, he defines the division's strategy within the guidelines provided by the Group. There is no specification on risk management responsibilities, but it must be assumed that he is the ultimate risk owner with regard to the division, and also regarding liabilities with the customers, depending on the contract provisions.

– **Do you hold Certifications (ISO)?**
The company is certified ISO 9001:2015 for quality and 14,000 for environment to remain on top of its game on a highly competitive market and meet the demands of customers. Other certifications include *JAR 145, JAR 21 G, QUALIFAS A, Confidential Defence, NATO, A.O.G.* (aviation spare certifications).

– **What are the specific regulations for air freight?**
The company must comply with the international air regulations and to the convention concerning cargo freight (Warsaw Convention, ADR – European Agreement concerning the International Carriage of Dangerous Goods by Road).

– **Is there a stated Group ethic?**
Be an economic partner for customers in a competitive world and acquire certifications.

– **How are we organised for crisis management efforts?**
The company is a subsidiary of an important Group but at the level of the relatively small entity no crisis plan is in place, nor has the Group provided guidance in this regard.

Conclusion of the Interview and on the Spot Advice

As MD, you are in charge and answerable to top group management, and you are expected to be present at all time. Do you have plans to delegate to your staff your missions should you be kept away for a period of time? No succession plan or replacement contingency is in place at this stage.

You should put in place actions to raise risk awareness in your staff through nurturing a culture of risk management and accountability in issues of safety and security. In spite of sound financial result and strong partner relationships, the lack of resolute action in risk management may weaken your competitive advantage in the long run and endanger your resilience.

Notes

Notes

www.ingramcontent.com/pod-product-compliance
Lightning Source LLC
LaVergne TN
LVHW020922180325
806137LV00004B/15